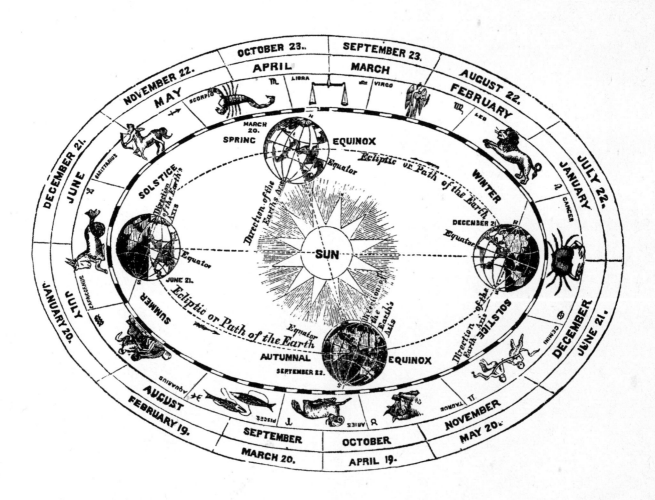

Astrology

The Worldwide Guide to Reading the Stars

Nancy J. Hajeski

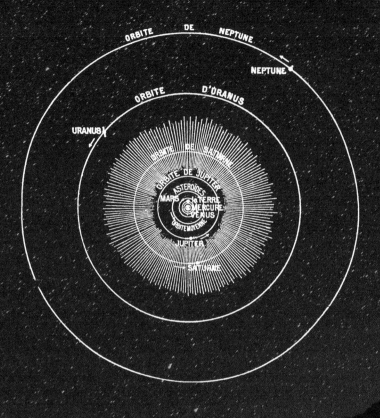

MOSELEY ROAD INC.
International Rights and Packaging
22 Knollwood Avenue
Elmsford, NY 10523
www.moseleyroad.com.

President **Sean Moore**
Editorial director **Lisa Purcell**
Art direction and design **Duncan Youel** at **oiloften.co.uk**

Printed in China

ISBN 978-1-62669-211-4

10 9 8 7 6 5 4 3 2 1 21 22 23 24 25

Contents

Chapter Four: The Modern Western Zodiac 132

Chapter Five: The Contemporary Chinese Zodiac 188

Chapter Six: Astrological Branches 224

Chapter Seven: Lessons from the Masters   236

Introduction

The future in our stars...

The night sky has always held a fascination for human beings. Those illuminated astral bodies moving through their stately seasonal arcs enthrall the viewer; the orbiting moon, looming so near at times, beckons to all. Planets align, come close, then appear to drift away. Meanwhile, the sun, lingering below the horizon, is anxiously awaited each dawn. While the earth feels finite, the sky is vast, limitless. It is no wonder, then, that early seers and prophets looked to the heavens for omens, and that earth's relationship with the moon, sun, planets, and stars furnished fledgling civilizations with both the means to calculate the passage of time and predict the future.

It is instructive to recall that for most of history, people could actually see the night sky in its star-spattered glory, that the light pollution modern societies endure did not exist for them. Based on these unobscured views, the Arabs systematically mapped the stars, furnishing names that are still in use, while the Egyptians and Greeks turned the observation of celestial bodies into a science, and the Romans named the visible planets after their gods.

Seasons and Shamans

Primitive forms of astrology, based on the movement of constellations and rooted in calendrical systems, were initially used to predict seasonal milestones, such as the times of yearly floods. These ancient people had no knowledge of what stars actually were, so it is not surprising they created legends and stories about them, assuming they were

gods or home to gods . . . and believing that priests or shamans were allowed some form of communication with the immortal ones.

Eventually astrology began to take on more weight, as an indicator of divine pleasure or displeasure and as a means to forecast how a person's life path might stretch out before them. The importance of astrology to certain civilizations cannot be understated; shaping their culture, their statecraft, or their religion, sometimes all three. It made sense to these people that there was a real correspondance between what was observed in the sky and what took place on the ground. "As above, so below" is a common theme echoed by occultists throughout history. Today, countries like China, India, and Nepal take birth signs and their corresponding traits quite seriously . . . to the point that some businesses discourage certain birth signs from applying for "unsuitable" jobs.

Horoscopic astrology, the ancestor—and foundation—of modern Western astrology, was born in the Mediterranean region, gestating in Babylonia, Egypt, Greece, and Rome. Hellenic astrology, as practiced by the Greeks and Egyptians, was influenced by Pythagoras, Plato, the Stoics, and the Hermetic tradition, which provided an intellectual basis and structural foundation for the discipline . . . and the mathematical calculations needed for accurate predictions.

Cosmic Connections

As the centuries passed, the passion for astrology rose and fell. Interest was limited during the early Christian era, waned during the Middle Ages, and was revived during the Renaissance. English astrology reached its zenith during the 17th century, with astrologers acting as theorists and researchers, and providing advice to everyone from crowned heads to streetsweepers. In addition to recommending the best time to take a journey or harvest a crop, they could diagnose physical or mental illnesses and even predict natural disasters. This era exemplified a world in which everything in heaven and on earth was understood to be interconnected . . . a time when astrology coexisted contentedly with religion, magic, and science.

At the dawn of the 20th century a renewed interest in astrology sprang up in many countries, including the US and Britain . . . an interest bolstered by the advent of the New Age movement of the 1970s. Today the discipline remains enormously popular—with at least 80 branches of astrology currently in use.

Within this book readers will become acquainted with the major aspects of astrology. They will trace its long history—its origins and evolution, explore the countries where it is still practiced today, and meet its many notable advocates who made their mark studying the stars and planets. Aspiring astrologers will discover the numerous indicators and placements that shape a horoscope and learn the basics of creating a birth chart based on Western astrology as well as how to determine character traits and the auspiciousness of upcoming events using the Chinese zodiac.

While some people still scoff at astrology and disparage it as a pseudoscience, the discipline can become a reassuring presence in a person's life—offering counsel, building confidence, and providing signposts toward a more productive and even prosperous future. Like multitudes before them, those who earnestly study the stars, ultimately come to understand that the wisdom revealed by the movement of celestial bodies can uplift the spirits, open the heart to new encounters, teach caution when needed, and inspire the adventurous to take destiny into their own hands.

Astrology and Religion

A Pew Research survey from 2018 determined that nearly one in three American adults (29 percent) believe in astrology. And, in spite of the Christian church's negative view of the practice, more than one in four Christians (26 percent) believe in it. This breaks down to 24 percent of Protestants, 33 percent of Catholics, and 18 percent of evangelicals and agnostics. Curiously, atheists, at 3 percent, are the least likely demographic to give it credence. The most likely group to believe, at 47 percent, are people who say their religion is "nothing in particular" followed by Protestants in historically black churches at 34 percent.

Star Points

In Europe the terms astronomy and astrology were used interchangeably until the 17th century. Astrology was taught in universities and considered part of a classical education. The modern distinction between astronomy—the scientific study of the motion, nature, and composition of stars, and astrology—the search for celestial significance in regard to earthly affairs, did not exist.

Chapter One

The Basics of Astrology

Branches of Astrology

Astrology is the belief that distant cosmic objects like the sun, moon, planets, and stars influence human lives. The study of astrology covers an enormous astrological system, encompassing many branches, schools of thought, and applied techniques. In spite of the many versions there are to pursue, most astrologers practice one or more of the following six main types:

Natal Astrology

This is the branch that people who read newspaper or magazine horoscopes are familiar with. Even more detailed information can be ascertained with the creation of a natal chart that shows the placement of various celestial bodies at an individual's time of birth. Astrologers then assess these charts for clues and indications: What is the potential for this person's character and path in life? What are their greatest strengths and weaknesses, their best opportunities or most perilous pitfalls? Natal astrology has been referred to as "a deep dive into the soul," and it certainly can be an effective tool for developing self-awareness. To get an accurate reading based on actual time of birth—as opposed to a "magazine" horoscope based only on a given sun sign—it makes sense to visit an actual astrologer, at least once. Some websites allow people to plot their own birth charts but, again, it takes an experienced astrologer to interpret all the nuances.

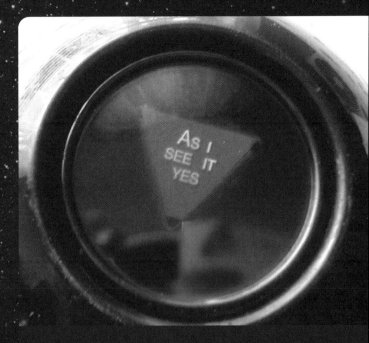

Horary Astrology

This ancient method of divination—it possibly goes back 10,000 to 30,000 years—supplies the answer to a yes or no question. It is used for fortunetelling, similar to divination methods like the Tarot or I Ching, and was popular in the Middle Ages. It appealed to those who did not know their exact day or time of birth for casting a natal chart. The astrologer must know the exact time and location of the question in order to give the most accurate reading. Generally, an answer is forthcoming, but if there is a "block" in the chart, it is possible the client is not supposed to know the answer. This branch is quite difficult for a novice to master, but a number of experienced astrologers continue to practice it.

Outlook Good

In the 1950s, Albert C. Carter and Abe Bookman invented the Magic 8-Ball, a fortune-telling novelty item that was a hit with both teens and adults at parties and family gatherings. Today it is produced by the toy giant Mattel. The Magic 8-Ball looks like a large black pool ball. After a question is asked, the plastic, liquid-filled sphere is shaken, and the answer floats up and appears in a clear triangular window. The 20 possible answers include: "As I see it, yes," "Cannot predict now," "Reply hazy, ask again," "Don't count on it," "Outlook good," and "It is decidedly so." Astrologically speaking, the Magic 8-Ball is a horary device.

Electional Astrology

Also known as event astrology, this field of study looks for the best time to hold an event or complete an action. Based on what will be going on in the sky, the astrologer pinpoints the optimum date to schedule that special occasion. Requests range from the best times to propose marriage, ask for a raise, meet a potential client, or buy a car to getting a pet or taking a college entrance test. A couple may want to avoid getting married while Venus is in retrograde, for example, which would put a damper on romance. Many astrologers specialize in this type of forecasting.

Mundane Astrology

This form of astrology predicts world events. It goes back thousands of years, to the days when astologers were less concerned with the fates of individual men and women, and more involved in guiding nations and their monarchs. Mundane astrologers need a strong grasp of history, as they look for patterns and observe cycles. For instance, Stephanie Powell of Astrology.com explains, "The last time Saturn and Pluto met, did we see other pandemics? Yes." Some countries even have their own birth charts, enabling astrologers to determine when treaties should be signed or other affairs of state should take place.

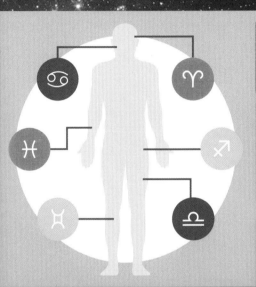

Medical Astrology

This is another ancient branch, one that associates various parts of the body and diseases with celestial objects. Each body part is ruled by a zodiac sign, while some planets affect certain organs. For instance, the sun sign Leo rules the heart, Mercury shows where there is action in the body, and Mars concerns energy levels. It would not be uncommon, then, for a person born with Mercury and Mars beside each other in Leo to have tachycardia—a faster-than-normal heart rate. While astrology may indicate certain medical tendencies, it is important to see a physician with any questions regarding health issues.

Relationship Astrology

This branch deals with how people get along, especially romantically. It is the reason many people seek out astrologers—the search for an enduring life partner. They usually want to know one of two things: their best time for meeting a potential partner and if a new partner is compatible, or "the one." They may also seek guidance on when to have a child, especially if they believe in the auspiciousness of certain dates or zodiac signs. There are six relationship dynamics between couples within the zodiac: same sign, one sign apart, two signs apart, three signs apart, four signs apart, five signs apart, and six signs apart.

What Is the Zodiac?

To ancient civilizations, who believed the earth was the center of the universe, the sun appeared to travel through the sky, its yearly journey taking it on a perceived elliptical path called THE ECLIPTIC. The route was so called because lunar or solar eclipses could only occur when the moon crossed it.

Within this ecliptic path, when viewed from the perspective of earth, lay a number of constellations. When the sun was "in" one of these arrangements of stars at the time of a person's birth, it became the familiar "sun" sign astrologers use to determine potential traits and upcoming events.

The concept of dividing the ecliptic into 12 sectors, each containing a constellation that bestows different characteristics to those born "under" those stars, is thought to have originated with the Babylonians during the first millenium BC. This tool of divination, called the zodiac, was subsequently adopted by Hellenistic Egyptian, Persian, Greek, Roman, Hebrew, and, to some extent, Asian astrologers. Centuries later this system would find its way to northern Europe and then to the New World.

The zodiac extends approximately 8 degrees north or south (measured in celestial latitude) of the ecliptic, which is the apparent path of the sun across the celestial sphere in the course of a year. Within this belt the paths of the moon and the visible planets can also be viewed. According to Western astrology, the 12 signs of the zodiac occupy 30-degree sectors of the ecliptic and roughly correspond to the following constellations; Aries, Taurus, Gemini, Cancer, Leo, Virgo, Libra, Scorpio, Sagittarius, Capricorn, Aquarius, and Pisces. These signs form a system of celestial coordinates, or more accurately, a system of ecliptical coordinates, using the ecliptic as the source of latitude and the sun's position at the vernal equinox as the origin of longitude. This equinox marks the start of the zodiac, known as the First Point of Aries.

Although the zodiac was the basis for the ecliptic coordinate system

The Ecliptic Path

An Expanded Zodiac?

The sun appears to travel through an additional two constellations along the ecliptic path: Ophiuchus, the Serpent Bearer, was a proposed thirteenth sign of the sidereal Zodiac, covering December 6 to 31. The constellation is situated behind the sun from November 29 to December 13. It was part of a 14-sign zodiac proposed by Steven Schmidt in 1970. The 14th sign—Cetus, the Whale—(May 12 to June 6), is located in the region of the sky that contains other water-related constellations like Aquarius and Pisces. A 13-sign zodiac, minus Cetus, was proposed by Walter Berg in a 1995 book. Mark Yazaki also supported the idea in Japan, where Ophiuchus is known as Hebitsukai-za. Ophiuchus offers protection from poison and is associated with doctors, physicians, and healers. In some cultures, Cetus represents storms and upheaval.

used in scientific astronomy (along with the equatorial version) to represent the apparent positions and orbits of Solar System objects, today the term zodiac and the names of its 12 signs are chiefly associated with horoscopic astrology. There are varied approaches to measuring and dividing the sky found in different types of astrology, yet the names of the zodiac and its totemic symbols are found in most forms. Western astrology calculates from equinox and solstice points (points that relate to the equal, shortest, and longest days in a tropical year). Vedic or Jyotisha astrology measures along the equatorial plane, a system called sidereal astrology.

The word zodiac...

...stems from the Greek *zōdiacus*, from the ancient Greek *zōidiakòs kýklos*, meaning a "cycle or circle of small animals." This early name indicates the prominence of the animals or mythological beasts that inhabit the zodiac. The word can also be used to describe the band containing the path of a given object in space: "the zodiac of the moon," say, or "the zodiac of a comet."

Astronomy & Astrology Contrasted

In the modern world, the term astronomy relates to the scientific study of the universe and its contents that lie outside the earth's atmosphere. Astrology, which is now considered a pseudoscience, evaluates how those same celestial spheres affect people and events on earth. Yet up until the 17th century in Europe, the terms astronomy and astrology were interchangeable.

In fact, many of the astronomical discoveries made by earlier cultures were actually in aid of creating more accurate astrological forecasts. This confluence ended during the late 1600s, when Newton demonstrated how earthly laws, like those that make an apple fall, also applied to the movement of stars and planets and other objects in space. From that point on, astronomy "got its wings" and moved into the realm of true science.

Early stargazers who lacked the assistance of telescopes were limited to viewing seven "planets"—the sun, the moon, Mercury, Venus, Mars, Jupiter, and Saturn. Many ancient civilizations imagined these planets inhabited by gods and so monitored their movements carefully. Eventually, these movements (recall that until the 16th century the earth was considered the center of the universe, with the sun "orbiting" around it) gained significance for humans, who imagined there were divine

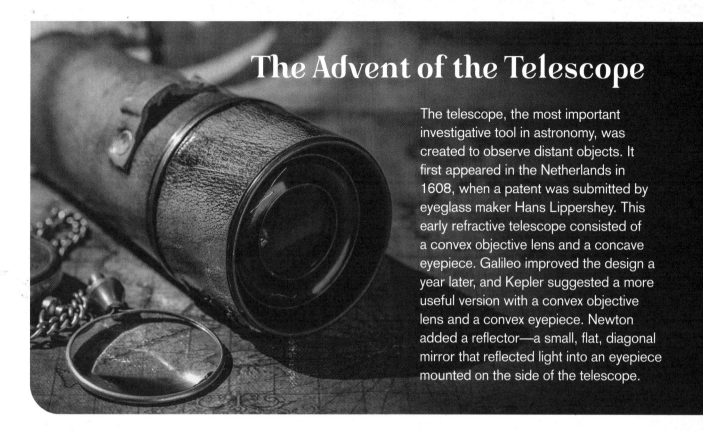

The Advent of the Telescope

The telescope, the most important investigative tool in astronomy, was created to observe distant objects. It first appeared in the Netherlands in 1608, when a patent was submitted by eyeglass maker Hans Lippershey. This early refractive telescope consisted of a convex objective lens and a concave eyepiece. Galileo improved the design a year later, and Kepler suggested a more useful version with a convex objective lens and a convex eyepiece. Newton added a reflector—a small, flat, diagonal mirror that reflected light into an eyepiece mounted on the side of the telescope.

intentions behind them. Thus, the framework of astrology was formed: planets and stars had relationships with one another that held clues to the fates of the humans living below. It was the responsibility of astrologers to suss out the portents and interpret them.

Astronomy, once legitimized, would evolve into the observation of celestial bodies and galactic phenomena, as well as the study of their origins, interrelationships, and future movements. This is not to say that objects in space do not affect earth; for example, the gravitational pull of the moon determines earthly ocean tides

and weather patterns. And when four or five planets align, many people on earth insist they feel lighter (by about the weight of a raisin, science reports). Most astronomers simply do not believe these distant objects affect human lives as directly as astrologers claim.

One feature both fields have in common is that they rely heavily on computers. This technology allows astrologers to formulate complicated star charts and uncover subjective evidence for their predictions. Astronomers use computers to perform complex mathematical functions and to find scientific proof that confirms their hypotheses.

Currently, astronomical exploration of distant galaxies and black holes has been made possible by powerful space telescopes; most astrologers, on the other hand, are content to focus on the 12 constellations identified with the zodiac . . . along with the sun, the moon, and the planets.

Astrology may not qualify as a science, but it does bear some of the same trappings: the use of mathematical calculations and charts and a specific terminology of its own. Scientists test out their theories, however, before drawing conclusions but astrologers perform no trials to confirm their speculations.

Planets

Ancient skywatchers were able to observe seven planets with the naked eye—Mercury, Venus, Mars, Jupiter, Saturn, the sun, and moon ... or five planets and two of what the Greeks called luminaries—the sun and moon.

A New Category

Our Solar System is home to a number of additional planets. Take Ceres, which lies between Mars and Jupiter and was discovered in 1801. Then in 2005 another planet, later named Eris, was observed out beyond Pluto. It was possibly a large KBO, or Kuiper Belt Object, icy bodies that orbit the sun en masse. Taxed with reassessing what the term planet actually meant, the International Astronomical Union created a new category in 2006— the dwarf planet. Into this category went Ceres, Eris, two more KBOs named Haumea and Makemake, and, alas, the former planet Pluto, now classified as the largest KBO.

Early astronomers were able to distinguish planets from stars by noting that planets moved back and forth against a backdrop of fixed stars. They also observed that some planets had moons similar to earth's. To these viewers it appeared that the other planets (as well as the sun and stars) orbitted around the home planet, an arrangement called the Ptolemiac System. This misconception was not corrected until the mid-1500s with the advent of the heliocentric—sun-centered—models of Copernicus.

Planets are defined as astronomical bodies orbitting a star or stellar remnant that are massive enough to be rounded by their own gravity but not large enough to cause thermonuclear fission and which have cleared their neighboring regions of planetesimals (solid objects made of cosmic dust). Planets give off no light; they are only visible due to the sun's light reflecting off them. In our Solar System, the inner planets are smallish and rocky, while the outer planets are gas giants or ice giants.

Astrologically, the planets embody the energy and inherent qualities of a specific sign of the zodiac. The inner bodies—the sun, moon, Mercury, Venus, and Mars—all move relatively quickly through the zodiac, meaning their effect is more intense and intimate.

Mercury, named for the messenger of the Roman gods, is the smallest planet and the one closest to the sun, which it takes 88 earth days to orbit. One day takes a surprising 176 earth days. It has no atmosphere, and temperatures range from 800 degrees F by day to -290 degrees F at night.

Venus, the morning star or evening star, is named for the Roman goddess of love. It spins in the opposite direction from most other planets. Its dense atmosphere creates a greenhouse effect making it extremely hot. One Venusian day equals 243 earth days, and one year equals 225 earth days.

Mars, named for the Roman god of war, has a thin atmosphere and a dusty, cold, desert climate. It gets its reddish color from iron oxide in the dirt. The visible canals on its surface were carved by ancient rivers, signs of its watery past. One day equals 24.6 hours and one year equals 687 earth days.

Jupiter, the largest planet, was named for the top Roman god, but not due to its size (which was unknown at that point), but rather because it was such a bright presence in the sky. Its atmosphere is hydrogen and helium, with cold, windy clouds of ammonia and water. A day lasts 9.93 hours and its trip around the sun takes 11.86 earth years.

Saturn, with its spectacular system of icy rings, is named for the father of Jupiter, the Roman god of wealth and agriculture. This gas giant, the second largest planet in our Solar System, is made mostly of hydrogen and helium. A days last 10.7 hours, while it takes 29 earth years to orbit the sun.

Uranus, an ice giant that rotates on its side, was the first planet discovered by telescope. The atmosphere is composed of molecular hydrogen and atomic helium with small amounts of methane. A day takes a speedy 17 hours, but orbiting the sun takes 84 earth years.

Neptune, an ice giant that was the first planet predicted mathematically before discovery, it was named for the Roman god of the sea. Its surface is dark and cold, whipped by supersonic winds. One full revolution takes 16 hours, but it takes 165 earth years to circle the sun.

Researchers now believe...

...there are more planets than stars in our galaxy, the Milky Way. The current count for our Solar System is eight, but some systems may have numerous free-floating rogue planets that do not orbit in addition to those that do orbit stars.

Astronomy Primer

Moons

Moons are defined as satellites that orbit around planets or asteroids. Our Solar System contains more than 200 moons—Mercury and Venus are the only planets that lack them.

Astrologically, the earth's moon represents emotions, a person's comfort zone, their nurturing side, and how they express feelings and vulnerability. When a person's ruling planet also has moons, especially a lot of moons, like Jupiter or Saturn, these could have some effect on the possible outcomes of a natal chart, just as the gravitational pull of the moons themselves can effect their host planet.

THE MOON

Earth's moon is the fifth largest natural satellite in the Solar System but the largest in relation to the size of the planet it orbits. It acts as a stabilizing force for earth, and its gravity affects both tides and landscape. Based on current data, it is the second densest satellite after Jupiter's moon Io. Due to "synchronous rotation" it always presents the same face to the earth; its visible side is marked by large dark plains (called volcanic "maria") that make up spaces between the bright, ancient crustal highlands and the prominent impact craters. In spite of its bright glow, the moon's surface is actually about as reflective as worn asphalt.

Theories abound on how the moon was formed, but the general consensus is that a planet the size of Mars slammed into earth about 4.5 billion years ago. The debris from this collision collected around the earth and gradually formed into a sphere.

PLANETARY MOONS

Mars has two small moons, Phobos and Deimos, which were only discovered in 1877. They are both lumpy and cratered and, like earth's moon, always present the same face to Mars.

Jupiter has 53 named moons and at least 26 without names. The four largest, called the Galilean satellites, are: Io, the most volcanic body in the Solar System; Europa, with a surface of watery ice and which may be able to sustain life; Ganymede, the largest moon in the Solar System (larger than the planet Mercury!), and ancient, cratered Callisto, which offers a glimpse into the history of the Solar System.

Saturn has 53 named moons and 29 awaiting confirmation and naming. The giant moon called Titan is larger than Mercury, while others may only be the size of a football field. These many moons shape, contribute to, and collect matter from Saturn's famous rings.

Uranus has at least 27 moons, which unlike other planetary moons are not named for mythological figures, but for characters taken from Shakespeare and Alexander Pope. Oberon and Titania are the largest and were the first to be sighted in 1787. The inner moons appear to be half water ice and half rock, the outer ones are likely captured asteroids.

Neptune was discovered by a Berlin observatory in 1846 and its largest moon, Triton, was discovered only 17 days later by amateur astronomer (and beer brewing magnate) William Lassell. There are 14 known moons circling Neptune, but only icy Triton rotates in opposition to its host planet's orbit.

Moony Over Names

Apparently a lot of parents-to-be are inspired to name their offspring after this familiar and beloved celestial body. There are more than 100 names from around the world that mean or relate to the "moon" including: Aidey (Kazakh), Alcmene, Menodore, Selene (Greek), Bulan (Indonesian), Chandra (Hindu), Dal (Korean), Ehann, Hilal (Arabic), Elatha (Celtic), Getsumei, Tsukiko (Japanese), Iah (Egyptian), Ilargi (Basque), Indumathi (Tamil), Jaci (Tupian), Jericho (Hebrew), Kuu (Finnish), Losna (Etruscan), Luna (Latin), Lusine (Armenian), Mahina (Hawaiian), Mahsa (Persian), Mani (Norse), Marama (M ori), Metzli (Nuhuatl), Monday (Old English), Mwezi (Swahili), Purnama (Malay), Rakesh, Purnima (Sanskrit), Tarkik (Inuktitut), and Tunkay, Feray, Nuray (Turkish).

Stars

Stars are the building blocks of galaxies . . . and arguably the most widely recognized objects in the night sky. They form inside the clouds of dust found in most galaxies, from examples like the Orion Nebula. Within these clouds, turbulence causes knots of sufficient mass that the gas and dust begins to collapse in on itself due to gravitational attraction. As this occurs, the material at the center of the mass begins to heat up, creating a protostar, the core of an actual star.

Often, these spinning clouds break up into two or more masses, explaining why the Milky Way is full of paired or grouped stars. Sometimes not all the space material is absorbed into the star and instead it becomes planets, comets, or asteroids.

Stars are fueled by nuclear fusion deep in their interiors, of hydrogen atoms fusing to form helium and creating enormous energy. This flow of energy provides enough pressure to keep stars from collapsing under their own weight and it also allows them to shine brightly. By studying the age, composition, and distribution of stars, astronomers can trace the evolution of a galaxy.

In ancient times, observers of the sky could not

know that stars were far distant luminous balls of gas—they most often ascribed myths or legends to their origins—but they did know that stars were fixed in the sky, unlike the "wandering stars" we now call planets.

Astrologically, the stars that form constellations are the chief indicators of traits and future paths (see the next spread), but there are some astrologers that also factor in fixed stars, such as Sirius or Aldebaran, believing that their positions can have an effect on a natal chart.

The Sun

The star at the heart of the Solar System is classified as a yellow dwarf. A star of this size takes roughly 50 million years to evolve, and will likely last another 10 billion. The sun's electric currents generate a magnetic field that is carried out into the Solar System by the solar wind, electrically charged gas that streams outward in every direction. The sun's interaction with earth is responsible for seasons, ocean currents, climate, weather, radiation belts, and the aurorae.

In astrology, the sun is considered the king of "planets" and is the ruler of fatherhood and the soul. The strength of a planet

The Origin of the Milky Way

Many cultures had stories to explain the vast field of stars that make up the galaxy. In the Kalahari Desert the people believed a lonely girl threw embers from a fire into the blank night sky and created the stars. The Cherokee explained that a mythological dog stealing cornmeal scattered it across the heavens. Finns called the Milky Way the "pathway of the birds." The Greeks believed Heracles was taken by his father Zeus to suckle from Hera, his wife, as she slept. When she awoke, she thrust the child away . . . and her milk became the stars. The Hindus thought of the stars as a dolphin swimming through the far reaches of space. In East Asia, the "river of Heaven" separated two lovers who were allowed to meet once a year.

Above: Tintoretto The Origin of the Milky Way, c.1575
National Gallery, London

on a person's birth chart can be affected by how distant that planet is from the sun. The sun is strongest when it is in Aries, Leo, and Sagittarius and it is also exalted in Aries at 10 degrees. It is weakest in Libra, where it is debilitated at 10 degrees.

According to Vedic astrology if the sun is strong in a person's birth chart (or kundali) they may become extremely powerful. Sun is benevolent to the moon, Mars, and Jupiter, but is hostile to Saturn and Venus; Mercury is neutral to sun.

Astronomy Primer

Constellations

Constellations are groupings of stars in the night sky that appear, as seen from the perspective of those on earth, to form the recognizable shape of a god, human, animal, bird, fish, or inanimate object. It is almost certain that our earliest ancestors made these connections between certain star patterns and stories from their own mythologies or beliefs.

Some scholars believe that a number of the 17,000-year-old cave drawings in Lascaux, France, portray the constellation Taurus and star patterns like Orion's belt.

Due to the vast distances that lie between stars in space, when stars appear near each other in a constellation, that relationship is an illusion. Some stars may be located closer to our solar system, others farther out in the universe. Some large stars may appear small and some smaller ones may appear unusually bright. The brightest star, according to astronomers, is Sirius (the Dog Star), which lies in the constellation Canis Major. Because stars exhibit independent, albeit incredibly slow, motion, eventually the configuration of

Above: Taurus and Orion's Belt in the Caves of Lasceaux; Opposite: **Planisphaerion Coeleste** (WikiCommons);

Stars Out of Sync

Due to the wobbling of the earth on its axis—a phenomenon called precession caused by the gravitational pull of the sun and moon—the start of the zodiac has moved. The first point of Aries, which lay at 0 degrees on the ecliptic 2,500 years ago, is now at 36 degrees. This means every sign in tropical astrology has shifted into the next month's sign. Cancer, which once started on June 22 now doesn't begin until July 20. Most Western astrologers intentionally overlook this shift, basing their findings on the zodiac positions of the past. In India's sidereal astrology, Jyotisha, the positions of the constellations are accurate.

constellations will change. After tens or hundreds of thousands of years, the outlines will become unfamiliar to viewers on earth.

To give visible objects in the sky a relationship with each other, astronomers and navigators "project" them onto an abstract backdrop called the celestial sphere. This sphere has an arbitrarily large radius and is concentric to earth; it may be centered upon earth or upon the observer. According to the equatorial coordinate system, the celestial equator divides the sphere into northern and southern hemispheres.

Through the passing centuries, sky watchers altered constellations in shape or size; some of them maintained popularity, others grew obscure. Different cultures or nations had

their own constellations, a few enduring into the modern age, until the recognition of these star formations was internationally standardized.

The 48 traditional Western constellations were established by the Greeks and were listed in poet Aratus's *Phenomena* and in astronomer Ptolemy's *Almagest*. As 15th century Europeans began to explore the southermost reaches of the planet, they added southern constellations, like Crux (the Southern Cross), to the list.

Today, there are 88 constellations, which were formally recognized by the International Astronomical Union in 1922. Any point in a celestial coordinate system, which helps tracks planets, moons, satellites, etc., will be found in a constellation. The

Bayer designation, originating with 16th-century German celestial cartographer Johann Bayer, gives each star a Greek or Latin letter followed by the genitive form of its constellation name—for instance the bright star Rigel is ß Orionis. The Flamsteed designation identifies a naked-eye star by assigning a number and the genitive name of its constellation—61 Cygni is a binary star system in Cygnus. John Flamsteed introduced this method in his book, *Historia Coelestis Britannica*.

The origins of the 12 constellations of the ancient zodiac, which straddle the ecliptic path that the earth, moon, and planets all traverse, are clouded, but the divisions were probably developed by Babylonian or Chaldean astronomers, c. 400 BC.

Planets in Retrograde

In recent years the warning, "Be careful, Mercury is in retrograde"—meaning things are really going downhill—has become quite prevalent. The phrase seems to auger some planetary thuggery on the part of this small rocky orb, something we must endure several times a year. During this period, for instance, small household objects tumble from shelves, keys and cell phones get lost, and day-to-day life becomes a challenge. A sullen, distasteful mood hangs in the air.

But what exactly is retrograde and does it effect other planets?

From an astronomical viewpoint, "apparent retrograde motion" occurs when a planet appears to be moving backwards. This is merely an illusion; called parallax, it is the apparent change of position of an object when viewed from different positions or distances. It is similar to when you start to accelerate after a stop light and the car beside you speeds away, making your car seem to move backward slightly. It is not, of course, but for an instant it feels that way. The retrograde motion of planets is simply created when earth passes a slower-moving planet farther out in orbit. All planets go retrograde, some more tellingly than others. Astrologers advise taking a breather from critical tasks during especially potent retrograde periods.

Mercury:

The planet with the bad press lies closest to the sun and goes retrograde for three weeks, three or four times annually. These "down" periods can make some people feel like their lives are going backward. This is not the time to start any new projects.

Reviewing your past endeavors and looking for life lessons makes more sense.

Venus:

The planet of love and money goes retrograde about every 18 months for about 6 weeks. This is the time to evaluate relationships and budgets. Old emotional wounds may reopen or bad financial habits could resurface. Use this period to improve your sense of self-worth.

Mars:

The ruler of physical energy, personal momentum, and the sex drive goes retrograde every two years for about two and a half months. This furnishes an opportunity to channel energy into productive or pleasurable endeavors. But be careful . . . sticky issues that have been back-burnered will undoubtled arise and should be dealt with once and for all.

Jupiter:

This space giant, the giver of luck and gifts, retrogrades about a third of every year, averaging 120 days of appearing to move

Main image: Mercury

Uranus:

Another long-hauler, Uranus is in a retrograde for 22 weeks or 40 percent of the calendar. At this time, the planet-driven need for freedom, change, and uproar is eased . . . and there is time to revisit and perhaps even accomplish older plans.

Neptune:

Neptune is retrograde for 23 weeks (43 percent of the calendar year), at which time it instructs people on how they deceive themselves, hold in fears, and create unhealthy attachments. On the plus side, it is always beneficial to view oneself more clearly. When Neptune is being direct, it has a habit of distorting reality into a falsely happy glow, so the planet is actually more useful while retrograde.

Pluto:

Even though Pluto has been scientifically reclassified as a planetoid, astrologers still

Wandering Stars...

The quirky track of retrograde motion is the reason planets got that name: *planetes asteres* means "wandering stars" in ancient Greek. Early astronomers naturally observed retrograde motion, but had no way to explain it.

backward. Fortunately, Jupiter produces one of the gentlest retrogrades, and is said to bring good fortune anywhere it appears in a chart. People must remember, though, not to coast through these times, but to understand that fulfilling dreams requires work.

Saturn:

Like its big brother, Jupiter, Saturn retrogrades for a third of a year. When the planet is direct, it can be quite a taskmaster—asking people to be focused on working hard, meeting goals, and leading a balanced life. Retrograde allows a time to take a break from discipline and lessons and look back at the things that were learned earlier.

consider it an influencer planet when calculating a birth chart. And no wonder . . . it is in retrograde for fully half a year or an average of 186 days. In retrograde, Pluto encourages the examination of one's relationship with power: Is it beckoning or frightening? Is it wielded to harm others? Are others wielding it against the querent? This might be the perfect time to accept one's inner power and help others to do the same.

Polarity and the Four Elements

The calculation of astrological indicators based on birth sign has traditionally included other factors that may affect outcomes and trends. These factors include polarity, the four elements, modality, and ruling planets.

Polarity

This relates to the concept that some birth signs identify more with the masculine, while others lean toward the feminine. These disignations have nothing to do with the gender of the person being charted, but rather with the alignment of the energy associated with each sign.

Masculine signs (also called positive or active, or *yang* in Chinese astrology) are more concerned with the external, outward world—business, finance, careers, ambitions, planning, innovating, etc. The signs are more extroverted in how they express themselves and their goals, motivated by those around them and their surroundings, and prompted by the idea of worldly rewards or success. Masculine signs are the odd-numbered divisions of the zodiac, the air and fire signs: Aries, Gemini, Leo, Libra, Sagitarius, and Aquarius.

Feminine signs (also called negative or passive, or *yin* in Chinese astrology) reflect the internal world—thoughts, emotions, reactions, aspirations, relationships, memories, etc. They tend to be more introverted, receiving inspiration from solitude and self-containment. Their goals may include using their innate talents or working at whatever gives them pleasure. Feminine signs are made up of the even numbered divisions, the water and earth signs: Taurus, Cancer, Virgo, Scorpio, Capricorn, Pisces.

Elements

In Western astrology, each sign of the zodiac is represented by one of four elements: fire, air, earth, and water. (In China these elements are wood, fire, earth, metal, and water.) Although each element is shared by three signs, the signs manifest the element's effects and traits in different ways. The elements also impact relationships: earth and water, as well as air and fire, get along, yet water douses fire, while air floats above earth.

 Fire: This element presents a duality—fire can heat a home or destroy it; a candlabra can illuminate a room or blind someone with its brightness. Even the adjective "fiery" can be spoken as a compliment or leveled as a criticism. Fire is also ritualized, used in many ceremonies and almost every religion, from lighting votives in church to eternal flames placed at gravesites. In Chinese astrology fire is a yang element called *huo*, symbolizing passion and strength yet countered with impatience and aggression. The three fire signs are Aries, Leo, and Sagittarius.

 Earth: Not surprisingly, those influenced by this element are grounded, practical, and steady. Earth signs deal with physical reality, the body, and tangible possessions, such as money. While they can be pessimistic, these signs are ready to offer sound advice and bring others down to ... earth. The three earth signs are Taurus, Virgo, and Capricorn.

Air: The element of air oversees thoughts, words, and communication. Air energy is logical, using active reasoning to make sense of the world. It is symbolized by human breath, a necessity for life. Air signs are powerful, adventurous and not restrained by boundaries, but they can suffer from abandoning reality and indulging in too much fantasy. They often prefer talking about a project over actually doing it. In the Chinese zodiac, air becomes *qi*, the ultimate force that can be found in everything. The three air signs are Gemini, Libra, and Aquarius.

 Water: This element deals with emotion and intuition, with wants and needs. Like water, these signs are able to flow freely around those near them and sense their feelings and requirements. They are private and mysterious, but can also be both sympathetic and empathetic. Yes, they are sometimes overly emotional, but make up for this by offering comfort during times of stress. The water signs are Cancer, Scorpio, and Pisces.

Modality and the Ruling Planets

Modality

Astrologers are also able to interpret the zodiac through a sign's modality, which furnishes an additional way to understand its energy or "vibe." There are three modalities, each represented by four signs.

Cardinal Signs: Each of these four signs—Aries (fire), Cancer (water), Libra (air), and Capricorn (earth)—initiates the seasons of spring, summer, autumn, and winter (or the opposite seasons in the Southern Hemisphere). They are called cardinal signs, originating from the Latin for "important," because they mark a seasonal turning point. Their stars are also related to solstices and equinoxes. Sometimes called reacting signs, they are known for stimulating action and producing results. No idle loiterers found here, but rather inspired go-getters with vision, motivation, and execution who believe if a person can dream it, they can achieve it.

Fixed Signs: These four signs—Taurus (earth), Leo (fire), Scorpio (water), and Aquarius (air)—are the persistant closers of the zodiac, determined, stable, and deep. They stick with their tasks to such an extent that their motto could be "Get 'er done." On the other hand, those with this astrological profile can be stubborn, inflexible, and opinionated: They typically need to be "right" and will fight for their beliefs, even if misguided. Once set on a course, they move doggedly forward, and little will draw them from their path.

Mutable Signs: These four signs—Gemini (air), Virgo (earth), Sagittarius (fire), and Pisces (water)—mark the end of the seasons in temperate regions. They represent the admirable qualities of adaptability, flexibility, and sympathy. These are the skilled mediators, known to be diplomatic and helpful, especially with those experiencing changes or transitions. The downside is that they can seem inconsistent and uncommitted and may even be perceived as unreliable.

Ruling Planets

Each sun sign has a ruling planet; that planet's "domicile" is the zodiac sign over which it presides. Not surprisingly, the planet exerts a more powerful effect when positioned within its sign. This is known as "domal dignity" and it is the strongest of the five essential dignities of a planet. (*See* Dignities in Chapter 4, Modern Western Astrology.)

Ruling Planets

Sun Sign/Rising Sign	Ruling planet	Traits
Aries/Aries rising	**Mars**	Leadership, action oriented
Taurus/Taurus rising	**Venus**	Seeks comfort
Gemini/Gemini rising	**Mercury**	Clever, communicative
Cancer/Cancer rising	**Moon**	Nurturing, emotional
Leo/Leo rising	**Sun**	Warm, creative
Virgo/Virgo rising	**Mercury/Chiron**	Healing, resourceful
Libra/Libra rising	**Venus**	Romantic, caring
Scorpio/Scorpio rising	**Mars/Pluto**	Deeply connected, passionate
Sagittarius/Sagittarius rising	**Jupiter**	Assertive, yearns to travel
Capricorn/Capricorn rising	**Saturn**	Mature, disciplined
Aquarius/Aquarius rising	**Saturn/Uranus**	Eccentric, humane
Pisces/Pisces rising	**Jupiter/Neptune**	Empathetic, idealistic

Ruling Planets for Days of the Week / Ruling Planet Gemstones

Day of the Week	Ruling Planet	Gemstone
Monday	**Moon**	**Moonstone** for intuition and purpose
Tuesday	**Mars**	**Ruby** for passion and energy
Wednesday	**Mercury**	**Emerald** for calm and balance
Thursday	**Jupiter**	**Yellow sapphire** for happiness and prosperity
Friday	**Venus**	**Diamond** for love and beauty
Saturday	**Saturn**	**Blue sapphire** for sincerity and faithfulness
Sunday	**Sun**	**Citrine** for abundance and radiance

In addition to a sun sign with a ruling planet, people also have what is called a rising, or ascendent, sign, based on which constellation was on the eastern horizon at their birth. Each rising sign has an accompanying ruling planet that oversees it. (See Chapter 4 for details.)

Many astrologers consider the ruling planets' contributions to a person's outcomes nearly equal to those of the sun signs. Some have even called them the "soul line that creates the script" of a person's life.

Originally early astrologers recognized seven "planets" in the geocentric field of vision—the sun, Mercury, Venus, the moon, Mars, Saturn, and Jupiter. When Uranus, Neptune, and Pluto (now reclassified as a dwarf planet) were discovered, some signs shifted rulership to these new additions to utilize the symbolism they represented. The result was that some signs have more than one ruling planet. It is up to the astrologer to determine which planet best fits their personality. Some modern astrologers apply co-rulership, using day and night designations for signs with two planets. For instance, Uranus may be designated the day ruler of Aquarius, while Saturn oversees the night. It helps to note when a specific planet is in retrograde or when it changes signs, because at those times people ruled by that planet will feel its effects more keenly.

Chapter Two

Ancient Origins

Babylonia

Most scholars of antiquity agree that the earliest practice of astrology occurred in the Middle East, in the fertile crescent known as Mesopotamia, the "land between two rivers"—the Tigris and Euphrates.

From the beginning of recorded history, the region was dominated by the Sumerian empire and the Akkadian empire, which included both the Babylonians and Assyrians. In 539 BC, Babylonia fell to Achaeminid—early Persian—invaders. It was then conquored by Alexander the Great in 332. Today this region is home to Iraq, Kuwait, and parts of Syria, Iran, and Turkey.

Arising during the second millennia BC, Babylonian astrology was the first organized system used to predict future events. In fact, one of the earliest historical records is the Venus tablet, featuring astrological observations and omens collected over 21 years, which was preserved from the reign of King Ammi-saduqa (1683–47 BC). Although there are indications that some form of astrology was practiced by the Sumerians in the 3rd millennium, BC, there is not enough evidence that the culture utilized a fully integrated theory. It is more likely that an organized system of celestial divination emerged with later Old Babylonian texts, from around 1800 BC, which continued through the Middle Babylonian and Middle Assyrian eras (c. 1200 BC).

In both Babylonia and its cultural offshoot, Assyria, astrology was one of the two ways priests (known as *bare*, or "inspectors") sought portents that indicated the intentions of the gods; the second method was studying the blemishes and marks on the livers of sacrificed animals.

The division of the zodiac into 12 units was first reported in a cuneiform inscription from 419 BC. How it evolved from the seasonal quarters of the year into this format has never been reconstructed, yet along with the planets, it has provided an enduring framework for astrology. Indeed, this early form of Babylonian astrology would eventually spread beyond Mesopotamia, carried directly or indirectly to Europe, Asia, and other regions of the Middle East. Initially, this version found its way to Greece and China, where it merged with the pre-existing forms of astrology found in those cultures.

Signs From the Gods

Just as they ascertained messages from the gods via liver divination, Babylonian priests also sought signs and indicators from planets and stars that were associated with specific gods.

Marduk
Patron god of Babylon; associated with the planet Jupiter

Ishtar
Goddess of love, beauty, war, and justice; associated with the planet Venus

Ninurta (Ninib)
God of farming; associated with the planet Saturn

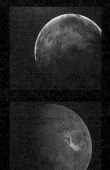

Nabu (Nebo)
God of literacy, scribes, and wisdom; associated with the planet Mercury

Nergal
God of war and pestilence; associated with the planet Mars

The activity of these five significant planets, along with that of the sun god, Shamesh, and the moon goddess, Sin/Selardi, was believed to determine occurrences on earth. Those skilled in reading these movements could then anticipate the intentions of the gods, possibly forestalling negative outcomes and thus gaining great prestige and influence. Astrologers used two methods for interpretating the skies: the collected writings of their predecessors recounting what events had occurred during celestial phenomena; and an association of ideas, where a past phenomenon was accompanied by a significant change in status quo. The traditional mariner's maxim "Red sky at night, sailors' delight. Red sky at morning, sailors take warning." is an example of this association of ideas.

 **Aries**
LUHUNGA

 Cancer
NANGAR

 Taurus
GUANNA or MUL

 Leo
U-RA

 Gemini
MASTABAGALGAL or MASH

 Virgo
ABSIN

By 1500 BC, the Babylonians had already created a zodiac consisting of 12 equal signs, which had familiar symbols—the Great Twins, the Lion, the Scales, etc., which were later incorporated into Greek astrology. The chart above and opposite draws a rough correlation between the Babylonian names for constellations and those of the Western zodiac.

Babylonians also believed in a form of astral medicine, whereby astrology determined which medications should be prepared on which dates to be most effective. The calendar and astrology were also deeply entwined: the calendar was often based on lunar cycles, and lunar omens were among the most prevelent, especially eclipses. Furthermore, because gods and goddesses were associated with certain times, months, and days, their festivals and celebrations had to be factored in as each year's calendar was created.

The Assyrians, who conquored Babylonia in 729 BC had also developed a system of constellations, and they placed great importance on the movement of the five key planets (and their godly inhabitants) into these constellations.

Libra
ZIHANITUM

Capricorn
SUHUR

Scorpio
GIA-TAB

Aquarius
GU or GULA

Sagittarius
PAH

Pisces
ZIB

The King's Library

Ashurbanipal was an Assyrian king in the 7th century BC. In Nineveh, he amassed a great library of cuneiform tablets that focused on astrology, mythology, history, and science. Two of his astrologers, Rammanu-sumausar and Nabu-musisi, became so adept at reading celestial omens that the king's couriers announced the details throughout the empire, and the king himself used the reports for his political advantage. When his kingdom fell to the Medes and Chaldean Babylonians, the library was destroyed and its tablets dispersed.

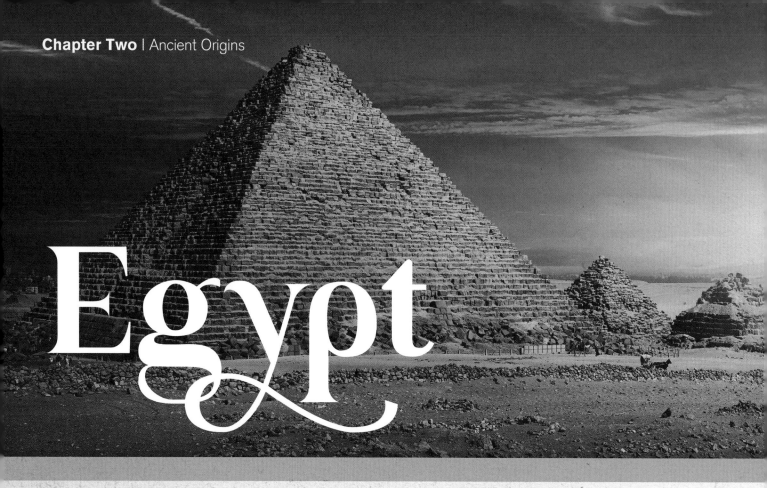

Egypt

Astrology formed a key part of the Egyptian belief system—it became perhaps as close to a religion here as astrology ever got—and as a result the country became a major contributor to its development and evolution.

Above: The Pyramids of Giza; Opposite, top: The Dendera Zodiac; Opposite, bottom: Petosiris's Circle

Astronomical observations certainly inspired ancient builders: the fifth millennium BC stone circles at Nabta Playa may have used astronomical alignments, while the pyramids were carefully aligned toward the pole star. Yet those early Egyptians also sought guidance from the night skies, believing that the star configurations people were born under influenced their personalities, lives, and destinies.

The Persians conquered Egypt in 525 BC, no doubt adding Mesopotamian influences to Egyptian astrology. The Alexandrian conquest of 332 BC brought Egypt under

Hellenistic rule, and around the late second or early first century BC, Babylonian astrology with its planetary emphasis became mixed with Egypt's Decanic practice, giving birth to "horoscopic" astrology. Decans were a system of time measurement employed by Egyptian astrologers and based on certain constellations; their risings were used to divide the night into "hours."

Of particular importance to horoscopic astrology was Claudius Ptolemy of Alexandria (c. AD 100–170). Both an astrologer and astronomer, Ptolemy wrote the *Tetrabiblos*, a foundation work of Western

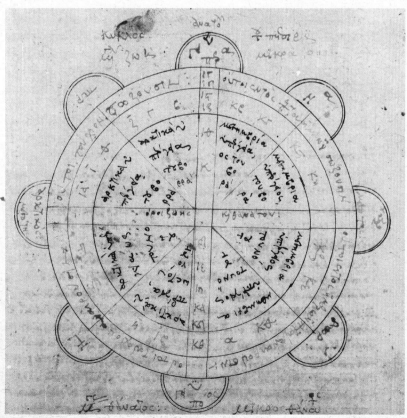

Star Points...

The ancient Egyptians spent so much time gazing at the heavens for signs that they actually practiced sharpening their vision by studying the movement of clouds.

astrology. Even a thousand years later, it was said to have a status similar to that of the Bible for astrological writers.

Many notable astrologers followed in the wake of Ptolemy: Paul of Alexandria, Hephaestion of Thebes, and Palchus. Ptolemy's work was also advanced and commented on by three mathematicians: the Alexandrians Pappus and Theon, and the Greek Proclus. According to Roman astrologer Firmicus Maternus, the Hellenistic (Greek) astrologers of Egypt traced the root of their discipline to Nechepso and Petosiris, a 4th century BC pharoah and his high priest, who first noted an ancient divination technique involving numerology, the lunar month, and a circular diagram.

The Nile
Qualities: Symbol of new starts; passion for life, avoids conflict, dreams big
Decans: January 1-7, June 19-28, September 1-7, and November 18-26
Greek influence: n/a

Amon-ra:
Qualities: Leaderlike, confident, motivating, encouraging
Decans: January 8-21 and February 1-11
Greek influence: April 26 – May 25

Mut
Qualities: Nurtering, logical, practical, maternal
Decans: January 22-31 and September 8-22
Greek influence: n/a

Geb
Qualities: Kind, sensitive, intuitive, consciousness of environment,
Decans: February 12-29 and August 20-31
Greek influence: n/a

Osiris
Qualities: Dual natured— strong and vulnerable, independent, enthusiastic
Decans: March 1-10 and November 27 – December 18
Greek influence: March 27 – April 25

Isis
Qualities: Direct, protective, energetic, playful
Decans: March 11-31, October 18-29, and December 19-31
Greek influence: February 25 – March 26

Thoth
Qualities: Problem-solving, good memory, romantic, stable
Decans: April 1-19 and November 8-17
Greek influence: August 29 – September 27

Horus
Qualities: Courageous, optimistic, ambitious, needs to be in charge
Using decans: April 20 – May 7 and August 12-19
Based on Greek influence: September 28 – October 27

Anubis
Qualities: Seeks solitude, introverted, passionate, even tempered
Decans: May 8-27 and June 29 – July 13
Greek influence: July 25 – August 28

Seth
Qualities: Perfectionist, needs to roam, good communicator
Decans: May 28 – June 18 and September 28 – October 2
Greek influence: n/a

Bastet
Qualities: Peacemaker, intuitive, insightful of others, motivator
Using decans: July 14-28, September 23-27, and October 3-17
Greek influence: n/a

Sekhmet:
Qualities: Down-to-earth, intelligent, authoritative, balanced
Decans: July 29 – August 11 and October 30 – November 7
Greek influence: November 27 – December 26

HORUS　　OSIRIS　　ISIS　　ANUBIS　　ECHNATON

The Egyptian Zodiac

There are 12 signs in the Egyptian zodiac, featuring Egyptian gods and the Nile, and 30 groupings of stars, or decans. Two people may share the same sign, but be born under different decans and have different paths foretold. This list also shows the date ranges for each sign based on Greek influence. Below are the additional gods and their date ranges used in the Greek-influenced Egyptian Zodiac.

Wadjet

Qualities: Loyal, rational, cautious, ambitious

**Greek influence:
October 28 – November 26**

Sphinx

Qualities: Adaptable, stern, shrewd, self-disciplined

**Greek influence:
December 27 – January 25**

Shu

Qualities: Humorous, creative, principled, conscientious

**Greek influence:
January 26 – February 24**

Hathor

Qualities: Charming, outgoing, romantic, expressive

**Greek influence:
May 26 – June 24**

Phoenix

Qualities: Seizes opportunities, optimistic, guarded, caring

**Greek influence:
June 25 – July 24**

The **Acropolis** in Athens; **Inset:** Delphi, in ancient times was a sacred precinct that served as **the seat of Pythia**, the major oracle who was consulted about important decisions throughout the ancient classical world.

Greece

The occupation of Greece by Alexander the Great's forces in 332 BC, followed by his conquest of Asia, exposed the Greeks to many new influences from the cultures of Syria, Persia, Babylon, and central Asia.

Meanwhile, Greek soon replaced cuneiform as the language of intellectual expression. And so when the Middle Eastern astrological texts were translated from cuneiform to Greek, it sparked Grecian interest in the study of the stars and their omens. Around 280 BC a priest of Bel named Berrossus moved to the Greek island of Kos in order to teach astrology and Babylonian culture to the Greeks. As this new pursuit swept the

Hellenic world, it gave rise to what historian and astrologer Nicholas Campion called an "innovative energy." This Eastern form of astrology was both complex and varied, with many different forms eventually emerging.

By the 1st century BC, two types of astrology had evolved in Greece. The first version dealt with a person's current life and required the reading of horoscopes to determine precise details about the past, present, and future. The second variation was theurgic, having to do with "god-work," and focused on the soul's ascent to the stars, a belief the Hellenic culture shared with the Egyptians. This version focused on personal transformation, with astrology allowing a sort of dialogue with the gods.

Affairs of State

Kings and military leaders and other wealthy patrons who could afford astrologers relied on horoscopes to advise them on matters of state, warcraft, finance, and personal relations. These predictions for the upcoming days, months, or even years were created in ways very similar to today, by calculating where in the sky an individual's particular constellation was located at the time of their birth. Astrology eventually became associated with three different philosophical schools— those of Plato, Aristotle, and the Stoics. All three schools of thought shared the concept that the cosmos was a single, living, integrated whole. That the stars and planets should foretell events on earth did not seem a foreign concept in the least. In fact, the science of mathematical astronomy developed in large part in order to bolster the accuracy of astrological predictions.

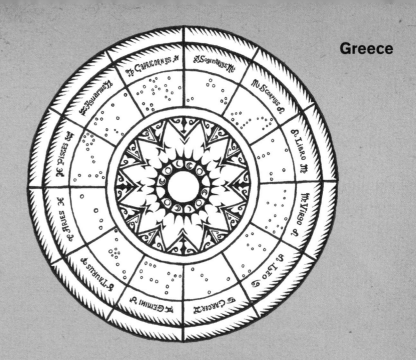

Naming the Zodiac

Greek poets and astronomers drew on the names of their gods and goddesses to identify the planets that shone in the night sky, while the constellations were given names that reflected the shapes they created. Twelve constellations were used to identify the signs that appear on the Zodiac circle. A 13th sign was listed by Ptolemy as Ophiuchus, meaning the "serpent holder" in Greek. It was not commonly used, however. Each sign was also assigned a "ruling" body, a planet, moon, or star.

English	Greek	Symbol	Ruling Body
Aries	**Krios**	Ram	Mars
Taurus	**Tavros**	Bull	Venus
Gemini	**Didimoi**	Twins	Mercury
Cancer	**Karkinos**	Crab	Moon
Leo	**Leon**	Lion	Sun
Virgo	**Parthenos**	Maiden	Mercury, Chiron
Libra	**Zygos**	Golden scales	Venus
Scorpio	**Skorpios**	Scorpion	Pluto
Sagittarius	**Toksotis**	Archer	Jupiter
Capricorn	**Aigokeros**	God with goat's body/fish tail	Saturn
Aquarius	**Ydrohoos**	Water bearer	Uranus
Pisces	**Ihtheis**	Pair of fish facing two directions	Neptune

Two key sites of **ancient Rome,** 'the eternal city': **The Imperial Forum**, and inset, **The Coliseum**

Rome

Astrology was a central feature of ancient Roman society, democratized to the point that it was practiced equally in the streets and in the imperial palaces. Noted astrologers were akin to rock stars, feted and in great demand.

Like much of Roman culture, astrology was yet another "contribution" from the Greeks. Both the Greeks and Romans so identified Babylonia and Chaldea with astrology that the term "Chaldean wisdom" came to mean divining the future through the planets and stars. Astrology was even considered a form of natural science, akin to the study of plants or animals.

Not surprisingly, the emperors of Rome used astrological findings to justify their decisions and to maintain their "divine" power over the populace. Ceasar Augustus, the first emperor, insisted his rise to the throne was foretold by his horoscope, and so he had his birth sign, Capricorn, struck onto Roman coins. Furthermore, Capricorn, the "father of the Zodiac," is controlled by the planet Saturn, which is the symbol of rules and rulers. The god Saturn was said to have overseen Rome's predecessor city during a golden age in the distant, mythological past. Some emperors themselves became avid students of astrology, as did celebrated figures of state, philosophers, and poets. These included the politician Cicero, the neo-Platonic philosopher Plotinus, and the poets Virgil, Ovid, and Horace. Marcus Manilius, a poet/astrologer who lived at the beginning of the common era, joined Alexandrian Ptolemy as a representative of learned astrology. From Manilius came the oldest surviving complete astrological textbook. Although his *Astronomica* was written in poetic form, it nevertheless systematically explained the cosmos using a Stoic metaphor—a divine order with its astrological laws.

The more radical astrologers of Rome insisted heavenly bodies neither influenced nor caused events on earth, but rather were timing devices that measured the rise and fall of humanity's doings. They held that the future already existed and that their task was to intervene and alter that future in favor of their clients. This meant astrology was a type of "participation mystique," where time and space were seen as one entity, and individuals could derive benefits from interacting with it.

Troubled Times

Around the 4th century AD, Western horoscopic astrology found itself facing a number of serious challenges: in addition to disputes over what exactly astrology could or could not do and the frequent lack of precision in the predictions, it also had to contend with the rise of Christianity and the decline of classical culture in Western Europe. As a result, interest in celestial divination began to steadily wane. It did manage to hang on in Persia, where it had a powerful influence on Indian astrology. From India it was conveyed to the Islamic world, when Hellenistic astrology was

Ancient Roman coin showing Capricorn on the obverse

revived in the 8th century. It eventually returned to Latinate Europe in the 12 century.

Notable Roman Astrologers

Nigidus Figullus: This scholar/occultist of the late Republic was friends with statesman and philosopher Cicero. He tried to revive the theories of Pythagoreanism, which included math, astronomy, and astrology. Medieval tradition portrayed him as a magician.

Julius Firmicus Maternus: A Roman writer and astrologer conversant in Greek, he lived during the reign of Constantine I and became a Christian apologist.

Marcus Manilius: This poet/astrologer was the author of the five-volume poem *Astronomica*.

Paulus Alexandrinus: This astrologer of the late Roman empire penned *Eisagokica*, or *Introductory Matters*, covering the astrological practices of his era.

Other notable astrologers of the Roman Empire include Teucros, Antiochos, Dorotheus, Manetho, Vettius Valens, Hediodoros, and Hephaiston of Thebes. (*See* Chapter Three: Fabled Astrologers)

Gods in the Sky

Nearly every early culture identified the five eye-visible planets that orbited closest to earth, and many believed they were dieties. Other cultures may have christened those wanderers of the night sky, but the names that have remained in use were the ones given to them by the ancient Romans and drawn from their pantheon of gods.

Those five planets, along with their more recently discovered brethren, remain major factors in the interpretation of birth charts . . . and the attributes of their namesake gods are firmly associated with the effects of the planets.

Above, center: Mercury, the multifaceted god; **Above, right: Mars,** the bringer of war; **Opposite, left:** The sun god **Helios** crosses the heavens in his chariot; **Opposite, right: Saturn** looking down on the plentiful Earth

Mercury

The first planet was named for the multifaceted god of financial gain, commerce, eloquence, messages, communication, travelers, boundaries, luck, trickery, merchants, and thieves. The name may derive from the Indo-European root merĝ, for "boundary" or "border." This fits the god's role as intermediary between the upper and lower worlds. Mercury was called Hermes by the Greeks.

Venus

The bright planet behind the morning and evening "star" was named for the Roman goddess of love and sexuality. The name stems from the Proto-Italic wenos, or "desire." She was revered as Aphrodite by the Greeks.

Mars

The fiery red planet was named for the Roman god of war (as was the often-turbulent month of March). Although his Greek equivalent was Ares, Roman Mars was more of a stabilizing force for peace as opposed to a destructive, destabilizing force like his Greek counterpart.

Jupiter

A powerful presence among celestial bodies, this large, glowing planet was named for the king of the Roman pantheon and the god of the sky and thunder. The Greek version, Zeus, was much more humanized in their myths.

Saturn

This spectacularly ringed planet was named for the god Saturn. He was the father of Jupiter and god of generation, dissolution, plenty, wealth, agriculture, and liberation. His popular festival, the Saturnalia, later coincided with the Christian Christmas and was noted for reveling, feasting, and gift giving.

Uranus

Identified in the late 18th century, the planet was originally called Georgium Sidus after King George III. Other astronomers called it Herschel after its discoverer. When it was decided to follow the style of other planets by using a mythological god, Uranus was chosen. Unlike the previous names, however, Uranus represents a Greek god, that of the sky. His Roman counterpart was called Caelus.

Neptune

First sighted in 1846, this distant ice giant was initially named for one of the two astromomer's who predicted its existence, Urbain Le Verrier. It was eventually given the name of the Roman god of the sea, brother to Jupiter and Pluto. His equivalent in Greece was the powerful Poseidon.

Pluto

Discovered in 1930, this planet (now a dwarf planet) inspired a host of possible names including Lowell, Atlas, Artemis, Perseus, Tantalus, Idana, Cronus, Zymal, and Minerva. Its eventual name, Pluto, based on the Roman god of the underworld, was suggested by Venetia Burney, an 11-year-old from Oxford, England.

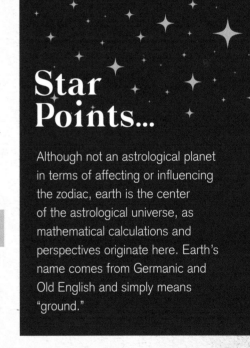

Star Points...

Although not an astrological planet in terms of affecting or influencing the zodiac, earth is the center of the astrological universe, as mathematical calculations and perspectives originate here. Earth's name comes from Germanic and Old English and simply means "ground."

The Middle East

Persia

The Persian or Achaeminid Empire was founded around 550 BC by Cyrus the Great in the region now known as Iran. Eventually stretching from Europe's Balkan Peninsula to the Indus Valley, it became one of the largest empires in history, and the world's first "super power."

Ancient Iran was home to the spiritual leader Zoroaster, who likely lived in the second millennium BC and founded Zoroastrianism, a monotheistic religion that became the state religion of the Persian Empire. The prophet reportedly incorporated astrology and sorcery into his teachings, a reputation fostered by much literature that circulated through the Mediterranean from the 3rd century BC until the early Middle Ages, and possibly beyond.

After Babylonia fell to the Persians in 539 BC, Persian rulers like Darius the Great encouraged the study of natural science, including astronomy. When a great Babylonian astronomer, Nabu-rimanni (Naburianus), was instructed to carry out a study of lunar eclipses, his calculations proved more accurate than those of Ptolemy and Copernicus. Yet the science of astronomy was still inevitably linked with—and in service to—astrology, to the point where astronomy texts made reference to connections between the stars and certain illnesses.

Although astrology lost favor in Rome sometime around the 4th century—and would disappear from Europe for many centuries, it gained new followers in the Middle East, especially during the 7th century, after the fall of

Alexandria to the Arabs, and with the rise of the Persian/Arab Abbassid Empire in the 8th century. The second Abbassid caliph, Al-Mansur, founded the city of Baghdad (near the former site of Babylon) to act as a center of learning. His civic plan included the construction of an impressive observatory and a library-translation center called Bayt al-Hikma, or "Center of Wisdom," which provided a major impetus for the ongoing translation of Hellenic astrological texts into Arabic.

Early translators included the Persian Jew Mashallah, who helped select the time for founding the city, and Sahl ibn Bishr, who influenced at least two European astrologers—Guido Bonatti in the 13th century and William Lilly in the 17th century. The scholar Abu Ma'shar (Albumasar) was considered

the reigning astrologer at the Abbassid court in Baghdad. His practical training manuals for astrologers, such as *Introductorium in Astronomiam*, greatly affected Muslim intellectual history, and after being translated, had a similar impact on the Western world and Byzantium. Al Khwarizmi, a brilliant mathematician, astronomer, astrologer, and geographer, was made head of the caliph's library.

Arabia

The Arabs were an ethnic group that arose around the 9th century BC, a tribal people found originally in the north of the Arabian Peninsula and in eastern and southern Syria. The term was at times applied to nomadic and settled Arabic-speaking Semites

found throughout the eastern Mediterranean. During the mandated Arab expansion of the caliphates (called the Muslim conquests), after the death of the prophet Mohammad, their influence extended from the south of France, throughout the Middle East and North Africa, all the way to the borders of China. With its emphasis on education and study, Arab culture contributed to many diverse fields: architecture, literature, language, philosophy, medicine, science, mythology, ethics, dance, cuisine, dress, sports, and warfare.

The Arabs were notable for increasing the world's knowledge of astronomy and named many of the most familiar stars: Aldebran, Altair, Betelgeuse, Rigel, and Vegaretain. There was also a healthy respect for the students of the stars, and astrologers were welcomed by many early rulers. As advancements in science continued apace, however, some Arabic scholars began to refute many of the claims

made by astrologers, pointing out that conclusions were typically conjectural and lacking proof, rather than empirical, i.e., confirmed by senses like observation and documentation. The naysayers also reminded advocates of astrology that the notion that the will of God could be known and predicted in advance went against strict orthodox views. These criticisms were aimed primarily at "judicial" astrology, which attempted to predict events by studying heavenly bodies and their relationship to earth, rather than at "meteorological" or "medical astrology," which were at the time viewed as aspects of natural science.

Above, left and right: Depictions of **Abu Ma'shar,** an early Persian Muslim astrologer, thought to be the greatest astrologer of the Abbasid court in Baghdad. His manuals for training astrologers greatly influenced Muslim intellectual history.

The unique heritage of **Thee Ain, Al-Baha, Saudi Arabia**

Astrology Banned

During the 7th century, the prophet Mohammad denounced the practice of astrology as haram, or a sin. In the 5th chapter of the Quran, Surah Al-Midah, it plainly says, "Forbidden also is to use arrows seeking luck or decision, all that is disobedience of Allah." Although some scholars argued that astrology should not be forbidden because it was neither an illusion nor a demonic practice, the ban was not overturned.

In spite of the edict against it, many Muslims maintained their interest in astrology because they felt spiritually connected to the heavens. This affinity was particularly strong in the nomadic Arabs who traveled the deserts at night and relied on reading the constellations in order to navigate. Thus, the stars became their guides and their signposts in more ways than one. Faithful Muslims also had to know how to direct themselves toward the Kaaba in Mecca for prayer and orient themselves inside their mosques, another reason to study astronomy—which in turn fostered the belief that astral movements affected earthly doings.

Abu'l-Rayhan Muhammad ibn Ahmad Al-Biruni (b. AD 973) was possibly the first first Muslim astrologer to propose a relationship between Islam and astrology. He created a chart in which he focused on the prominence of Mercury, the ruler of the ascendant, and with Gemini, on the cusp of the tenth house. He based his chart on the 12 houses in which he focused on the universe, human beings, and their relationship with astrology. He followed a logical path, incorporating geometry, arithmetic, astronomy, and geography. Because Islamic culture valued science, Al-Biruni's chart likely influenced enough people so that the study of astrology never faded from the Arab world. This science-based approach to the discipline was eventually imported into 12th-century Europe, where it became the basis of Renaissance astrology.

Israel & The Jews

The debates among Jewish scholars on the relationship of early Judaism to astrology have gone on for more than 2,000 years. It cannot be denied that astrological practices made their way into Jewish culture, but likely not until the beginning of the third century AD, when Jewish laws and theology were first being compliled into the Talmud. During the earlier eras of ancient Israel, the First Temple (1200–586 BC) and Second Temple (516BC–AD 70) periods, the attitude of the scriptures was clear:

"You shall not practice divination or soothsaying." (Leviticus 19:26) "When you enter the land that the LORD your God is giving you, you shall not learn to imitate the abhorrent practices of the nations. Let no one be found among you who . . . is an augur, a soothsayer, a diviner, a sorcerer, one casts spells . . . . For anyone who does these things is abhorrent to the LORD . . ." (Deuteronomy 18:9–12)

During the Second Temple period, however, historian Josephus censured the populace for ignoring what he believed were celestial signs that foretold the destruction of the Temple.

It is interesting to note that, in spite of the prohibitions against astrology, awareness of the Babylonian zodiac is reflected in the Old Testament. The animals that appear in the Book of Ezekial have been interpreted to represent aspects the zodiac. Thus the lion becomes Leo, the bull becomes Taurus, man is Aquarius, and the eagle is Scorpio. The arrangement of the 12 Tribes of Israel around the exterior of the Tabernacle possibly echoes the order of the zodiac. Author Thomas Mass even attributes characteristics of each of the 12 zodiac signs to the 12 Tribes in his novel *Joseph and his Brothers*.

The Babylonian Talmud, which was completed around AD 500, makes many references to astrology; furthermore, astrological statements were considered worthy of debate by Torah scholars. Not surprisingly, this period of Jewish history saw a loosening of the prohibitions against the practice.

Some rabbis preached that the stars determined the fates of nations and men; others believed that different periods of time could be categorized as lucky or unlucky. Rabbi Yehoshua ben Levi felt that certain days of the week were more propitious to be born on than others, and Rabbi Hanina declared that character traits were determined by the planet one was born under. Samuel of Neharia, a physician and astrologer, taught that it was dangerous to bleed a patient on a Tuesday due to the influence of Mars; others believed bleeding should not take place under a new moon, on the third of the month, or the day before a festival. According to modern Judaic scholar Jacob Neuser, "magic, astrology, and occult sciences . . . were regarded as advanced science." For the Jews to have rejected them meant rejecting all the "technological attainments of contemporary civilization."

Centuries later, scholars in the Geonic era (AD 589–1038) proposed that, while astrology may give a person certain inclinations, he or she has the power to overcome those desires and thus maintain the free will gifted to them by God.

A misconception arose during the Middle Ages that European Jews, with their heritage arising from the East, were the heirs of the Chaldeans and, therefore, masters of astrology. Unfortunately, this perceived power over the destinies of men led to Jews being regarded with awe, and often fear, factors that in later centuries led to them being further persecuted, ghettoized, and even murdered.

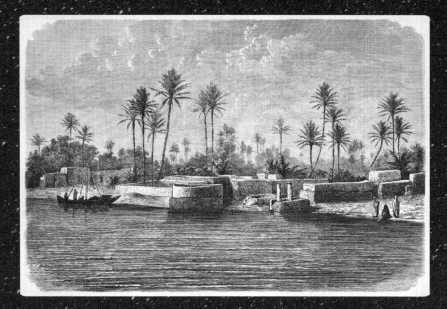

Left: An early engraving of the Eastern shores of **the Mediterranean Sea**, for thousands of years a key trading hub for the many peoples of the region; **Right:** A 19th Century French engraving of **Levantine Hebrews**

The Levant

The east coast of the Mediterranean—sometimes called the Levant—included the Western Asian countries of Syria, Lebanon, Israel, Palestine, Jordan, and Turkey and furnished a bustling trade center dating back to the time of the ancient Phoenicians.

Such hubs of commerce were naturally also cultural crossroads, where new ideas, philosophies, and trends were discussed, dissected, and disseminated. Historical influences on the astrology practiced in the region doubtless included Babylonian, Assyrian, Persian, Hellenic Egyptian, and Greek methodologies.

In much of the Levant, astrologers could be found plying their skills in bazaars and marketplaces, formulating horoscopes and predictions for passersby, while their more elevated brethren advised rulers and military leaders on critical matters of state or upcoming campaigns.

During the Middle Ages, Muslim astrologers typically employed three tools, which novices learned about from their masters while also studying astronomy and mathematics.
The astrolabe, a hand-held device able to tell the time based on the position of the sun or some other visible star;

The ephemeris, a table that was able to give the position of astronomical objects at a given time;
The dust board, a tablet covered with sand upon which calculations could be noted and then erased.

Images from the zodiac were considered to have talismanic protective powers and so were often incorporated into the art and architecture of this region, including Muslim mosques and Jewish temples. The images were also used to decorate household items, including bowls, mortars, platters, candlesticks, basins, ewers, flasks, pen boxes, and inkwells. Most often, the Greek representations of the figures of the zodiac were the versions used.

The symbol of Islam, a crescent moon and star, might seem to have astrological connotations, but modern scholars believe the emblem was chosen simply because Islam had no representative symbol, like the Hebrew Star of David or the Christian cross. Originally, the Ottoman Empire had used the crescent and star on their official flag.

India

The practice of Indian astrology is known as *Jyotisha*, a term based on *jyotish*, meaning light, such as that of the sun, moon, or other celestial bodies.

Jyotisha was one of the six disciplines, or Vedangas ("limbs of the Vedas"), used to support Vedic rituals, which included sacrificial ceremonies, rites, and chants. The Vedas are religious texts written in Sanskrit, the oldest examples in the world. Over time the Vedic culture blended with shramanic (ascetic, austere) beliefs like Jainism and Buddhism, along with many local

customs, to form the basis of modern Hinduism.

Indian astrology likely developed about the same time as the Babylonian discipline, around 3,000 BC, with earlier primitive forms perhaps extending back to 5,000 BC. The Atharva Veda, c. 1,000 BC, is a collection of 20 books that covers aspects of everyday life; they contain astrological entries in the parts known as "Mahopanishat" or "Jyothishmati." The foundation of Jyotisha is a concept called bandhu, connections that link the inner and outer worlds, the microcosm and the macrocosm. Jyotisha is reputedly the most widely practiced form of astrology in the world.

Indian astrologers believe that every occurrence in an individual's life is determined by the position of the constellations, planets, and the moon at the time of birth. Because Vedic philosophy embraces reincarnation—the concept that a living being starts a new life in a different physical body after biological death—it likewise became a factor in Indian astrology, and so the spiritual journey from past lives to present life is also taken into account. Other influences include the effects of karma (the concept that like actions cause like effects) on present life, doshas (energy patterns around the body that determine thinking and behavior), and remedies. It is thought that a supreme power oversees humanity and that, based on past karma, this force decides when a person is to be born in order for him or her to have the life for which they are best suited.

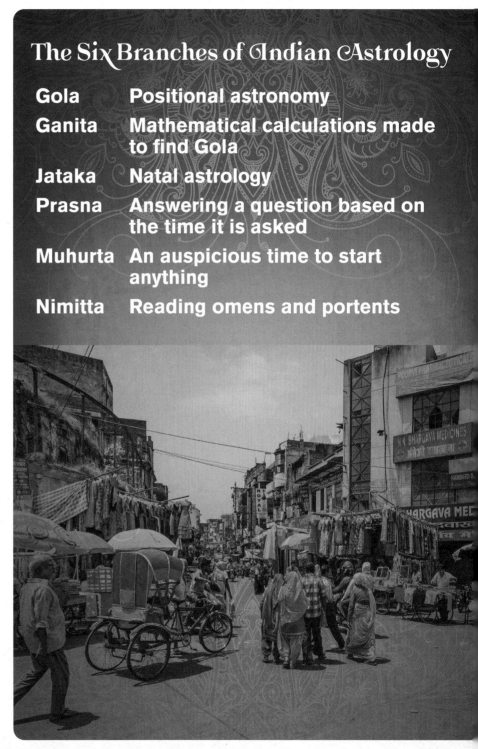

The Six Branches of Indian Astrology

Gola	**Positional astronomy**
Ganita	**Mathematical calculations made to find Gola**
Jataka	**Natal astrology**
Prasna	**Answering a question based on the time it is asked**
Muhurta	**An auspicious time to start anything**
Nimitta	**Reading omens and portents**

Opposite: Varanasi, Banaras, Uttar Pradesh, on the banks of the Holy Ganges; **Center left:** Wall carvings in the ancient temple at **Udaipur; Above: Chandni Chowk** market, in old Delhi

The temple on Gadi Sagar lake in Jaisalmer, Rajasthan, India; **Right, inset:** The Kite Festival in **Ahmedabad, Gujarat, India**

By using these six tools, and based on the place of birth and the celestial positionings at that moment, the traits of a person can be determined, as well as their compatibility with a potential marriage partner. Indian astrology views the sun as the source of life, as well as spirituality and intelligence. The moon controls fertility cycles and influences the emotions. Other mindful practices, such as yoga, mediation, and prayer, are also considered a valuable part of astrology, helping the individual lead a spiritual and upright life, until the soul achieve its final destination, which is god.

Historical evidence supports the theory that horoscopic astrology as practiced on the Indian subcontinent arose from two sources: Hellenic astrology, post-dating the Vedic period; and from the Vedanga Jyotisha, an astrology text written in the final centuries BC. Scholars still argue whether Jyotisha developed independently or was influenced by the Hellenic (Greek) practices.

Today, astrology plays a significant part in the folk beliefs of many contemporary Hindus. Children are named based on their Jyotisha chart, or Kundali, while calendar events and holidays are still organized based on astrological signs and positionings. Major life decisions, such as marriage, moving, or changing jobs, are also seen to be affected by the stars and planets.

Kite Festival

This popular and exhuberent celebration, called Makar Sankranti, is held thoughout India. It usually takes place in January, marking the sun's passage into Capricorn (Makara), and heralds the auspicious period Uttarayan. As part of the festivities children and adults fly wildly decorated kites. It is possible kite flying was encouraged because it got people outdoors, exposed to beneficial vitamin D, ridding them of any winter illnesses. Philosophically, it is a time of great spiritual healing when Enki the Sea Goat is eager to impart new knowledge and people are able to put their pasts behind them and start over.

Symbols of the Indian Zodiac

For the most part the Indian zodiac uses the same symbols as the Western zodiac.

Western name	Indian name	Symbol
Aries	Mesh	Ram
Taurus	Vrishabh	Bull
Gemini	Mithun	Twins
Cancer	Karka	Crab
Leo	Simha	Lion
Virgo	Kanya	Maiden
Libra	Tula	Scales
Scorpio	Vrishchika	Scorpion
Sagittarius	Dhanush	Archer
Capricorn	Makara	Goat (also Crocodile)
Aquarius	Kumbh	Water bearer
Pisces	Meena	Fish

Medieval and Renaissance Europe

During the Middle Ages, astrology in the Arab world flourished. Though still evolving as it assimilated its mingled influences of India, Persia, and Islam, it managed to overcome a religious ban and remain highly visible.

Meanwhile, European astrology had become fragmented and crude. There was no longer access to Greek astronomy, for one thing. For another, the Catholic Church condemned the practice, with advocates facing strong sanctions, including excommunication.

Yet by the late 10th century, Latin translations of Arabic texts on astrology were beginning to make their way to Spain. By the 12th century this influx had gained enormous momentum. Ptolemy's masterwork, the *Tetrabiblos*, was one of the first astrological texts to be circulated in medieval Europe after being translated from Arabic into Latin by Plato of Tivoli (Tiburtinus) in Spain in 1138.

The medical community in Europe was regularly referring to astrology texts by the 13th century, as physicians combined the wisdom of 2nd-century Greek healer, Galen, with their own observations of the stars. In the 1500s, it was illegal across much of Europe for doctors to perform risky procdures like surgery or bleeding without calculating the position of the moon. One English astrologer, Richard Trewythian (b. 1393), left details of his practice in a notebook, indicating a wide range of clients hailing from all walks of life. This journal deomonstrated that in the 14th century a relationship with astrology was not confined to the scholars, doctors, priests, or politicians.

Aries.leo.sagittarius.sunt
calida et sicca collerica
masculina. Orientalia.

Taurus.virgo.capricornus.
sunt frigida et sicca melanco
lica feminina. occidentalia.

Aries.

Taurus.

Geminus.

Cancer.

Leo.

Gemini
aquarius
libra.sunt calida et
humida masculina
sanguinea.occidentalia.

Cancer.scor
pius.pisces.
sunt frigida et humi
da flemmatica feminu
na.Septentrionalia.

61

New Contributors

Inevitably European astrologers began contributing to the collected wisdom: British monk Johannes de Sacrobosco penned a number of influential works in the 13th century as did Italian astrologer Guido Bonatti, a highly placed civil servant who acted as adviser to Holy Roman Emperor Frederick II. Bonatti's c.1277 textbook, *Liber Astronomiae*, was pronounced "the most important astrological work" of the century.

Even the literature of the age reflected the growing interest in celestial movements, and many authors incorporated astrological symbols into their work. Dante Alighieri used planetary associations when describing the architecture of the *Inferno, Purgatorio, and Paradisio* ... as when the seven layers of Purgatory's mountain purge the seven deadly sins that correspond to astrology's seven classical planets. Geoffrey Chaucer's writing, replete with astrological allegories and planetary themes, indicates an easy familiarity with the discipline. He even wrote a *Treatise on the Astrolabe*—a handheld model of the universe used for making astronomical calculations—for his son. During the early modern period, astrological references were also freely employed by William Shakespeare and John Milton.

The Renaissance

Arguably, the greatest scientific upheaval of the age was the discovery that, contrary to many centuries of learned writings, the sun was the unmoving center of the universe and not the earth. During the 16th century, Polish astronomer, mathematician, and church canon Nicolaus Copernicus spent many years honing his theory of heliocentricity. When he finally presented a heliocentric model in his book *De revolutionibus orbium coelestium*, it was met with astonishment by the scientific community, the Church, and the populace—and resulted in the Copernican Revolution. (In the 4th century BC, Greek mathematician and astronomer Aristarchos of Samos had made a similar deduction about the sun, but for the most part he was ignored by his successors.)

Not surprising for the time, many of Copernicus's brilliant proponents, including Tycho Brahe, Galileo Galilei, and Johannes Kepler, were also practicing astrologists. Later observations by William Herschel, Friedrich Bessel, and others acknowledged the sun as the center of our "solar" system, but not of the entire universe.

As in imperial Rome, Renaissance astrologers prepared horoscopes and studied the movement of stars and planets in order to advise monarchs and men of rank, thus earning themselves prestige and, often, considerable wealth. But as the end of the Renaissance neared, astrology again slid from favor. Contributing to this fall off was the breakdown of Aristotlean physics, which had once placed earth at the center of the universal spheres, and the loss of the distinction between the celestial (heavenly) and sublunar (earthly) realms, upon which so much of astrology had depended. By the 18th century, there was little intellectual investment left to continue buoying up the discipline and as a result its standing was greatly diminished.

Liberal Arts and Astrology

For students attending a medieval university, the curriculum was typically divided into seven subjects, or liberal arts, each with a ruling planet assigned to it based on descending planetary speed. Grammar was represented by the moon, the speediest celestial body, while dialectic was assigned to Mercury, rhetoric to Venus, music to the sun (which was believed to orbit like a planet), arithmetic to Mars, geometry to Jupiter, and astrology/astronomy to the slowest planet, Saturn.

Grammar (Moon)

Dialectic (Mercury)

Rhetoric (Venus)

Music (Sun)

Arithmetic (Mars)

Geometry (Venus)

Astrology/Astronomy (Saturn)

The Return of the Fire Festivals

The study of cosmology harks back to simpler eras, when signs in the sky served as an indicator to pre-Christian or pagan communities of when to plant and harvest. In recognition of this tradition, a number of groups, including Neopagans and Wiccans, have revived many of the celebrations that accompanied these vital dates. Furthermore, many towns and villages that hold these festivals have seen a steep rise in tourism over the past few decades.

The traditional Wheel of the Year displays eight Fire Festivals, each signifying a major shift or event in the agrarian calendar. Solar Fire Festival days include the solstices and the equinoxes. Lunar Fire Festivals, or cross-quarter days, are the four points that lie between equinox and solstice; they occur when the sun reaches the middle of the Fixed Signs: Taurus, Leo, Scorpio, and Aquarius. These days once marked the start of each season for earlier cultures, especially the Celts. Astrologically, the Solar Festivals occur at 0 degrees in their signs, while the positions of the Lunar Festivals have shifted slightly (rearranged by the Romans).

Solar Fire Festivals

Spring Equinox (Ostara): 0° Aries, March 20th–22nd

This day once heralded the "new year." The stars shift into Aries, first sign of the zodiac, which favors new beginnings and is emblemized by the trailblazing Ram. Aries is a Cardinal Sign, which indicates a turning point in the zodiac: a new season. This day also honors the festival of Eastre, Germanic goddess of spring connected with rabbits and eggs.

Summer Solstice (Litha): 0° Cancer, June 20th–22nd

As the zodiac shifts into Cancer, it is time to focus on issues in the home and assess the effects of the past. Once known as Midsummer (when May 1 kicked off summer), many earlier cultures acknowledged it with festivals, bonfires, dancing, church services, and processions.

Autumnal Equinox (Mabon): 0° Libra, September 20th–22nd

The onset of Libra offers a time for personal reflection and the opportunity to change. Mabon's emblem is the horn of plenty, symbolizing a good harvest and the storing of produce for winter. The Christian feast of Michaelmas in late September looks to the onset of fall, while the lively Asian Mid-Autumn Festival is celebrated with lanterns and rich mooncakes.

Winter Solstice (Yule): 0° Capricorn, December 20th–22nd

Capricorn brings a time to contemplate former goals and to feel a sense of accomplishment. The traditional festive Yule season runs from December 21 to January 1 and includes Christmas, often Hannukah and Kwanzaa, and the New Year holidays.

Lunar Fire Festivals

Beltane (May Eve): 9° Taurus, May 1st, traditional start of summer

This pagan Sabbat, representing sexuality, fertility and life renewed, is also known as May Day, Walpurgisnacht, Rood Day, Rudemas, and the Festival of Tana. As tactile Taurus

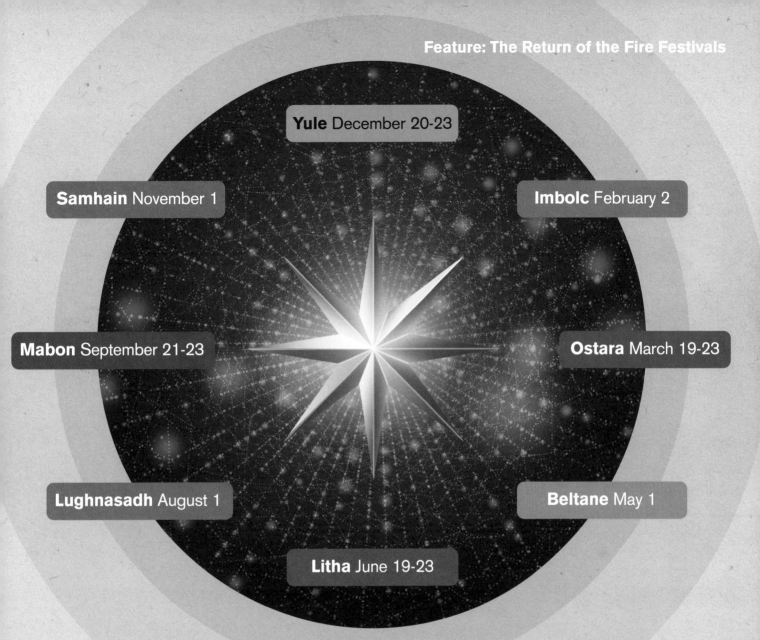

Yule December 20-23

Samhain November 1

Imbolc February 2

Mabon September 21-23

Ostara March 19-23

Lughnasadh August 1

Beltane May 1

Litha June 19-23

reigns, revelers indulge in bright colours, weave ribbons around the Maypole, and honor the festival of Flora and Ma by donning floral crowns or bringing baskets of flowers to loved ones.

Lughnasadh (Lammas):
9° Leo, August 1st,
traditional start of fall

This is the first of three traditional harvest festivals along with Mabon and Samhain. It was originally associated with Lugh, the god of light, and his foster mother Tailtiu, who both introduced agriculture to the Celts; a corn dolly image of the god is baked in bread, which is eaten as a symbolic sacrifice.

Samhain (Hallowe'en):
9° Scorpio, October 31st–
November 2nd,
traditional start of winter

An ancient Celtic festival set on the eve of the spiritual new year, throughout the world the day is set aside to honor ancestors. Situated in Scorpio, a sign that resonates to darkness and death, Samhain is nevertheless a light with bonfires and lanterns.

Imbolc (Candlemas):
13° Aquarius, February 2nd–7th,
traditional start of spring

This day honors St. Brigid (also the pagan goddess Brigid of the Eternal Flame), and signals the time to emerge—like the groundhog—from the darkness of winter. Imbolc means "in the belly," relating to the start of lambing season.

China

The study of astrology, known as known as Sheng Xiao or Shu Xiang, was highly esteemed in ancient China. Confucius, that profound and influential 5th-century sage, accorded astrologers great respect, pronouncing, "Heaven sends down its good or evil symbols and wise men act accordingly."

The animal-based Chinese zodiac with its six-decade cycle has been documented at least as far back as the Shang dynasty (ca 1766 BC–1050 BC). Oracle bones—an ox's shoulder blade or turtle's plastron—from that era have been unearthed bearing the 60-year marks upon them as well as the name of the divining astrologer and the topic being investigated. As occurred in other early cultures, the nation's best astrologers were drawn into

elevated court circles and were often asked to forecast political events or military outcomes. Around 300 BC, astrologer Tsou Yen wrote: "When some new dynasty is going to arise, heaven exhibits auspicious signs for the people."

Similar to Western astrology, the Chinese or Mandarin zodiac is divided into twelve signs, but each sign represents an entire year rather than a four-week period. This system, which repeats every 12 years was drawn from the 11.85 orbital cycle of Jupiter. It is based on calendars and the native astronomy that flowered during the Han Dynasty (200 BC to 200 AD).

Astrologers must also know the element for a person's day of birth to give an accurate reading. The Chinese zodiac recognizes five elements, each with its own

motivating force. Each one gets matched to the 12 yearly zodiac signs, resulting in an astrological cycle that lasts 60 years—and then recurs.

- Fire (huo): inspired by excitement
- Earth (tu): motivated to secure foundations
- Metal (jin): driven to create order
- Water (shu): compelled to form emotional bonds
- Wood (mu): born with a desire to explore

The Four Pillars
Chinese astrology also incorporates a daily reading based on the animal of the day, or "true animal." Identifying true animals can be done using the Four Pillars of Destiny, or Ba-Zi, which date to the Han period and were refined during the Tang and Song dynasties. The

"pillars"—representing the day, week, month, and year of birth—are each assigned one of the 10 Celestial stems and one of the 12 Terrestrial branches. These elements form a sexagenary cycle of 60 years, the span historically used to reckon time in early China. (This type of astrological method is also used in Japan and Korea.) For a Chinese astrologer to prepare a chart, he or she must know the person's "true animal" and the element for their day of birth. This can be very difficult to calculate—the ancient Chinese week contained ten days—and typically requires someone with a mastery of the discipline. There are also online calculators that can provide this information.

Philosophical Influences

There is a distinct connection between Chinese astrology and Chinese philosophy, especially in relation to the three harmonies: heaven, earth, and water, and the principles of yin and yang (the concept of dualism, that contradictory forces may actually be complementary), concepts not often found in Western astrology.
(*See* Chapter 5: The Contemporary Chinese Zodiac)

Above right: Statue of the 5th-Century philosopher **Confucius**

Early Chinese coin depicting the figures of the zodiac. Coins such as this inspired the famous maple leaf coins of Canada, as well as coins issued by Australia, South Korea, and Mongolia.

Japan

Shukuyo is the name given to the Japanese system of divination, which dates back more than 3,000 years. Around 1,000 BC it was influenced by the Indian Buddhist saint Monju-Bosatsu; four centuries later Chinese monk Fuki-Sanzo studied his methods while traveling in India and brought the discipline home to China.

Here, his gathered information was placed into a book on Shukuyo scripture. This book was later carried to Japan by a Japanese monk named Kukai, a disciple of Fuki-Sanzo. After devising ways to interpret the Shukuyo scriptures, Kukai began making astrological predictions. They proved to be so accurate that people grew frightened. It is believed the practice was even banned for a time.

Shukuyo features 27 "Shuku" signs based on the nightly placement of the moon over its roughly 27-day cycle of waxing and waning. The term shuku means "hotel," an indication that Japanese astrologers believed the moon "checked in" to a specific place in the night sky.

A person's sign is determined by the day and year of their birth. Due to the shifting of the lunar calendar, however, a baby born on March 4 may have a certain Shuku sign one year, and one born on that date the following year will have a different sign.

Shukuyo incorporates the fundamental beliefs of Buddhism as well as concepts of Eastern spirituality: karma, self-realization, and honesty. Today it remains one of the most popular divination systems in Japan, one that sheds light on both life paths and relationships as well as revealing emotional character, the special province of the moon that oversees each sign.

Lunar Birth Charts

The 27 Shuku signs, reflecting monthly phases of the moon, are typically placed in a chart with three rows of nine signs. Japanese astrologers place great emphasis on the relationship between the signs and how they affect each other. In order, the 27 signs are as follows. The signs that use the same names have different corresponding pictographs. Rou, I, Bou, Hitsu, Shi, Shin, Sei, Ki, Ryu, Sei, Chou, Yoku, Shin, Kaku, Kou, Tei, Bou, Shin, Bi, Ki, Tou, Jyo, Kyo, Ki, Shitsu, Heki, Kei.

Animals of the Japanese Zodiac

The year-based Chinese zodiac is also quite popular in Japan, where it was introduced to the island nation in around the 4th century. Known in Japan as Juunishi, it utilizes the same animal symbols and reflects the same birth years as the zodiacs in China and Korea.

	Western	Japanese	Traits
	Rat	**Nezumi**	Hardworking, charming, ambitious
			Year: 1924, 1936, 1948, 1960, 1972, 1984, 1996, 2008
	Ox	**Ushi**	Patient, mentally alert, inspiring
			Year: 1925, 1937, 1949, 1961, 1973, 1985, 1997, 2009
	Tiger	**Tora**	Sensitive, stubborn, courageous
			Year: 1926, 1938, 1950, 1962, 1974, 1986, 1998, 2010
	Rabbit	**Usagi**	Persuasive, virtuous, admirable
			Year: 1927, 1939, 1951, 1963, 1975, 1987, 1999, 2011
	Dragon	**Tatsu**	Energetic, excitable, inspirational
			Year: 1928, 1940, 1952, 1964, 1976, 1988, 2000, 2012
	Snake	**Hebi**	Wise, quiet, lucky with money
			Year: 1929, 1941, 1953, 1965, 1977, 1989, 2001, 2013
	Horse	**Uma**	Talkative, financially skilled, moody
			Year: 1930, 1942, 1954, 1966, 1978, 1990, 2002, 2014
	Sheep	**Hijtsuji**	Artistic, outdoorsy, spiritual
			Year: 1931, 1943, 1955, 1967, 1979, 1991, 2003, 2015
	Monkey	**Saru**	Clever, inventive, original
			Year: 1932, 1944, 1956, 1968, 1980, 1992, 2004, 2016
	Rooster	**Tori**	Devoted to work, direct, self-critical
			Year: 1933, 1945, 1957, 1969, 1981, 1993, 2005, 2017
	Dog	**Inu**	Dutiful, honest, confident
			Year: 1934, 1946, 1958, 1970, 1982, 1994, 2006, 2018
	Boar	**Inoshishi**	Brave, inwardly strong, volatile
			Year: 1935, 1947, 1959, 1971, 1983, 1995, 2007, 2019

Korea

Chinese astrology, which was the basis for Korean astrology, began more than 2,000 years ago. Like most other forms of the zodiac, the Korean discipline assigns 12 animals, called Sibijisin, to represent the divisions. Sibijisin comes from the words sibi, or "twelve," and jisin, which means "gods of the earth."

In more primitive times, these animals were seen as guardians that kept evil spirits at bay. Each day was also divided into 12 two-hour blocks and one of these guardians was assigned to each block. The time time between 5:00 and 7:00, for instance, was Myosi, or the time of the Rabbit. These protective animals were so revered by the Korean people that large statues of them were erected near many royal sites.

All the ways of predicting the future in Korea have to do with the concepts of yang and um: yang reflects positive, bright, active outcomes, while um reflects negative, dark, passive results. It is understood by most people that a combination of the two is best. There is also the notion of tee to be factored in, which is based on the basic nature of an individual. Tee means understanding what being born under a certain totemic animal means in relation to the current year's animal. A rabbit-year person might face obstacles during the year of the Ox, making big plans but getting little done. Tee can also help determine if two people are compatible; couples who are both born under stubborn or volatile signs might not have the smoothest relationship. And, depending on gender, some years are considered more auspicious than others. Yet there are no bad signs; all offer a variety of possibilities, especially if there is attention paid to balancing yang and um.

In Korea, the animals of the zodiac are frequently personified as guardians of the culture.

Animals of the Korean Zodiac

According to one fanciful legend, Buddha invited all the animals in the world to call on him, but only 12 honored him with a visit. These then were chosen to represent the zodiac. Another tale relates that 12 animals competed in a race across a river, with the gods ordaining that the order in which they finished would determine their ranking in the zodiac. Supposedly the rat rode across the water on the ox's back and then jumped ashore, capturing first place. Whatever the story of their origin, each of these animals is believed to lend distinct character traits and tendencies to those born in their year.

	Western	Korean	Traits
	Rat/Mouse	**Jui**	Imaginative, sociable, agile
			Year: 1924, 1936, 1948, 1960, 1972, 1984, 1996, 2008
	Ox/Cow	**So**	Trustworthy, patient, efficient
			Year: 1925, 1937, 1949, 1961, 1973, 1985, 1997, 2009
	Tiger	**Horangi**	Adventurous, independent, competitive
			Year: 1926, 1938, 1950, 1962, 1974, 1986, 1998, 2010
	Rabbit	**Tokki**	Rational, hardworking, intellectual
			Year: 1927, 1939, 1951, 1963, 1975, 1987, 1999, 2011
	Dragon	**Yong**	Generous, arrogant, lucky
			Year: 1928, 1940, 1952, 1964, 1976, 1988, 2000, 2012
	Snake	**Baem**	Intuitive, calm, charismatic
			Year: 1929, 1941, 1953, 1965, 1977, 1989, 2001, 2013
	Horse	**Mal**	Individualistic, stubborn, faithful
			Year: 1930, 1942, 1954, 1966, 1978, 1990, 2002, 2014
	Sheep	**Yang**	Friendly, considerate, adaptable
			Year: 1931, 1943, 1955, 1967, 1979, 1991, 2003, 2015
	Monkey	**Weonsungi**	Stern, confident, versatile
			Year: 1932, 1944, 1956, 1968, 1980, 1992, 2004, 2016
	Rooster	**Dak**	Sensitive, impatient, intelligent
			Year: 1933, 1945, 1957, 1969, 1981, 1993, 2005, 2017
	Dog	**Gae**	Devoted, pugnacious, passionate
			Year: 1934, 1946, 1958, 1970, 1982, 1994, 2006, 2018
	Pig	**Dwaeji**	Honest, impulsive, brave
			Year: 1935, 1947, 1959, 1971, 1983, 1995, 2007, 2019

The Chinese Influence

The Chinese zodiac has had a widespread effect on the astrological practices of a number of other Asian nations or regions. In some cases this occurred in countries under the direct influence of China; in other instances it was a matter of proximity or cultural appropriation. Many countries followed the general format established in China, but used different animals.

The Korean zodiac includes the Sheep (yang) instead of the Goat (yeomoso), although the Chinese source of yang may refer to a goat-antelope.

The Japanese zodiac includes the Sheep (hitsuji) instead of the Goat (yagi), and the Wild Boar (inoshishi, i) instead of the Pig (buta). Unlike the Chinese, the Japanese celebrate the start of the new year on January 1, following the Gregorian calendar.

In the Vietnamese zodiac the second animal is the Water Buffalo instead of the Ox, and the fourth animal is the Cat instead of the Rabbit.

The Cambodian zodiac is nearly identical to the Chinese although the dragon is interchangeable with the Neak (nāga), the Cambodian sea snake. Sheep and Goat are interchangeable as well. Unlike in China, Cambodians start their new year in April rather than in January/February.

The zodiac of the Cham people of Cambodia uses the same order as the Chinese zodiac, but replaces the Monkey with the Turtle, known locally as kra.

The Malay zodiac replaces the Chinese Rabbit with the Mousedeer (pelanduk) and the Pig with the Tortoise (kura). The Dragon is normally equated with the nāga, but it is sometimes called Big Snake (ular besar) while the Snake sign is called Second Snake (ular sani).

The Thai zodiac includes a nāga in place of the Dragon and begins either on the first day of the fifth month in the Thai lunar calendar or during the Songkran New Year festival (April 13–15).

The Gurung zodiac of Nepal includes Cow instead of Ox, Cat instead of Rabbit, Eagle instead of Dragon, Bird instead of Rooster, and Deer instead of Pig.

The Bulgar zodiac calendar, in use since the 2nd century, has only been partially reconstructed, but it uses a 60-year cycle of 12 animal-named years similar to the Chinese. It includes Mouse (somor), Ox (shegor), possibly Tiger/Wolf (ver?), Rabbit (dvan[sh]), possibly Dragon (ver[eni]?), Snake (dilom), Horse (imen[shegor]?); Ram (teku[chitem]?); probably Monkey; Hen or Rooster (toh), Dog (eth), and Boar (dohs).

The Old Mongol calendar uses uses the Mouse, the Ox, the Leopard, the Hare, the Crocodile, the Serpent, the Horse, the Sheep, the Monkey, the Hen, the Dog, and the Hog.

The Volga Bulgars, Kazars, and other Turkic peoples replaced some Chinese animals with local fauna: Leopard instead of Tiger, Fish instead of Dragon, Crocodile instead of Dragon, Hedgehog instead of Monkey, Elephant for Pig, and Camel for Mouse.

In the Persian version of the Eastern zodiac carried to the West by Mongols during the Middle Ages, the Chinese word lóng and Mongol word lū (both meaning Dragon) was translated as nahang, meaning "water beast." This may refer to any dangerous aquatic animal both mythical and real (crocodiles, hippos, sharks, sea serpents, etc.). In the 20th Century nahang is used almost exclusively for Whale, thus switching Dragon for Whale in the Persian variant.

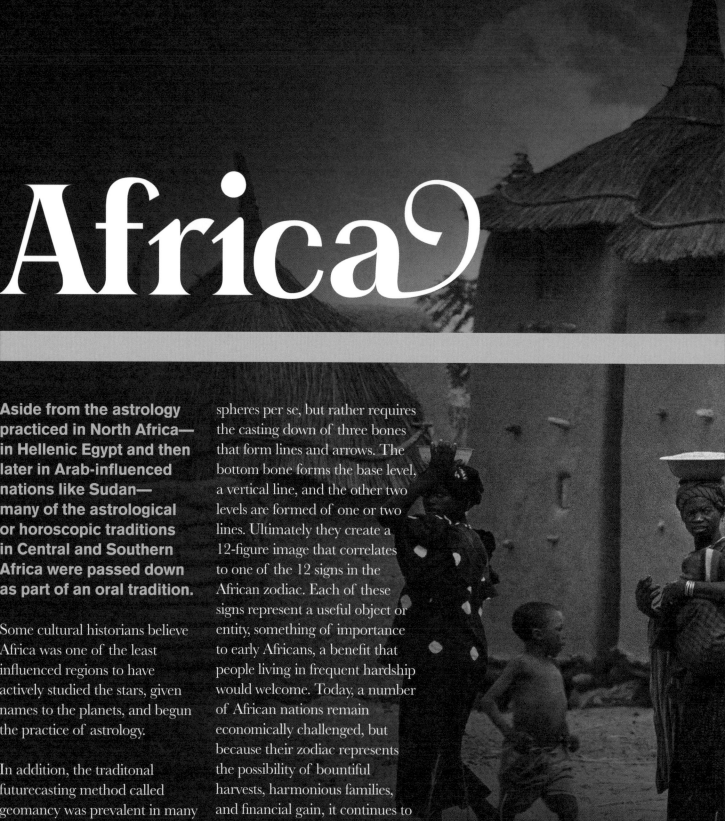

Africa

Aside from the astrology practiced in North Africa—in Hellenic Egypt and then later in Arab-influenced nations like Sudan—many of the astrological or horoscopic traditions in Central and Southern Africa were passed down as part of an oral tradition.

Some cultural historians believe Africa was one of the least influenced regions to have actively studied the stars, given names to the planets, and begun the practice of astrology.

In addition, the traditonal futurecasting method called geomancy was prevalent in many places. This type of divination does not involve the celestial spheres per se, but rather requires the casting down of three bones that form lines and arrows. The bottom bone forms the base level, a vertical line, and the other two levels are formed of one or two lines. Ultimately they create a 12-figure image that correlates to one of the 12 signs in the African zodiac. Each of these signs represent a useful object or entity, something of importance to early Africans, a benefit that people living in frequent hardship would welcome. Today, a number of African nations remain economically challenged, but because their zodiac represents the possibility of bountiful harvests, harmonious families, and financial gain, it continues to instill hope.

African Geomancy

Another traditional form of African geomancy consists of throwing handfuls of dirt in the air and observing how the dirt falls. It can also involve a mouse as the agent of the earth spirit. Ifá, a Youruba religion and system of divination, is one of the oldest forms of geomancy. It originated in West Africa,and uses the same sixteen geomantic figures found in Arabic and Western geomancy but with different meanings and names.

A Dogon village in Mali, West Africa. The Dogon people are thought to be the progeny of ancient Egyptians. They were accomplished astronomers who believed extraterrestrials from the Sirius system visited earth in the form of mer-creatures.

The Twelve Signs

The Boabab Tree
January 4–February 3
Favorable day: Thursday
Sensitive body part: Liver
Sense: Smell
Element: Air
Successful months:
January, May
Key traits: Honest, liberal, thoughtful

Like the determined boabab that seeks sustenance from the earth, this sign has the ability to find opportunity and maintain a strong sense of self. Anxiety can sabatage speed and optimism.

The Wealth of Amber and Silver
February 4–March 5
Favorable day: Wednesday
Sensitive body part: Nervous system; **Sense:** Sight
Element: Air; **Successful months:** February, June
Key traits: Intolerant to differences, emotional, temperamental

This sign produces quick-witted, nervous people who are susceptible to strong positive and negative emotions. They hold tight to their beliefs and resist temptation.

Family
March 6–April 4
Favorable day: Tuesday
Sensitive body part: Lungs
Sense: Smell
Element: Earth
Successful months: March, July; **Key traits:** Selfless, giving, honest

Warmth and acceptance typifies those born under the Family sign, but they can also be reserved. They are often called upon to play diplomatic or mediating roles due to their inner wisdom and lack of duplicity.

Small Services to the Neighborhood
April 5–May 4
Favorable day: Saturday
Sensitive body part: Medullary
Sense: Hearing
Element: Earth; **Successful Months:** April, August
Key traits: Dependable, creative, affectionate

Although this sign offers reliable counsel, it is often delayed until the moment of crisis. There is a continuing search for affection and connection, and many relationships may result, yet often they are fleeting.

The Market
May 5–June 4
Favorable day: Sunday
Sensitive body part: Veins and throat; **Sense:** Touch
Element: Fire; **Successful months:** May, September
Key traits: optimistic, dramatic, humane

This sign of duality can provide a sense of harmony and tranquility, but always with a hint of danger and difficult trials to come. There also needs to be caution about wasting emotions and time on relationships that cannot evolve.

The Ancestor
June 5–July 4
Favorable day: Monday
Sensitive body part: Head
Sense: Taste
Element: Water
Successful Months: October, June
Key traits: Perceptive, fair, leadership qualities

Fairness, nobility and strength create leaders, champions, and teachers, although egotism combined with a need to show off can create difficulties. Fortunately, there is an innate ability to self-correct.

The Judge
July 5–August 4
Favorable day: Tuesday
Sensitive body part: Kidneys
Sense: Touch
Element: Fire
Successful months: July, November
Key traits: realist, magnetic, generous

These charismatic, empathetic personalities often inspire and influence others; deeply root spirituality allows them to improve morale, while leading and strategizing with confidence.

The Kola Nut
August 5–September 3
Favorable day: Wednesday
Sensitive body part: sexual organs; **Sense:** Taste; **Element:** Earth; **Successful months:** December, August
Key traits: Sensual, brave, haphazard

A free spirit that gravitates to powerful signs, the Kola Nut often irritates more mild signs. Unstable energy and rampant sexuality is balanced by a thirst for knowledge; eventually wisdom overcomes youthful follies and the need for pleasure.

The Traveler
September 4–October 3
Favorable day: Thursday
Sensitive body parts: Feet and joints; **Sense:** Sight
Element: Air; **Successful months:** January, September
Key traits: Sensitive, tends to wander, misunderstood

These complex nomads, who yearn to explore new vistas, find that people sometimes mistrust their intentions. Yet their travels often bring them enlightening experiences and opportunities for interior growth.

The Distance
October 4–November 3
Favorable day: Friday
Sensitive body part: Heart
Sense: Hearing; **Element:** Water; **Successful Months:** February, October
Key traits: Spontaneous, creative, inwardly strong

Creativity can suffer from lack of patience in this sign of dreamers and revolutionaries, while anxiety can make commitments feel risky, leading to a nonconformist lifestyle. Once engaged emotionally, however, inner strength creates a lasting bond.

Child of the World
November 4–December 3
Favorable day: Saturday
Sensitive body part: Viscera
Sense: Taste; **Element:** Fire
Successful months: March, November
Key traits: Generous, opportunistic, devoted

With a gentle, easygoing attitude, this Child draws in good fortune and opportunities. An excess of pride can surface, however, causing an equal measure of misfortune. An upbeat nature makes this individual popular and a trusty friend.

The Harvest and the Granary
December 4–January 3
Favorable day: Tuesday
Sensitive body part: Skin and bones; **Sense:** Hearing
Element: Water; **Successful months:** December, April
Key traits: Generous, loyal

Always seeing the bright side of things, this sign may suffer from a false sense of security. They often end up as trailblazers, but their vanity and love of the spotlight can cause problems with romance if they don't develop sincerity and serenity.

North America

Long before European explorers "discovered" the New World, the indigenous peoples of North America—the Inuit and other native groups in the far north and the Indian nations of the plains, woodlands, mountains, and deserts of the more temperate regions of the continent—were forming legends about the night sky and creating their own methods for interpreting its movements.

Inuit

The Inuit peoples who live in the polar reaches of North America have had plenty of time to study the night sky—they are exposed to it continuosly for four and half months each year. Oddly, this has not resulted in the acquiring of a great deal of astronomical data. This lack is partly due to the moonlight, which, when reflected off the ice and snow, impedes a clear view of the stars. Icy, windswept snow particles often collect in the atmosphere, creating a haze. Clouds and the aurora borealis can also obscure the stars. Finally, the bitter cold makes long-term outdoor observation nearly impossible.

Still, Inuit religions and beliefs often alluded to events in the night sky, including the flaring of the auroras, but were based more on happenings that took place in the sea and on land. The ancient Inuit believed the earth (called *Nunarjuaq* in the Inuktitut language) to be a flat and stationary body at the center of the universe. The moon (*Taqqiq*) was seen as a flat disk of ice and the sun (*Siqniq*) as a ball of fire. The disappearance of the winter sun below the horizon for several

Opposite: Dream Lake and Hallet Peak, Rocky Mountain National Park, Colorado; **Inset: Native Americans** of the Southwest, photographed in 1899. Many of these desert tribes told stories explaining the origins of the planets and the stars.

months was taken as a sign that it was so weighted down with the cold and frost that it could no longer rise into the sky.

The planets were viewed as large stars, and the distant stars as holes in the celestial dome. Improbably, the North Star—the polar star that remains in a fixed position in the sky and around which all the other stars appear to revolve—seems to have been unknown to these people. The ancient Inuit acknowledged 33 stars, seven of which were given names, and of these several were used to help them navigate during hunting trips or migrations. This was key in a land with few landmarks or reference points. For the most part, the Inuit did not actually utilize a system for reading signs in the stars; rather, the moon, sun, and their 16 constellations became the basis for many of their myths and parables.

Native American

Many American Indian tribes incorporated astrology into their early cultures and traditions— and some have continued to do so into the 21st century. One of the consistant themes of their philosophy has been to view human existence through the lens of the natural world. This is in sharp contrast to the European attitude, which placed humans at the center of the world and relegated nature to one of mankind's possessions. In addition to striving for harmony with nature, Native Americans also value both the seasons and animals.

The Plains Indians

A number of Native American clans of the Great Plains, including the Pawnee, Shoshone, Arikara, and Wichita, had complex belief systems that incorporated the use of a star chart and observation of astral bodies. The Cherokee, for example, accepted that everything on the planet was an earth impression of the stars.

The Pawnee believed that stars were gods who once lived on earth and were changed into stars after death. The Skidi tribe of the Pawnee referred to one particular ring of stars as the "Council of Chiefs" and believed this was a celestial reflection of their own elders resolving matters and making wise decisions for their people; they even left openings at the tops of their lodges so they could gaze upon the council at night. This constellation is also known as the Corona Borealis, the "Crown of the North." Other celestial phenomena—comets, asteroids showers, and novas—were viewed as signs of extraordinary disasters. The tribes also used the stars to set agricultural patterns and influence their social rituals, and images of a Pawnee star chart show conspicuous heavenly body designs, possibly used to flag seasons and occasions of the year.

Ancestral Puebloans

At Peñasco Blanco, in Chaco Canyon, New Mexico, there is an Ancestral Puebloan pictograph on a rock face that appears to depict a supernova explosion [see overleaf]. Based on the orientation of a crescent moon and stars, researchers believe the art may represent the birth of the Crab Nebula, which was formed in 1054 AD by supernova— an event recorded as a "guest star" by Chinese and Japanese observers, but apparently not noted in Europe or the Arab world.

The Ancestral Puebloans, once known to the Navajos as the Anasazi, were cliff dwellers of the American Southwest who emerged around 100 AD, established large, lasting communities, and who then left their habitations in the 12th and 13th centuries AD to disperse throughout the region. Yet even though many details of their culture remain clouded, archeologists have found numerous examples of their pit houses, built with precise astronomical alignments, indicating that a familiarity with the stars was integrated into their way of life. The sun was especially important to these people, who not only observed it in the sky, but also crafted keyholes and windows in their homes and kivas (round ceremonial chambers), where it shone in at crucial or significant times of the year. Like many other early cultures these peoples devised ways to observe and record celestial events in order to give their lives order, balance, and predictability.

The Crab Nebula, a six-light-year-wide expanding remnant of a star's supernova explosion. Native Americans observed and recorded this spectacular event in AD1054. *See* pictures opposite

Prehistoric pictographs in **Chaco Canyon, New Mexico,** and **right:** In **Canyonlands National Park, Utah**

Navajo and Hopi

Both the Navajo and Hopi cultures of the Southwest contain many stories explaining the origin of the stars and sun. One Navajo legend tells of the Four Worlds that had no sun, and the Fifth World, which was earth. The people of the Fifth World were given four lights, but complained that it was not enough light. After many attempts to please them, First Woman created the sun for light and warmth, and the moon to provide coolness and rain. These two heavenly objects were carved from quartz, and the leftover stone chips were tossed into the sky to make the stars.

The Hopi also believed there were worlds previous to the current one, the modern era being the Fourth World. Accordinng to the legends, each preceding world came to an end when the "blue star" appeared. Certain Hopi carvings seem to indicate the presence of aliens during these "worlds," a belief that is still part of American culture today. In New Mexico and Arizona, several Southwestern pueblo cultures, including the Hopi, still gather to mark the winter solstice, the shortest day, while a number of rituals tied to the rising and setting of the sun also mark the waning of winter and eventual arrival of the spring planting season. These ancient ceremonies, based on events in the sky, have been passed down through many generations.

Horizon Calendars

Knowing when to plant seeds or harvest a crop was vital to agrarian communities like the Pueblos and later the Navajo and Hopi. This knowledge could be acquired by using horizon calendars.

Astroarcheology...

...is the study of how early humans observed, tracked, recorded, and began to understand the movement of celestial objects. Some cultures left behind only subtle hints of their exploration of the stars, but the peoples of the Southwestern pueblos reflected their fixation on the heavens in both their architecture and in images cut into stone walls.

I-ah-to-tonah, or **Little Woman Mountain,** and son **A-last-Sauked,** or **Looking-away-off,** Nez Perce, photographed in 1909. This tribe had a myth about the "lost" sister in the Pleiades that mirrored one from ancient Greece.

Native American Birth Signs

Native American astrologers typically split the year into four clans—Butterfly, Frog, Turtle, and Thunderbird—which were further split into three sections each. Together these divisions formed what is known as the Medicine Wheel, the circle being a symbol for unity or convergence. This breakdown of 12 sections marches neatly with the 12 signs of the zodiac brought to America by Europeans and other cultures. Rather than star signs, however, totems representing indigenous animals were used in Native American astrology.

These totems are not to be confused with an individual's spirit animal or spirit guide—a teacher, mentor, guardian, or messenger—that appears to them during a dream or vision quest ceremony.

The Four Clans

Thunderbird (Hawk) Clan

Element: Fire; **Medicine:** Messenger
Traits: Leadership, gets things done, open with feelings; Signifies: Renewal, power, understanding

Frog Clan

Element: Water **Medicine:** Cleansing
Traits: Feels deeply, gift of healing, empathatic; Signifies: Calm, protection of water, flushing away obstacles

Turtle Clan

Element: Earth **Medicine:** Mother Earth
Traits: Loyal, stubborn, methodical, practical; Signifies: Roots, growth, stability

Butterfly Clan

Element: Air **Medicine:** Transformation
Traits: Physically, mentally, and emotionally active, fresh thinker, serves others; Signifies: Change, may indicate manipulation

Totemic Animals

Opposite is a chart of the Native American totems with their clans, their corresponding zodiac signs, and a brief list of positive and negative traits associated with each animal. There are also four spirit keepers that influence totem animals: White Buffalo (Waboose) oversees Snow Goose, Otter, and Wolf; Golden Eagle (Wabun) oversees Red Hawk, Beaver, and Deer; Coyote (Shawnodese) oversees Woodpecker, Salmon, and Brown Bear; and Grizzly Bear (Mudjekeewis) oversees Raven, Snake, and Owl.

Totem	Clan	Zodiac Sign	Traits
RED HAWK	**THUNDERBIRD**	Aries	Passionate, energetic, innovative, intrepid; impatient, may be unaware of obstacles
BEAVER	**TURTLE**	Taurus	Practical, steadfast, reliable, sensual; faithful to tested formulas, may lack initiative
DEER	**BUTTERFLY**	Gemini	Alert, inquistive, on the go, keen intelligence; needs stimulation, must keep moving
WOODPECKER	**FROG**	Cancer	Sensitive, homeloving, nurturing animals, plants, people; smothering, trouble letting go
SALMON	**THUNDERBIRD**	Leo	Strong, passionate, shows great determination; may become obsessed, too dug in
BROWN BEAR	**TURTLE**	Virgo	Practical, dutiful, smart, inquisitive, joiners; Overly analytical, cautious, introverted
RAVEN	**BUTTERFLY**	Libra	Peacemaker, seeks harmony, convivial; Unsettled by conflict, too selfless
SNAKE	**FROG**	Scorpio	Feels deeply, private, mysterious, transformative; emotionally remote, can spiral down, inspire fear
OWL	**THUNDERBIRD**	Sagittarius	Philosophical, broad-minded, wise, intuitive; inattentive to detials, may overlook greater meaning
SNOW GOOSE	**TURTLE**	Capricorn	Practical, organized, meticulous, leadership potential; may lose touch with emotions
OTTER	**BUTTERFLY**	Aquarius	Friendly, neither leaders nor followers, eccentric; may find fitting into society difficult
WOLF	**FROG**	Pisces	Sensitive, intuitive, eager for spiritual enrichment; may become too dependent

The Astrology of Places

According to many astrologers it is not only human beings who have ruling sun signs, but also countries, geographic regions, and cities. As with people, these signs are based on the date that the country or city was founded. For instance, the United States was officially formed on July 4, 1776, so it is overseen by the zodiac sign of Cancer.

Aries

Countries that are ruled by the optimistic sign Aries include Palestine, England, China, Germany, Poland, Syria, Israel, Lithuania, Senegal, Sierra Leone, and Zimbabwe.

Cities that are ruled by Aries include Birmingham, Cape Town, Leicester, Florence, Krakow, Naples, Utrecht, Marseilles, and Georgia.

Taurus

Countries that are ruled by loyal Taurus include Cyprus, Tasmania, Ireland, Capri, Rhodes, the Greek Islands, Cuba, East Timor, Serbia, Tanzania, South Africa, and Yemen.
Cities include Lucerne, Eastbound, Eastbourne, Hastings, Palermo, Leipzig, St. Louis, and Dublin.

Gemini

Countries ruled by the enthusiastic, energetic sign of Gemini include Iceland, Sardinia, Morocco, Belgium, Wales, Eritrea, Guyana, Kuwait, Norway, Montenegro, Sweden, and Tonga.
Cities include Nuremberg, Tripoli, San Francisco, London, Melbourne, Plymouth, and Cardiff.

Cancer

Countries overseen by nurturing, compassionate Cancer include the United States, Paraguay, Scotland, Holland, the Bahamas, Bahrain, Belize, Burundi, Cape Verde, Columbia, Comoros, Democratic Republic of the Congo, Croatia, Djibouti, Kiribati, Laos, Liberia, Madagascar, Malawi, Mozambique, Rwanda, Slovenia, Solomon Islands, Somalia, and South Korea.
Cities include Manchester, New York City, Stockholm, Tokyo, Venice, York, Amsterdam, Milan, and Algeria.

Leo

Countries ruled by the charismatic birth sign Leo include Afghanistan, India, Italy, Macedonia, Romania, Sicily, Ecuador, Zanzibar, Bhutan, Bolivia, Central African Republic Chad, The Ivory Coast, Gabon, Indonesia, North Korea, South Korea, Kyrgyzstan, Malaysia, Maldives, Nicaragua, Pakistan, Mongolia, Seychelles, Singapore, Ukraine, and Madagascar.
Cities include Bristol, Bombay, Chicago, Madrid, Los Angeles, Philadelphia, Rome, and Bath.

Virgo

Countries ruled by multitalented Virgo include Crete, Brazil, Greece, Switzerland, Turkey, Uruguay, West Indies,

Armenia, Azerbaijan, Belarus, Brazil, Costa Rica, El Salvador, Estonia, Guatemala, Honduras, Mali, Moldova, Qatar, and Tajikistan.
Cities include Athens, Paris, Toulouse, Corinth, Lyons, Boston, and Mexico City.

Libra

Countries that are ruled by the balanced and fair sign of Libra include France, Argentina, Austria, Burma, Canada, Japan, Siberia, Botswana, Equatorial Guinea, Fiji, Iraq, Israel, Lesotho, Nigeria, Palau, Saint Lucia, Saudi Arabia, Tuvalu, and Uganda.
Cities include Lisbon, Frankfurt, Copenhagen, Nottingham, and Antwerp.

Scorpio

Countries or regions ruled by passionate Scorpio include Angola, Morocco, Queensland, Korea, Syria, Norway, the Transvaal, Bavaria, Antigua, Barbuda, Cambodia, Dominica, Latvia, Lebanon, Micronesia,

Panama, Turkey, Turkmenistan, and Zambia.
Scorpio cities include Cincinnati, Liverpool, Newcastle, Washington DC, Vienna, Baltimore, and New Orleans

Sagittarius

Countries ruled by independence-minded Sagittarius include Spain, Australia, Chile, Hungary, Saudi Arabia, Bangladesh, Barbados, Cameroon, Kazakhstan, Kenya, Libya, and Mauritania.
Cities include Budapest, Johannesburg, Naples, Nottingham, Sheffield, Sunderland, Stuttgart, and Toronto

Capricorn

Countries ruled by the ambitious and resourceful sign of Capricorn include India Bulgaria, Mexico, Great Britain, the United Kingdom, Albania, Afghanistan, Lithuania, Bosnia, Brunei, Czech Republic, Haiti, Nauru, Slovakia, and Sudan.
Capricorn cities include

Brandenburg, Brussels, Delhi, Port Said, Oxford, and Ghent.

Aquarius

Countries that are overseen by free-spirited Aquarius include Iran, Finland, New Zealand, Russia, Sweden, Syria, Ethiopia, The Holy Vatican City, and Sri Lanka.
Cities ruled by Aquarius include Brighton, Hamburg, Helsinki, Moscow, Salzburg, St. Petersburg, and Bremen.

Pisces

Countries or regions ruled by the imaginative, creative sign of Pisces include Normandy, North Africa, Portugal, Samoa, Egypt, Scandinavia, Mauritius, Morocco, Namibia, and Tunisia.
Cities ruled by Pisces include Warsaw, Alexandria, Grimsby, Jerusalem, Bournemouth, Seville, and Cowes.

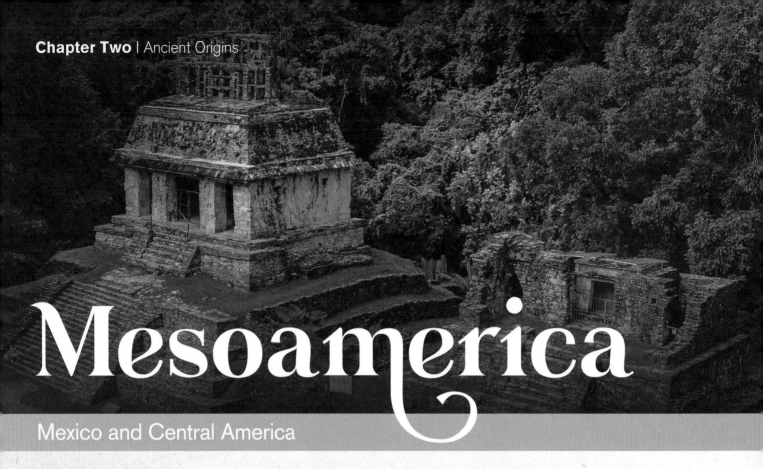

Mesoamerica

Mexico and Central America

The ancient cultures of Mesoamerica—the area encompassing Mexico and Central America—were no different from other emerging civilizations around the globe: they held deep beliefs in multiple gods, mythical beasts, and supernatural happenings, and, like the Egyptians, Greeks, and Romans, believed that the stars and planets could indicate character traits and foretell future events.

Above: Palenque/Lakamha (Big Water), a Mayan UNESCO World Heritage site; **Opposite:** A modern casting of an ancient **Aztec calendar**

The early forms of Mesoamerican astrology evolved as the cultures matured, becoming more powerful, if not yet sophisticated. These advancements occurred in spite of their astrologers lacking the two millennia of astrological foundation that European and Asian practitioners could draw from.

A number of indigenous groups dominated the region from around 1000 to 1500 AD. The Olmecs, who settled along the Gulf Coast, were the earliest inhabitants. It was likely they who created the 260-day astrological calendar, which would become the core of Mesoamerican astrology. They were followed by the Maya, Toltec, Zapotec,

and finally the Aztec cultures. Each of these peoples elaborated on the astrological themes of the previous culture. It certainly helped that they shared the same astrological forms, ideas regarding time counts, symbolic images, a belief in mundane— world-based—astrology, and the study of planetary phenomena, especially Venus.

Many of their guiding principles were based on the sun and the day, which is the sun's creation. (In the Mayan language the word *kin* means "sun," "day," and "time"—there is no distinction.) They valued both astronomy and numerology, and because they believed a sequence of 20 had great import, they created 20 totems which were then grouped

into sets of 13, resulting in a combined cycle of 260 days. They also believed that certain time periods had special meaning, something modern doctors compare to the study of biorhythms.

Unfortunately, far too little of the astrological knowledge of Mesoamerica was preserved after the Spanish conquest—the invaders their burned books and banned astrological practices, so information could only be passed along orally. What historians know today on the subject has been pieced together from the oral tradition and the few remaining documents the Spanish did not destroy, as well as the work of Spanish chroniclers, often priests, who wrote down first-hand accounts of indigenous life and culture.

The Mayans

The Mayan civilization arose in the tropical rain forests of the Yucatan, predominately in what is now Belize and Guatamala. Its dominion extended across three main time periods: Pre-Classic (2000 BC to AD 250), Classic (250 to 900) and Post-Classic (900 to 1519), although it was well past its peak by the time the Spanish invaded in the early 1500s. These conquistadors eventually destroyed much of the culture, which had been notable for its art, architecture, mathematics, and astronimical study, along with the development of a sophisticated logosyllabic script, similar to Egyptian heiroglyphics. Only remote villages that escaped Spanish notice were able to keep their traditions alive. Fortunately, many examples of their architecture have survived in the form of pyramids and other ceremonial structures.

Mayans incorporated both astronomy and astrology into their religion, which led to the development of a divine calendar of 260 days, the *Tzolk'in*. There was also a civil lunar calendar, the *Haab*, of 365 days. Their multiple dieties were linked to the Tzolk'in and to the cosmos, with their behavior varying based on the movement of celestial bodies. This allowed priests to determine which dieties required ceremonies or ritual sacrifices, including occasional humans. Gods that ruled the skies included Itzamna, the sun creator; K'inich Ahau, god of the day sun; the Jaguar, god of the night sun in the Underworld; and Ix Chel, the moon goddess.

Mayan astrology, however, was not based so much on the movement of planets and stars, but rather on the energy rhythms of the universe. A person's horoscope was determined not monthly or yearly, but daily, and each day had its own name and sign. For instance, if a calendar cycle began on the first totem, Crocodile-1, it would end at the 13th totem, Reed-13. The next grouping would begin as Jaguar-1 and end 13 totems later as Deer-1. This calendar cycle ends when every totem has served to begin a 13-day cycle, with the process totaling 260 days. The Mayan respect for creation is reflected in this number—it coincides with the average length of human gestation as well as the germination span of maize (corn) from sowing to harvest.

The End of the World...

During the late 20th century, while many cultural historians were studying the astronomical findings and astrological beliefs of ancient civilazations, the Mayan calendar came under scrutiny. Imagine the shock when these students of antiquity realized the current Mayan Long Count calendar was winding down ... and seemed to be predicting the end of the world on December 12, 2012. The Mayans, widely influenced by numerology, structured their days into units: one day was a kin, 20 days was a uinal, 360 days a tun, 7,200 days a katun. Twenty katuns formed a baktun; 13 baktuns formed a creation epoch, which equaled 260 katuns, or a period of about 5,126 years. Once this Long Count was over, the universe was believed to reset itself and start over . . . in other words, a doomsday scenario was approaching. Happily, the date in December came and went, and the world went on spinning.

The Twenty Mesoamerican Totems

English	Mayan	Mayan Tribe	Aztec	Action
Alligator/Crocodile	Imix	Red Dragon	Cipactli	Nurture
Wind	Ik	White Wind	Ehecatl	Communicate
House	Akbal	Blue Night	Calli	Dream
Lizard	Kan	Yellow Seed	Cuetzpalin	Target
Serpent	Chicchan	Red Serpent	Coatl	Survive
Death	Cimi	White World-Bridger	Cimi	Equalize
Deer	Manik	Blue Hand	Manik	Know
Rabbit	Lamat	Yellow Star	Tochtli	Beautify
Water	Muluc	Red Moon	Atl	Purify
Dog	Oc	White Dog	Itzcuintli	To love
Monkey	Chuen	Blue Monkey	Ozomahtli	Play
Grass	Eb	Yellow Human	Malinalli	Influence
Reed	Ben	Red Skywalker	Ben	Explore
Ocelot/Jaguar	Ix	White Wizard	Ocelotl	Enchant
Eagle	Men	Blue Eagle	Cuauhtli	Create
Vulture	Cib	Yellow Warrior	Cib	Question
Earthquake/Earth	Caban	Red Earth	Ollin	Evolve
Knife	Etznab	White Mirror	Tecpatl	Reflect
Rain/Storm	Cauac	Blue Storm	Cauac	Catalyze
Flower	Ahau	Yellow Sun	Xochitl	Enlighten

This page: Maya stela (statue) at the ancient city of Tikal;
Opposite: Pyramid of the Sun, Mexico

The Aztecs

The Aztecs were a group of fierce warriors, the Nahua people, whose empire flourished from around 1100 until the incursion of the Spanish in the early 1500s. The capital, Tenochtitlan, lay in Central Mexico and was set on an island in Lake Texcoco. It is now the site of Mexico City. Their religion was woven around calendar rituals and the worship of many dieties. This included the local favorite, Quetzalcoatl, the Feathered Serpent, the god of wind, sky, and stars. The center of the Templo Mayor, in the capital city, was where the four directions of the universe supposedly originated. The temple itself was considered the embodiment of a living myth where sacred power was concentrated. As with other Mesoamerican cultures, two different calendars were used simultaneously—*tonalpuhualli*, one of 260 days used for divination and to mark rituals, and a solar calendar of 365 days called *xiupohualli*. These calendars converged every 52 years and a new cycle began.

Among Aztec records are references to soothsayers and readers of day signs, called *tlapouhqui* or *tonalpouhqui*. Mind-altering substances such as peyote or morning glory would sometimes be employed to help the prophecy or answer gel. Maize kernals could also be tossed into the air, and the patterns they formed were then interpreted. In addition to soothsayers, other ritual specialists who could divine information from the gods were the priest-astronomers, who kept records of the movement of stars, and the rulers, who could summon dead ancestors or petition gods for advice.

The Aztecs believed that all people were protected by the gods from birth, which was the date that determined their character, tendencies, talents, and future path. They felt that an individual must discover his or her "power" in life in order to achieve personal victories and to contribute successfully to the community.

South America

In pre-Columbian South America, the numerous indigenous peoples were keen observers of the sky. In these mostly agrarian societies, the cycles of the sun, moon, and stars were faithful indicators of the annual seasonal weather shifts, so critical for successful planting and harvesting.

With this came a certain respect for any portents or indicators that might also be offered by celestial bodies, especially those occurring on or around a birth date. It was not uncommon for priests to be the interpreters of astrological indicators.

The Incas

The Incas oversaw the largest empire in pre-Columbian America. It arose around the 13th century and fell when the region was conquered in 1572 by the Spanish. As a society without many civilized "trappings," including the wheel, draft animals, awareness of iron or steel, and a written language, it still managed to conquer a large portion of western South America. It was known, however, for its monumental stone architecture, network of roadways, vibrant textiles, and agricultural innovations. Inca rulers enforced the worship of sun god Inti, also called Apu-punchau, over other religions, and considered their king the "son of the sun."

The Quecha people not only identified various stars and constellations, they assigned a purpose to each of them, primarily the protection of different animals. This interconnectedness was a strong part of their belief system. They

Opposite: To the Incas, **the Milky Way** was seen as a river, with the dark areas of **the Great Rift** representing living animals. **This page: Machu Pichu,** the Incan citadel, was astrologically positioned in both Leo and Capricorn and used as a celestial observatory.

even laid out their temples and pillars so that heavenly bodies like the sun would pass over them or shine through their windows on certain days, such as solstices.

In addition to inanimate, "connect-the-dots" constellations made of visble stars, the Incas also identified certain dark nebulae in the Great Rift. (This was a series of dark patches in the Milky Way that were more visible in the Soutern Hemisphere.)

The Incas gave animal names to these "dark cloud constellations," believed they were alive, and associated them with seasonal rains. In keeping with the Incan conviction that all things in the universe were connected, they believed that the dark animals of the Great Rift had relationships with their namesakes on earth and lived in harmony with each other. This was a departure from the way most other cultures viewed constellations, which was

as separate, remote entities that did not interact with each other.

Sadly, after the fall of the Incan empire and the arrival of European colonists to the continent, many of the customs—and the rituals that depended on the study of the stars—were lost. Still, a number of Europeans, including Catholic priests, took the time to chronicle the local traditions and beliefs, helping to preserve them for posterity.

The Incan zodiac incorporated indigenous animals, including the Tinamou bird and that invaluable beast of burden, the Llama.

The major dark constellations identified by the Incas included:

Mach'acuay the Serpent, which emerges in August and was said to oversee all snakes on earth, protecting them, and ensuring procreation.

Hanp'atu the Toad, who arranges the croaking of frogs and toads to be foretellers of rain; his appearance in the night sky also signaled the start of planting season.

Yutu the Tinamou, a clumsy bird similar to a partridge, chases Hanp'atu in the sky, the way birds pursue frogs on the ground.

Urcuchillay the Llama emerges next, in November. This is another dark constellation, although the stars Beta and Alpha Centauri served as its eyes.

Atoq the Fox is positioned at the foot of the Llama, where it poses little threat. The sun passes through the constellation in

December, the time when fox kits are born on earth.

Fortunately, the Incan connection to and respect for the cosmos and the influence of the dark constellations was able to survive the advent of the Spanish overlords and centuries of forced assimilation ... and remains part of the Quecha-speaking culture of the central Andes today.

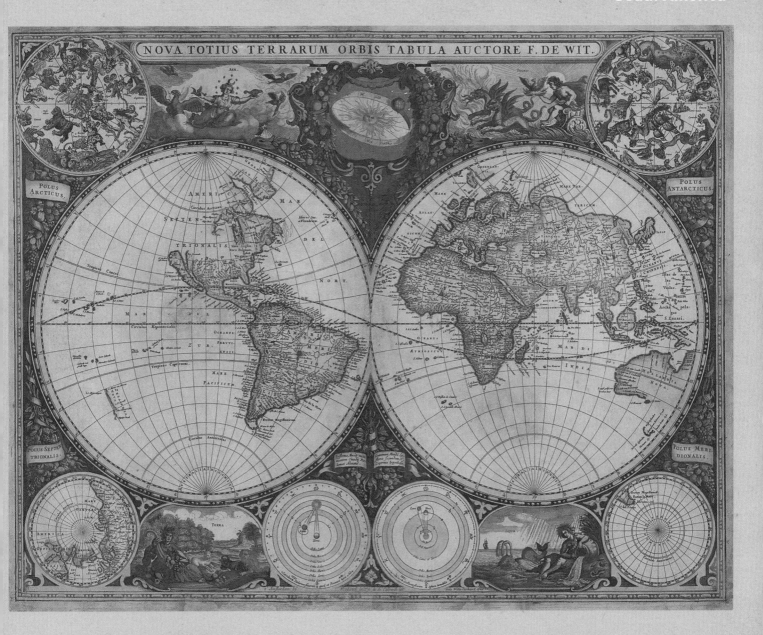

NOVA TOTIUS TERRARUM ORBIS TABULA AUCTORE F. DE WIT.

The Zodiac Below the Equator

When in the Northern Hemisphere, astrologers most often look to the south. This is because the sun and the culminating degree of the zodiac (a person's midheaven astrology sign or MC) are found in a southerly direction. The planets are also mostly seen in the southern sweep of the sky. But for those who live below the Equator, it is the reverse: the sun culminates in a northern direction as does the MC; this is also the part of the sky where most planets

can be seen. Additionally, the zodiac runs clockwise here and the 12 constellations are seen as mirror inversions. It has been suggested that because the seasons are reversed, that signs in southern regions should match the proper seasons. Thus those born in Aries (spring in the north, but fall in the Southern Hemisphere) should have Libra as their sun sign below the Equator. Most astrologers from those regions reject this idea, however.

Chapter Two | Ancient Origins

Australia & New Zealand

Australia

The First Nations of Australia, the Aboriginals and Torres Strait Islander peoples, possess a culture that stretches back more than 65,000 years, making them the longest continuing culture in the world, as well as the oldest astronomers.

Above: Uluru, or Ayers Rock, in Australia's Northern Territory is located on a major planetary grid point and is believed to be home to the ancestral spirits of the Aborigines.

They not only developed ways to observe the sun, moon, stars, and planets to aid navigation, help create calendars, and predict weather, they also assigned meaning to celestial events that had a bearing on their laws and societal structure. Plus the better they were at reading the sky, the better they could predict there when to hunt, fish, harvest, and come together. These astral phenomena also influenced the songs, stories, oral traditions, and artwork passed down by the elders for many millennia.

Like the Mayans and Incas of Mesoamerica, the Aborigines of Australia also discerned dark cloud constellations in the Great Rift, a series of dark patches in the Milky Way that is more visible in southern regions. The most prominent of these is Gugurmin, the Emu in the Sky, whose head is formed by the dark nebula known as Coalsack. Its story arose from the lore of the Wiradjuri people of central New South Wales. This Emu has even been commemorated on a unique one dollar silver coin featuring Gugurmin floating in the sky with three Aborgine men dancing below.

Regional Beliefs

Aboriginal communities are scattered throughout many parts of Australia. Each has developed their own set of myths or legends about the human relationship with celestial bodies. Some

of Dreamtime, the Aborigine version of the creation story, when the first ancestors walked the earth. They resembled plants and were half human, but were responsible for creating the landscape of earth, all the animals, as well as air, water, and fire, and the sun, moon, and stars. Dreamtime also represents a psychic state wherein the "dreamer" can make contact with ancestral spirits. Similar to many native Americans, these indigenous people feel that all natural creatures on earth are part of one unchanging network of relationships that can be traced to the Great Spirit Ancestors of Dreamtime.

The Wardaman communities of the Northern Territory relate that during the Dreamtime Buwarraja, when the spiritual world gave way to the current natural word, the shadows of

the Spiritual People, especially the major Spiritual Ancestors, went up into the black spaces of the Milky Way. These entities—Bowonin, Nardi, Dungdung, and Rainbow Gorrondolmi—gaze down at earth each night to make sure the humans are caring for the land.

Luritja country, situated west and south of Alice Springs in the Outback, extends around the edge of Arrernte country. Here scientists found Aboriginal rock art with symbolism that confirms that early Aborigines had a strong understanding of astronomy and our planet's role in the Solar System. The stars and other celestial objects formed the basis of many of their origin stories.

At Lake Tyrrell in Victoria state, research revealed that the now-lost Boorang Aborigine community may have lived there for 30,000 years, or a thousand generations. They identified more than 40 constellations based on local birds, fish, and animals, which had been catalogued by Englishman William Stanbridge in the late 1800s after speaking with the Boorangs.

The *Kamilaroi* and *Euahlayi* peoples and their neighbours, the *Murrawarri* and *Ngemba*, are an

Aboriginal cultural grouping of New South Wales. Their sky lore includes myths about the moon, the Milky Way, the Pleiades, the Southern Cross, Orion, and the Small and Large Megellanic Clouds—with the SMC being the *Wiringin*, "the clever man" who separates the deceased into initiated and uninitiated, those who are reborn.

Delving into Deep Space

The Wajarri Yamatji people of Western Australia have a long tradition of skygazing, but they also now have the ability delve into deep space and explore the universe. The region over which they hold title claims is home to the Murchison Radioastronomy Observatory, which was constructed in 2009 and comprises the Square Kilometer Array, the Australian Ska Pathfinder, and the Murchison Widefield Array. The leasees agreed to respect the cultural traditions of the Wajarri, who are allowed to move across the land providing they maintain the radio silence. Radio telescopes are specialized antennas and radio receivers that have the ability to detect radio frequency radiation emanating from extraterrestrial sources like stars, galaxies, and quasars.

A clear night sky in the Southern Hemisphere, showing **The Milky Way** over the Pacific

New Zealand

Like the indigenous people of Australia, the Māoris of New Zealand were also masters of observing the movement of objects in the sky. They believed that an understanding of cosmology augmented the spiritual, social, and practical aspects of life and was thus linked to all elements of their culture. The heavens also furnished source material for a rich history of mythmaking and legends.

The Māori saying, that "knowledge flows like a waterfall from the stars," can be taken beyond the limits of practical advice—the stars telling humans when it was time to plant or reap—into the realm of what is spiritual and healing, that which fosters growth.

This close relationship with the stars also enabled them to use celestial navigation on the open waters between islands, vital for trade with communities living miles distant from each other. The question historians asked was, could that type of primitive navigation have guided the first Māori explorers to New Zealand? Fortunately, Sir Hector Busby had an answer. Busby (or Heke-nuku-mai-nga-iwi Puhipi) was a Māori/Pākehā navigator and builder of wakas, traditional canoes. In 2012, after a 5,000 nautical mile journey from New Zealand his craft, *Te Aurere*, arrived in Rapa Nui (Easter Island), thus re-establishing the effectiveness of celestial navigation and substantiating the theory—based on their similar language—that the Māori people originated there. In addition to utilizing star positions to establish location at sea, celestial navigation also factors in currents, cloud formations, wave patterns, and the behavior of birds and marine life.

There was a reflowering of interest in Māori astronomy and astrology in the 1990s, perhaps not coincidentally around the same time that Project Hindsight, a 1993 translation project aimed at interpreting the surviving Hellenic astrology texts, had a similar effect on reviving Western astrology.

The Maori Creation Myth

According to legend, the ancestral world of the Maori began with a dark void, then moved to a supreme god, Lo-Matua-Kore, followed by emerging light, and then the creation of the physical world and two primeval parents, Ranginui and Papatuānuku. After the birth of their children, they are forcibly split apart— Rangi as the sky father that provides rain, Papa as the earth mother that represents the land and nourishment. The sun, moon, and stars were perceived as celestial beings, grandchildren of the primeval parents and parented by Tangotango and Wainui. The humans were also their grandchildren, fathered by Tānemāhuta. Humans were taught that they could reach back along this ancestral lineage by the pursuit of star knowledge.

A group of Hawaiian Tikis including **Maui the Trickster**

Polynesia

The ancient Polynesians were accurate trackers of celestial bodies through the night sky, especially the the seafaring inhabitants of the many South Pacific island groups.

Using the stars to navigate allowed them to determine their latitude and longitude in open water, both essential for the long-distance travel between different islands required for trading, social visits, and the occasional raids. Along with the ever-present sea, the movement of the cosmos also supplied inspiration for their myths and legends. According to their beliefs, this was where many of their gods dwelled and they were known for interacting with the stars. For instance, the

demigod/folk hero Maui the Trickster was said to have lassoed the sun to slow its passage across the sky and used a fishhook made from Scorpio's tail to raise the Hawaiian Islands from the depths of the sea.

In Hawaii the eastern star was called Manalo and the evening star Na-holo-holo. The first appearance of the Pleiades, the star group also called the Seven Sisters, in the autumn evening sky marked the beginning of the calendar year; it was called Makahiki and greeted with celebration. Other Polynesian groups started their year when the Pleiades appeared in the morning sky, sometime around June. The Hawaiian year was called Makahiki, and it was broken down into 12 lunar months, starting with the new moon. In Tahiti, each night of the 29/30-day month was assigned a different name based on the phase of the moon.

Navigation Revival

HOKULE'A IMAGE © POLYNESIAN VOYAGING SOCIETY
PHOTO © 'OIWI TV — PHOTOGRAPHER: SAM KAPOI

After Captain Cook's arrival in Hawaii the islanders were exposed to more scientific tools for navigation such as sextants, compasses, and charts . . . and the old ways fell out of use. But since the 1970s, there has been a revival of interest in Polynesian navigation and astronomy. Native Hawaiian Nainoa Thompson studied the ancient art and was also a leader in reconstructing a traditional, double-hulled voyaging canoe, the Hokule`a. He was the first Hawaiian since the 14th century to practice this traditional form of navigation when he sailed to other Polynesian nations without Western instruments.

Hawaiian Zodiac

The Hawaiian form of the zodiac corresponds with the Western zodiac in terms of dates and totemic symbols.

Western	Hawaiian	Traits
Aries	**Nana**	Instigator, crusader
Taurus	**Welo**	Builder, producer
Gemini	**Ikiiki**	Artist, inventor
Cancer	**Kaaona**	Prophet, teacher
Leo	**Hilinaehu Ku**	Leader, controller
Virgo	**Mahoe Mua Pele**	Craftsperson, critic
Libra	**Mahoe Hope**	Statesman, manager
Scorpio	**Ikuwa**	Overseer, inspector
Sagittarius	**Welehu**	Sage, counselor
Capricorn	**Makalii**	Ambassador, researcher
Aquarius	**Kealo**	Truth seeker, scientist
Pisces	**Mahimahi Kaulua**	Idealist, philosopher

Chapter Three

The Fabled Astrologers

Biography

Names: Zarathustra, Zarathushtra Spitama, Ashu Zarathushtra
Status: Founder, theologian, prophet, astrologer
Lived: Second millenium BC, or possibly 700–600 BC
Era: Persian Empire

Right: Zoroaster. Zoroastrianism, also known as *Mazdayasna* by the Iranian people, dates back to the second century BC and emerged from the teachings of the reforming prophet Zoroaster.

Zoroaster

Zoroaster, upon whose teachings the religion called Zoroastrianism is based, was one of the most influential figures to arise from the region of ancient Iran.

Although little is known of his origins, some scholars believe he lived in the second millennium BC, while others place him later, around 700 or 600 BC, in the time of Cyrus the Great or Darius. A speaker of Old Avestan, he is credited with composing the *Gathas* as well as the *Yasna Haptanghaiti*, a collection of hymns written in his native dialect and which formed the liturgy of his religious services. Most of what is known about his life was culled from these texts.

He likely trained to become a priest starting at age seven, was ordained at 15, and at 20 left his home to seek wisdom from other priests and teachers. At 30 he experienced a revelation during a spring festival ... a shining being on a riverbank revealed himself to the young man as Vohu Manah (Good Purpose) and told him about Ahura Mazda (Wise Lord) along with five other radiant beings. Zoroaster was also made aware of two primal spirits, including Angra Mainyu (Destructive Spirit), which opposed Asha (order) and supported Druj (deception). At this point he felt compelled to spend his life encouraging the search for Asha. His teachings, which challenged traditional beliefs of Indo-Iranian religion, were collected into the *Gathas* and the *Avesta*, and eventually became the predominant religion of ancient Persia.

Zoroaster's doctrines on individual judgement, Heaven and Hell, the resurrection of the body, the Last Judgement, and everlasting life being offered to the reunited soul and body were most likely borrowed by the Abrahamic religions, but much of his original context was lost. In addition to Zoroastrianism, today his teachings are venerated by a number of other religions, including Manichaeism, Bahá'í Faith, Mithraism, and Ahmadiyya.

Zoroaster's reputation as a sorcerer and astrologer was likely accurate, as it was normal for priests of that time factor in astral and planetary influences as part of their religious divination. Reinforcing this image of a holy magician was a "mass of literature" supposedly written by him and translated into multiple languages that made its way throughout the Mediterranean region from the 3rd century AD onward, even beyond the end of antiquity. Another pseudo-book said to be written by Zoroaster, the *Asteroskopita* (or *Apotelesmatika*), ran to five papyrus rolls and was purportedly an astrological

handbook for the making of predictions. His acolytes, known as the Magi, were astrologer/priests, perhaps best known for their Biblical journey to Bethlehem to acknowledge the birth of Christ. Surviving Zoroastrian texts indicate that the Magi used astrology as a method of measuring historical and calendrical time. They also used it as a means to date key events in Indo-Iranian history.

"The Twelve Ones"

In the Middle Persion language, the constellations of the Zoroastrian zodiac are called *Dwazdah-Akhtaran* or the "twelve ones." These groupings of stars were considered *bayan*, bringers of beneficence, while the planets were viewed warily as portents of harmful change, capable of reducing the positve effects of the constellations. Although this system was similar to the Greek zodiac, it used several different symbols and separated Western Pisces into two signs.

Zoroastrian Zodiac Signs

Western name	Zoroastrian name	Symbol
Aries	**Varak**	Ram
Taurus	**Gav**	Bull
Gemini	**Dopatkar**	Twins
Cancer	**Karzang**	Crab
Leo	**Shagr**	Lion
Virgo	**Hushag**	Ear of grain
Libra	**Tarazuk**	Scales
Scorpio	**Gazdum**	Scorpion
Sagittarius	**Nimasp**	Centaur
Capricorn	**Vahik**	Goat
Aquarius	**Dul**	Water pail
Pisces (Feb 14–Mar 15)	**Mahik**	Fish
Pisces (Mar 16–Mar 20)	**Hamaspath-maidyem**	Mid-path of all

Biography

Name: Pythagorus of Samos
Status: Philosopher, mathematician, astronomer, astrologer, founder
Born: 569 BC; Samos, Greece
Died: c.495 BC; Metapontum Village, Italy
Era: Archaic Period of Greece

Pythagorus

Pythagorus was an Ionian Greek philosopher, a "man of surpassing knowledge," who founded a school in Crotone, Italy. As a result, his teachings became well known throughout Greece and Southern Italy and went on to influence Plato, Aristotle, and much of Western philosophy.

He was already known for the mathematics discovery that in a right-angled triangle the square of the hypotenuse is equal to the sum of the squares of the other two sides, which in modern times is called Pythagorean theorem. (It is possible this formula was known to the Babylonians a thousand years earlier, but Pythagoras got the name cred.) He also pointed out that music had mathematical foundations and was acknowledged by his peers for identifying musical intervals, the differences in pitch between two sounds.

Philosophically he advocated for metempsychosis or the "transmigration of the soul"—the belief that each soul is immortal and that after death it enters a new body. He may have also been the originator of a doctrine called *musica universalis*, which proposes that planets move according to mathematical equations and produce an inaudible symphony of music. Pythagoras was also an astrologer and numerologist; he is considered have originated the concept of aspects, the angles which planets make with each other in the horoscope. His belief in sacred geometry, that numbers had qualities that could be experienced, expanded the reach of mathematics to include an occult dimension that could stimulate healing. He valued the numbers 1, the monad; 2, the dyad; 3, the first true number standing for knowledge, shaped into the triangle; 4, the solid foundation, shaped into the square; and 6, the perfect number containing 1, 2, and 3. The number 12 represented the spheres of the universe—God, seven planets, earth, air, fire, and water—as well as the 12 signs of the zodiac.

Berossus was a Hellenic-era priest of Bel (Marduk) and a contemporary of Alexander the Great. He is credited with bringing Babylonian astrology to the Greek-speaking world. As a young man in Babylonia, he doubtless received a traditional classical education, and this was supplemented at some point after the Macedonian conquest when he acquired the ability to read and write Greek.

Biography

Name: Berossus
Status: Priest, astronomer, astrologer, chronicler
Born: c.350 BC; Babylon
Died: after 281 BC
Era: Hellenic

Berossus

Berossus is perhaps best known for leaving Babylon and settling on the island of Kos off of Asia Minor, where he taught Babylonian astrology under the sponsorship of the king of Egypt. If he was not precisely the first to do this, he was at least the first to establish a school for translating the ancient cuneiform texts into a contemporary language. And even though many of the technical and theoretical details of pre-Hellenistic Babylonian astrology in Greece have been reduced to a few tablets, the doctrine of *apokatastasis*——or eternal recurrence——was attributed to Berossus by the Roman philosopher and statesman Seneca. In later life Berossus compiled a three-book history of Babylon, *Babyloniaca*,

possibly meant to correct Greek misconceptions about his homeland. It was based on ancient texts and records that have since been lost. And although very little of his book remains, as well, fragments were preserved in the works of Jewish historian Flavius Josephus and Christian historian Eusebius, enough to give a clear idea of the book's content. It has been

suggested that this book was one of several sources for the Biblical Book of Genesis. An additional accomplishment may have been the invention of the semi-circular sundial carved from a cubical block (according to Roman architect Vitruvius). A statue was erected to Berossus in Athens, likely as a testament to his abilities as a historian and an astronomer/astrologer.

A False History

In 1498, an official of Pope Alexander VI named Annius of Viterbo claimed to have found the lost books of Berossus. These turned out to be carefully crafted forgeries. Oddly, this fact did not stop these works from becoming an influence on Renaissance attitudes toward population and migration—the forged books included a list of kings from Japhet onward, filling in a gap in the Bible following the tale of the Great Flood.

Biography

Names: Hipparchus of Nicaea, Hipparchos
Status: Astronomer, mathematician, geographer
Born: c.190 BC; Nicaea, Bithynia, Greece
Died: c.120 BC; Rhodes, Roman Republic
Era: Hellenistic period

Hipparchus

Hipparchus was a Greek mathematician, astronomer, and geographer who is considered by many to be the top astronomer of classical antiquity.

Known as the "father of trigonometry," he not only compiled the first known trigonometry table, he also calculated the length of the solar year within 6.5 minutes and could calculate the time and location of eclipses. Arguably his greatest discovery was the precessional movement of the equinoxes, which is the movement of the celestial equator with regard to the fixed stars and the ecliptic path of the sun as viewed from earth. Hipparchus determined that the equinoxes were moving through the zodiac at a rate of not less than 1 degree per century. The modern value is 1 degree in 72 years.

He made studies of the motion of the moon and closely estimated the distance from the earth to the moon to be between 59 and 67 earth radii; the actual distance is 60 radii. His star catalogue contained at least 850 entries and was likely the first such compilation in the Western world. He calculated and proposed a heliocentric universe but then abandoned the notion when he realized the orbits of the planets would not be circular, as the science of the time demanded they be. He was also the first Greek to apply the Babylonian technique of dividing a circle into 360 degrees and 60 arc minutes. He is believed to be the inventor of the astrolabe, a handheld astronomical device for measuring altitudes and for calculating latitudes during navigation. It is not surprising he is considered the originator of scientific Greek astronomy after transforming it from a theoretical affair to a practical, predictive discipline.

Although there is no record of Hipparchus ever writing about astrology, his many astronomical discoveries and predictions have become invaluable to astrologers. As Roman natural historian Pliny the Elder wrote, Hipparchus can "never be sufficiently praised, no one having done more to prove that man is related to the stars and that our souls are a part of heaven."

In the second and third centuries coins commemorating his achievements and showing him holding a globe were circulated in Bithynia.

Roman Emperor Tiberius

An Egyptian of Greek descent, Thrasyllus's family origins are unknown, but he eventually rose to become court astrologer to the powerful emperor Tiberius, as well as a personal friend.

Thrasyllus

Biography

Names: Tiberius Claudius Thrasyllus, Thrasyllus of Mendes, Thrasyllus of Alexandria
Status: Astrologer, grammarian, philosopher
Born: c.1st century BC; Mendes or Alexandria
Died: AD 36
Era: Early Roman Empire

This connection is corroborated in the *Annals* of Tacitus and *The Twelve Caesars* by Suetonius. The two men met during Tiberius' voluntary exile on the Greek island of Rhodes, possibly 2 BC to AD 4, and the Egyptian became a valued companion, engaing Tiberius in the study of astrology and exposing him to the philosophy of the Stoics.

It was Thrasyllus who predicted that Tiberius would be recalled to Rome as the successor to his stepfather, Augustus, the first emperor. He accompanied him back to Rome and became his valued counselor both in the capital city and on the island of Capri, where Tiberius went to take the sea air. As a reward for his faithful service, Tiberius granted Thrasyllus and his family Roman citizenship. Being a trusted member of the court had its disadvantages, however. The astrologer sometimes had to foil plots against the emperor, but when a number of innocent Roman nobles appeared to be at risk from a suspicious Tiberius, Thrasyllus told the emperor he would outlive them all, thus saving their necks. The astrologer died before Tiberius, and so never saw the fulfillment of his prediction that the monstrous Caligula would succeed his friend.

Thrasyllus was also a literary scholar and a self-professed Pythagorean who had studed in Rhodes. Because he wrote on Platonic and Pythagorean philosophy, it might be assumed that his theory of astrology represents Middle Platonism from the early 1st century (the complex philosophical concept that there is a singple, supreme source of goodness and being in the universe from which all other things descend, and that man has free will, but that once a path is chosen, his fate is set.) Yet his summary of his own work also indicates his use of earlier sources, especially the writings of Nechepso and Petosiris, and Hermes Trismegistus. In effect, his astrological character was shaped by a mixture of Hermetic and Pythagorean elements.

Early Chinese Astrologers

In spite of the continuing popularity of the Chinese zodiac, especially in Asia where it has been widely adapted, the actual astrologers who originated and then expanded on this knowledge do not seem to be spotlit by Chinese history. There are, however, some exceptions, men of science and other scholarly pursuits, who also believed in the power of the stars and planets to influence the destinies of those dwelling below. Famous—or notorious—Chinese astrologers include the following:

Gan De

Gan De, born in the 4th century BC in the State of Qi, was an astronomer and astrologist. Along with Shi Shen he is the first known person to compile a star catalogue. He was preceded by the many unknown Babylonians who collected such lists and followed by the Greek Hipparchus, who was the first identified person in Western-based Hellenic astronomy to have done so. Gan De recorded his observations of the planets, especially Jupitier, and he may have been the first to describe one of the Galilean moons of that planet, usually invisible without the aid of a telescope. A fragment of his work that survived into the 20th century identified a naked-eye observation of either of the planet's two largest and brightest moons, Ganymede or Callisto.

Shi Shen

Shi Shen, a contemporary of Gan De and also an astronomer and astrologer, was born in the Chinese State of Wei. In addition to cataloguing the stars, he made the first surviving report on the presence of sun spots, erroneously believing they were eclipses that began at the sun's center and would expand. Nevertheless, he correctly identified them as solar occurrances. His writings include *The Rocks of Space, Celestial Map, and Star Catalogue of Shi*. Only a few examples of his crucial writings have been preserved.

Xu Fu

Xu Fu, a somewhat infamous opportunist, was an alchemist born in 255 BC in the ancient State of Qi. He was appointed the personal doctor of the first emperor of China, Qin Shi Huang, and when the emperor expressed a desire to live forever, Xu told him of an overseas god who possessed this secret. The emperor sent him off to this imaginery realm with bountiful supplies and several thousand virginal teens of both sexes. When Xu returned two years later, he reported the failure of the mission due to a large fish or whale. On the next voyage he sailed with a group of archers to kill the monster. This time he encountered a welcoming land with a tropical climate and

friendly inhabitants. He and the virginal teens all settled there, where he taught the locals how to farm and fish, declaring himself king. Historian believe he cleverly invented this tale of the "elixir of life" in order to escape the despotic rule of the emperor.

Zhang Heng

Zhang Heng, born AD 78 in Nanyang, China, was a polymath and statesman of the Han dynasty. His pursuits, in addition to astrology, included astronomy, math, engineering, cartography, art, poetry, and philosophy. With his extensive knowledge of mechanics, he was able to invent a water-powered armillary sphere to assist astronomical observation, a device that later aided astrologers and engineers. He also improved the inflow water clock by providing an additional tank and created the first seismoscope that could detect the cardinal direction of earthquakes from over 300 miles away. He calculated Pi to 3.1466, identified 2,500 stars, and formed theories about the nature of the moon's visible and hidden sides, and its relationship to the sun. Zhang died in AD

139 in Luoyang, but received many posthumous honors, including comparisons to the Greco-Roman master, Ptolemy.

Zu Chongzhi

Zu Chongzhi, courtesy name Wenyuan, was born c. AD 429 and died AD 500. Both an astrologer and engineer, he calculated Pi to between 3.1415926 and 3.1415297—a record held for 800 years, predicted four eclipses by studying the number of overlaps made by the sun and moon, made a close-to-accurate calculation of the length of Jupiter's year, and created a formula for the volume of a sphere that is equivalent to the modern formula. As an astrologer he differentiated the sidereal year from the tropical year and introduced the Daming calendar in 465. Unfortunately, during Zu's lifetime the Liu Song and Southern Qi dynasties officially adopted Confucianism, which viewed occultists and shamans with suspicion. As a result many astrologers became marginalized.

Ruins of Sidon Castle in the Lebanon

Biography

Name: Dorotheus of Sidon
Status: Astrologer, writer
Lived: c. late first century AD;
Sidon, Lebanon
Era: Hellenic

Dorotheus

This influential Greek astrologer lived in the late first century AD, possibly in Alexandria at some point.

He may have been a Lebanese from Sidon or hailed from Egypt or merely traveled to that country, as well as to Mesopotamia, in search of astrological doctrines as was the custom for that time. He admitted in his own prefaces that he was a frequently compiler of information from the foremost authorities.

Dorotheus is best known for writing a five-volume instructional poem on Hellenic astrology that is sometimes referred to as the *Pentateuch*. This textbook would go on to have a huge impact on the astrological practices of the Hellenistic and Medieval eras. Alas, the entire book has not survived the passage of time, but there are English translations based on Arabic translations—dating from around 800 AD and carried out by Omar Tiberiades—of a Persian version that was taken from the original Greek source. Other fragments of the work in Greek and Latin were also preserved by astrologers.

Although his astrological preferences are never made clear in his work (recall that its Arabic translation was bound to be several times removed from the original text), it is thought that he followed the same modified Stoicism as Valens and the other noted astrologers from the first and second centuries AD. Dorotheus is unique, however, in that he wrote an entire work of electional astrology, to wit: using astrological principles to determine the most propitious time to begin a new venture or project. This would indicate he did not believe that a person's fate was set in stone like the strict Stoicists, but thought more like the Middle Platonists or neoplatonists, that once a choice was made, the fate of the undertaking was determined at that moment of decision.

In later eras, Dorotheus was said to have influenced Manetho (2nd century), Anubio (2nd century) and Maximus (4th century), all three of whom also published books on astrology written in verse.

Biography

Name: Julia Balbilla
Status: Poet, courtier
Born: AD 72; Rome, Italy
Died: after AD 130; Athens, Greece
Era: Early Roman empire

Julia Balbilla

While it was not common in the ancient world for women to become astrologers, there is little doubt that many females who visited astrologers began to study the discipline on their own.

A few select women may have even risen to become notable in their own right. One who had an opportunity to accomplish this was Julia Balbilla, although it remains clouded as to whether she she ever practiced astrology, even if it was a notable part of her heritage.

Babilla was a member of the royal family of the Kingdom of Commagene in modern-day Turkey, and her ancestry included Greek, Egyptian, Armenian, Median, Syrian, and Seleucian elements. Brought up in Rome by her paternal grandparents, she and her brother received a classical Greek education. As a young woman she traveled in the highest circles and was court poet and friend to Emperor Hadrian. She also served as a companion to his wife, Vibia Sabina and was meant to prevent the empress's affairs with the learned men in her retinue.

Balbilla hailed from a lineage of astrologers: her maternal grandfather, after whom she was named, was Tiberius Claudius Balbilis, an astrologer and scholar and the son of Emperor Tiberius's personal astrologer, Thrasyllus of Mendes; Julia's own efforts as an astrologer have never been attested, but it is hard to imagine the descendant of Thrasyllus and Balbilis not applying her familiar knowledge of the stars and planets in a court so swept up by astrology as that of Hadrian and his wife. Plus her surviving poetry references the sun and the heavens.

In AD 129 Julia accompanied the imperial couple to the Valley of the Kings in Egypt and was commissioned to memorialize the group's return visit in November, 130. She thus inscribed three epigrams in Aeolic Greek on the Colossi of Memnon, which may have reminded her of the large sculptures found on Mount Nemrut, Turkey. (Although she was heeding a request from the emperor of Rome, her inscriptions on this earlier work of art fall perilously close to graffiti.)

Balbilla eventually left Rome to settle in Athens, where she married an aristocrat but died without issue.

Biography

Names: Claudius Ptolemy of Alexandria,
Claudius Ptolemaeus
Status: Mathematician, astrologer, astronomer,
naturalist, philosopher
Born: c. AD 100; Egypt, Roman Empire
Died: c. AD 168; Alexandria, Egypt, Roman Empire
Era: Roman Empire

Ptolemy

During the second century, as astrology continued to increase in popularity, two Alexandrian writers of differing philosophical viewpoints came to the fore: Claudius Ptolemy and Vettius Valens.

Unlike Valens, who employed practical techniques based on established traditions, Ptolemy was more scientific, concerned only with theories that had a sound basis. For instance, he dismissed the numerological significance of names as being unreliable.

Ptolemy, in spite of his Latinized name and Roman citizenship, was believed to be either Greek or a Hellenized Egyptian. Considered one of the intellectual Titans of his time, he was accomplished in math and the natural sciences, referenced Greek philosophers and wrote in ancient Greek, and reached back to Babylonian astronomical observations and lunar theory. A prolific writer, he contributed to such varied fields as astronomy, epistemology, music, geography, optics, as well as astrology. He compiled a star catalogue of more than 1,000 entries and improved on Hipparchus's table of trigonometric functions by calculating values at 30' increments.

He established mathematically that an object and its mirror image must make equal angles to the mirror. His first major book on astronomy, the *Almagest*, was a collection of his observations over 25 years, and it included a description of the ecliptic, the celestial band that includes the constellations of the zodiac. His scientific writings represented the zenith of Greco-Roman achievement, synthesizing the Greeks' knowledge of the universe. His research allowed astronomers to accurately predict planetary positions as well as solar and lunar eclipses. The acceptance of his work by scholars led to his theories being promoted in Europe as well as the Byzantine and Islamic worlds for more than 1400 years. Ptolemy accepted Aristotle's notion that the sun and the planets revolve around a spherical earth, in what is known as a geocentric view. Ptolemy's earth-centric model of the universe—expressed in his book *Planetary Hypothesis*—was known as the Ptolemiac system and became the main source of the cosmology that dominated the West until the age of Galileo.

Defined by its Limitations

Ptolemy's four-volume book on astrology, known as *Tetrabiblos*, attempted to promote that discipline as an inexact yet legitimate science that describes the effect of heavenly spheres on earthly life. In fact, he wanted to define astrology precisely by pointing out its limitations, and so focused only on astronomical data he believed was reliable. Akin to the practice of medicine with its variables of race, country, or upbringing, he believed that astrology was conjectural in that it also had too many variables, i.e., the exact positions of heavenly bodies at the time of birth. As a result, he posited that both were useful but not to be relied on completely.

Furthermore, he noted that the difficulty of the art of astrological prediction was what made critics believe it to be useless, yet he pointed out its helpfulness and usefulness. It is bad practitioners, he insisted, who are to blame for the failings of astrology. When observing the influence of the sun, moon, and stars on natural phenomena like weather and the seasons he admitted to the possibility than men can likewise be affected in temperament due to this natural ambience. The additional factors of time and place of birth contributed to character and temperament. He added to this upbringing, custom, and culture as additional "accidental" factors that contributed to a person's destiny.

Claudius Ptolemy, Astronomer, mathematician, and geographer of Alexandria.

Three Benefits

Ever a champion of astrology, Ptolemy maintained it was a beneficial pursuit because:

• **The astrologer gains knowledge of both the human and the divine**
• **When people are armed with foreknowledge, their souls are calm**
• **It is helpful to know there are causes for human behavior other than divine necessity. In effect, although the supralunary movements are perfect and destined, the sublunary are imperfect, changeable, and subject to influence from additional causes.**

Biography

Name: Vettius Valens
Status: Hellenistic astrologer, Stoic
Born: c. AD 120; Antioch, present-day Turkey
Died: c. AD 175
Era: Roman Empire

The ancient city of **Alexandria**

Vettius Valens

Vettius Valens was born in second-century Antioch, but traveled widely throughout Egypt, first in search of teachers and then in search of specific astrological doctrines that would support his theories.

In Alexandria he found remnants of the earlier traditions, astrologers who practiced Babylonian, Greek, and Egyptian forms of astrology. He collected the wisdom of these astrologers into the *Anthologiarum* (compiled between AD 152–162), an important work that cites earlier authorities like Nechepso and Critodemus, and immortalizes others, like Teucer of Babylon, who would never have been heard of otherwise. It also offers a look into the actual, practical astrological techniques of his era and allows scholars to contrast his observations with those of another master astrologer like Ptolemy, who was more concerned with theoretical models than hands-on astrology. Valen's work is also celebrated for indicating a regional variety of astrological techniques, key details not found in other texts from that time.

The author tested many of the methods he documented, and so was able to judge them after "much toil and experience." He also implored his readers to swear not to reveal the astrologers' secrets to the uneducated or uninitiated and to pay homage to their own teachers. The three manuscripts of the *Anthologiarum* currently available all date from the fourteenth century, but they appear to be reliable and complete, if somethwat disorganized.

A Fateful Outcome

Valens ultimately decided that traditional religion had little meaning for him, placing his trust in fate, while viewing astrology as a religious practice. According to the Stoic philosophy, adapting to one's fate and living in harmony with it was within a human's power. And even if people could not change the ultimate outcome of their lives, they could control how they played the part they were given. An acceptance of predestination, he emphasized, meant freedom from anxiety and offered a sense of salvation.

This Persian polymath is sometimes referred to as the "father of algebra" and the "grandfather of the computer."

Al-Khwarizmi was a brilliant mathematician, prolific author, and avid skywatcher during Persia's cultural peak. Perhaps his most notable scholastic contribution was the introduction of Hindu-Arabic numerals and the concepts of algebra to Western mathematics. Latinized versions of his name and of his most famous book gave the world the terms "algorithm" and "algebra."

Not much is known of his early life, not even the exact location of his birth. As an adult he lived in the fabled city of Baghdad and worked in caliph Al-Ma'mūn's House of Wisdom—or *bait al-hikma*, a library and scientific research and teaching center. There he acquired and translated scientific and philosophic documents along with continuing his own research on the many subjects he had mastered.

Around 830, he published *The Compendious Book on Calculation by Completing and Balancing*, which presented the first systematic solutions to linear and quadratic equations. The book was

Biography

Names: Muhammad ibn Musa al-Khwarizmi, Mohammad ben Musa Khwarazmi, Algorithmi
Status: Astrologer, astronomer, mathematician, geographer
Born: c. AD 780; possibly Khwarizm, modern Uzbekistan
Died: c. 850; Baghdad, Iraq
Era: Islamic Golden Age

Muhammad ibn Musa al-Khwarizmi

later translated into Latin and welcomed by mathematicians for its novel systematic and demonstrative approach to the subject. It has been said that he influenced mathematics more than any other medieval writer. He also worked on improvements to the sundial and wrote two books on the astrolabe.

As an astronomer Al-Khwarizmi's masterwork was his c. 833 *The Image of the Earth*, which offered the coordinates of locations in the known world based on, and improving upon, the *Geography* of Ptolemy. He supervised 70 geographers in the

creation of a world map for the caliph and worked on a project to determine the circumference of the earth (long known to be spherical by Islamic scholars).

Al-Khwarizmi exemplifies how a man dedicated to science and math would not hesitate to study astrology. One reason was that the practice still carried weight in the Muslim world—it aroused significant interest in the populace, while rulers used it to help them govern. Al-Khwarizmi wrote a number of books on astrology, referencing Persian and Babylonian astrologers as well as Indian and Greek sources.

Biography

Name: Theophrastus von Hohenheim
Status: Physician, philosopher, Hermeticist, prophet, astrologer
Born: November 11, 1493; Egg, Switzerland
Died: September 24, 1541; Salzberg, Austria
Era: German Renaissance

As Above

So Below

Paracelcus

Something of a paradox, Paracelsus was a notable Renaissance physician who rejected many previously accepted (and incorrect) medical methodologies, and so moved the science of medicine forward . . . yet he was also a prophet who, in his *Astronomia Magna*, wrote about astrology, divination, Hermeticism, and demonology.

Along with most physicians of his time, who combined the study of science with a belief in the mystical, Paracelsus was a practicing astrologer. He produced astrological talismans for curing disease and created a system of markings, the Alphabet of the Magi, which was used to engrave angelic names on talismans.

As a prophet, his *Prognostications* were studied in the 1600s by the Rosicrucians. This spiritual and cultural movement believed there were keys to discovering the mysterious knowledge of the ancients, secrets that combined the Kabbalah, Hermeticism, alchemy, and Christian mysticism.

A Medical Revolution

As a physician, Paracelsus was an advocate for a medical revolution that cast away many teachings of the Greek Galen, instead combining observation with acquired wisdom. He believed a well-rounded doctor should have a strong academic background, including the natural sciences, especially chemistry. Considered the "father of toxicology," the study of poisons, he was one of the first physicians to effectively use poisons in medicine. He proposed the then-radical notion that substances that could kill in large doses might save lives or effect cures in small doses. He proposed that diseases were caused by poisons brought by the stars, but, again, not all poisons were negative. He was thought responsible for the introduction of opium to Western Europe and was probably the scientist who gave the element zinc (zincum) its modern name.

As a Hermeticist, he understood the need for a balance between humans (the microcosm) and nature (the macrocosm). With his deep conviction that science and religion were indivisible, he felt the earnest search for spiritual salvation was often reflected outwardly by the body's flourishing health. He also detailed four elemental beings: Salamanders, which corresponded to fire; Gnomes, which corresponded to the earth; Undines (water nymphs), corresponding to water, and Sylphs, corresponding to the air.

After his death, an early medical movement called Paracelsianism became attractive to those who wished to subvert Galenic medicine, and so his teachings became more widespread. Although much of his published work was lost, his unpublished writings were translated, reprinted, and widely read during the 16th and 17th centuries. His reputation as a prophet or occultist remained controversial, but his medical writings were esteemed throughout Europe. In the late 16th century, there occurred a spate of pseudo-Paracelsian offerings, including letters, which muddied the waters as to his authentic output and still confounds scholars today.

Paracelcus, Germanic physician, Hermeticist, prophet and astrologer

The Roots of Hermeticism

This philosophical system is based on the teachings of Hermes Trismegistus, a legendary Hellenic figure who was a combination of the Greek messenger god, Hermes, and the Egyptian god, Thoth, patron of wisdom, science, magic, and art. Hermes Trismegistus was said to be the "author" of the collected philosophical texts called the *Hermetica*, a diverse work that covered a range of topics, including many aspects of astrology, like the relationship of earthquakes and astrological signs, and contained numerous Arabic entries on astrology, such as the "Secrets of the Stars." (Even today, the study of astrology and alchemy are described as "Hermetic arts.") The system was also closely associated with the revelation of divine wisdom, a sort of "ancient theology" that was given to the first humans by God. Some scholars have argued that the reverence for Hermetic tradition displayed during the Renaissance played a large part in the evolution of modern science.

Biography

Names: Michel de Notredame or Nostredame
Status: Astrologer, prophet
Born: December 14, 1503; Saint-Rémy-de-Provence, France
Died: July 2, 1566; Salon-de-Provence, France
Era: French Renaissance

Nostradamus

This French astrologer and physician is arguably the best-known prophet outside the Bible and certainly the most widely read seer of the Renaissance.

Nostradamus was born to a family that likely converted from Judaism to Christianity and attended the University of Montpelier until the plague caused it to close. In spite of having no medical degree—it was said he was expelled from medical school—he began practicing medicine as an apothacary healer in Agen, in southwestern France, around 1530. After a move to Salon in 1544, he became renowned for his innovative treatments of plague victims in Aix and Lyon.

He also earned money as an astrologer, casting horoscopes and making predictions for wealthy or noble patrons. His skill as an astrologer and study of the occult no doubt played a part in the next chapter of his life: sometime in the mid 1550s he began making prophecies about future events. He eventually collected these and published them in 1955 as *Centuries*. (This mystic, cryptic work was produced in rhymed quatrains, or four-lined poems, and each block of a hundred was called a century.) After some of his predictions came true, his fame as a seer—a person who could see into the future— began to spread. He was invited to the court of Queen Catherine de Médicis, consort of Henry II. In 1564 he was made physician-in-ordinary to King Charles IX.

In 1566 another book, *Les Prophéties*, was published and became his most timeless work. His prophecies, at least those that could be deciphered, were often targeted by critics. Yet contrary to a common myth, he was never condemned by the Catholic Church's Congregation of the Index, which examined books and manuscripts. Still, his mysterious words continued to invite controversy. His advocates believe that among his 6,338 quatrains, he predicted many real historical events, including the French Revolution in the 18th century. They also claim the quatrains that make no sense are predictions that have yet to occur. Statistically, his websites indicate his forecasts are 70 percent accurate. Due to the obscure nature of most of the quatrains, however, those who interpret them sometimes take liberties, stretching the meaning to match a prediction to an event.

Nostradamus, the French astrologer and prophet

The Predictions of Nostradamus

No doubt the people who suffered through lockdown, quarantine, illness, and the other rigors of pandemic-influenced 2020 don't want to know that the seer offered few upbeat predictions for 2021 and beyond. Here is only one example, believed to presage a drought or famine: "After great trouble for humanity, a greater one is prepared, / The Great Mover renews the ages: / Rain, blood, milk, famine, steel and plague, / Is the heavens fire seen, a long spark running." Probably better to review his collection of "greatest hits" about the past ... and one major miss.

The Great Fire of London in 1666 | **The conquests of Napoleon Bonaparte** | **The lifesaving work of Louis Pasteur** | **The rise of Hitler and the Third Reich** | **The atomic bombings of Hiroshima and Nagasaki** | **The assassinations of President John F. Kennedy and Robert Kennedy** | **The Moon Landing in 1969** | **The terrorist attack on the World Trade Center on 9/11:** "Earthshaking fire from the center of the Earth / Will cause tremors around the New City. / Two great rocks will war for a long time, / Then Arethusa will redden a new river." | **An asteroid passing close by or hitting earth.** On Christmas Day in 2014, Asteroid 2014 SD224 did shoot past earth. | **An increased risk from climate change, religious trends, and military technology** | **A major earthquake for California:** "The sloping park, great calamity, / Through the Lands of the West and Lombardy / The fire in the ship, plague, and captivity; / Mercury in Sagittarius, Saturn fading." **The astrological event cited takes place in November 2021.** Nostradamus also predicted that a battle between living humans and the half-dead will end the world, but there is no date given for this version of the zombie apocalypse.

Biography

Names: John Dee, Doctor Dee
Status: Astrologer, mathematician, cartographer, alchemist
Born: July 13, 1527; Tower Ward, London
Died: December 1608/1609; Mortlake, Surrey
Era: Elizabethan England

John Dee

If any man in Tudor England had a claim to being viewed as a wizard, it was Doctor John Dee, an Anglo-Welsh astronomer, astrologer, mathematician, occultist, and alchemist.

As the son of a courtier of Henry VIII, young Dee attended Cambridge, where his astounding stage effects for a production of Aristophane's *Peace* brought him lasting acclaim as a magician. After studying in Brussels and Paris with various cartographers and mathematicians, he returned to England with a collection of mathematical and astronomical instruments. An avid bibliophile, he amassed one of the largest antiquarian libraries in England.

In spite of being arrested for the crime of "calculating" horoscopes for the Tudor princesses, he eventually served as court astrologer to Queen Mary I and Elizabeth I and also acted political advisor to Elizabeth. It was Dee who enouraged the settlement of the colonies in the New World and was credited with coining the term "British Empire."

Bad Company

When he left the queen's service it was to explore more deeply the world of the occult, yet on his travels through Europe he often fell into company with charlatans or disreputable characters. He was even accused of spying for the British crown. On his return to England he found that his home and library had been vandalized. He rejoined the queen's court, but was dismissed after James I became the British monarch. Dee spent much of his last years working with spirit medium Edward Kelley—likely a fake—trying to commune with angels, hoping to learn the universal language of creation, called Enochian, in order to establish a "pre-apocalyptic unity of mankind." Dee died in poverty, and his gravesite is unknown.

Like other learned men of his era, Dee made no distinction between his scientific studies and his pursuits of astrology and alchemy. In spite of his repute as a mathematician, astronomer, and expert in navigation—who trained many of those who would embark on England's voyages of discovery—he also immersed himself in sorcery and the supernatural. Yet it was his academic work that often brought him into conflict with the Church of England, which felt higher mathematics was akin to witchcraft.

The statue of Galileo Galilei
outside the Uffizi Gallery, Florence

Biography

Name: Galileo di Vincenzo Bonaiuti de' Galilei
Status: Astronomer, astrologer, physicist, engineer
Born: February 15, 1564; Pisa, Italy
Died: January 8, 1642; Tuscany, Italy
Era: Italian Renaissance

Galileo Galilei

Like many astronomers of his era, Galileo studied astrology and, while teaching in Padua, often cast horoscopes for patrons to help support his family. In 1604, this brought him unwanted attention from the Venetian Inquisition.

It was not his work as an astrologer, however, that affected the fate of astrology; it was his championing of—and the eventual worldwide acceptance of—the Copernican theory of heliocentrism. The notion that the earth revolved around the sun shocked much of the astrological community. Critics wondered how astrologers, those keen watchers of the sky, missed that detail of celestial movement. As the physics of Aristotle and Ptolemy were undermined and the the lines between heavenly and earthly realms blurred, two bulwarks of astrology eroded . . . and the rise of pure science loomed.

Facing the Inquisition

Galileo's defense of Copernicus brought him into conflict with the Catholic Church as well as some astronomers. In 1615, the Roman Inquisition determined that heliocentrism was absurd and also heretical because it contradicted the Bible. Galileo defended his views in *Dialogue Concerning the Two Chief World Systems* but this was thought to attack Pope Urban VIII, thus alienating both the pontiff and the Jesuits, Galileo's former supporters. He spent the rest of his life under house arrest.

Astrology Under Fire

Astrology is not a religion. It is more accurately described as a mathematical science that links the movement of universal bodies to human experiences on earth. Yet over the passing centuries plenty of religious institutions have weighed in on the practice.

In general, their judgements were mixed: some faiths, such as Zoroastrianism, incorporate astrology; other faiths that believe in reincarnation, such as Buddhism and Hinduism, are more tolerant of it. Chinese astrology remains unconnected to any religions like Confucianism or Taoism. The attitudes of Jewish leaders varied; Philo of Alexandria and various Jewish pseudepigraphical writers condemned the practice of astrology, while other texts accepted portions of it and even depicted Biblical figures such as Abraham and Noah as astrologers.

Initially, a number of early Christians, such as Marcion

and Basilides, incorporated some aspects of astrology into their belief systems, but both Christian and Islamic clergy eventually rejected the study of cosmic portents. They insisted that the actions or divine will of God or Allah cannot be anticipated—or altered—by humans, and that to believe otherwise was blasphemous.

St. Augustine dabbled in astrology as a youth, yet protested against it in his books *Confessions* and in *The City of God*, writing: "Why, in the life of twins—in their actions, the events that befall them, their professions, arts, honors and other things pertaining to human life, as well as in their very deaths—is there often so great a difference hat, as far as these things are concerned . . . many entire strangers are more like them than they are like each other?" Likewise, in his *Summa Theologica* St. Thomas Aquinas argued that astrology could neither predict the future nor define personality: "It is impossible for heavenly bodies to make a direct impression on the intellect and will . . ."

Even the astrological importance of the Star of Bethlehem at the birth of Christ (and the subsequent visit of three astrologers from the East) was denied by the Church. Although the Gospel writers included the "myth" of the Star, Christians interpreted the phenomenon not as an astrological portent of "glad tidings," but as a symbol of Christ transcending the previous cosmic order.

Foremost among the reasons Christian leaders condemn astrology is that it conflicts with the Biblical prohibition against divination. It also has no basis in empirical observation, t attributes to celestial forces some actions that should be attributed to Providence, and it eeks to find God's hidden will n the movement of the stars. The Catechism of the Catholic Church further states that

divination, including predictive astrology, is incompatible with the Catholic belief in free will: "All forms of divination are to be rejected: recourse to Satan or demons, conjuring up the dead or other practices falsely supposed to 'unveil' the future. Consulting horoscopes, astrology, palm reading, interpretation of omens and lots, the phenomena of clairvoyance, and recourse to mediums all conceal a desire for power over time, history, and . . . other human beings." (It should perhaps be noted that the modern Catholic Church has the largest astrological library in the world.)

A Confusing Stance

During the Middle Ages, most Christian, Islamic, and Jewish clergy spoke out against astrology as an occult practice. Meanwhile, the law instructed Christian physicians to be guided by the moon, certain eminent rabbis felt astrology was a science compatible with the Jewish faith, and many Islamic rulers appointed a court astrologer, or vizier, to guide their statecraft. Again, here was that dichotomy: astrology forbidden, astrology

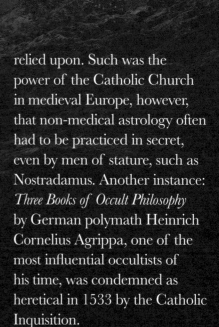

relied upon. Such was the power of the Catholic Church in medieval Europe, however, that non-medical astrology often had to be practiced in secret, even by men of stature, such as Nostradamus. Another instance: *Three Books of Occult Philosophy* by German polymath Heinrich Cornelius Agrippa, one of the most influential occultists of his time, was condemned as heretical in 1533 by the Catholic Inquisition.

These widely differing responses, starting with early religious leaders and continuing until the Modern Era, were certainly a factor in the see-sawing popularity of horoscopic astrology after it emerged from Greece in the 1st century BC

Biography

Name: Johannes Kepler
Status: Astrologer
Born: December 27, 1571; Weil der Stadt, modern-day Germany
Died: November 15, 1630; Regensburg, Germany
Era: German Renaissance

Johannes Kepler

Kepler's Supernova

In October 1604, a strange, new star blazed in the constellation Ophiuchus. Astrologically, 1603 had marked the start of an 800-year cycle of great conjunctions. The two previous periods marked the birth of Christ (1600 years earlier) and the age of Charlemagne (800 years earlier). Astrologers now expected great events. For his part, Kepler felt the star undermined Aristotle's doctrine of heavenly immutability—that celestial spheres were perfect and unchanging. The birth of this star proved that the heavens were variable.

Born during the scientific revolution of the 17th century, Kepler was an outstanding German mathematician, astronomer, and astrologer. His laws of planetary motion helped provide a foundation for Newton's theory of universal gravitation.

As a child Kepler was impressed by the Great Comet of 1577 and a lunar eclipse, cementing his interest in the night sky. At the University of Tübingen, he earned a reputation as a brilliant mathematician and skilled astrologer, casting horoscopes for fellow students. It was there he became a dedicated Copernican and defender of heliocentricity.

While teaching mathematics at a Protestant seminary in Graz, he published his first book, *The Cosmographic Mystery*. After an epiphany in Graz while demonstrating the conjunction of Jupiter and Saturn in the zodiac, he set out to uncover God's geometrical basis for the universe. The book was his attempt to justify his theory. After assisting noted astronomer Tycho Brahe in Prague, in 1601 he was appointed imperial mathematician—court astrologer—to Holy Roman Emperor Rudolph II and his successors Matthias and Ferdinand II.

Like his peers, Keplar did not distinguish between astronomy and astrology. He tried to incorporate religious arguments into his work, believing that God created the universe according to "an intelligible plan . . . accessed through the use of reason." He called this new type of astronomy "celestial physics."

A re-enactment of **the Fire of London** of 1666, using a model town

Biography

Names: the "English Merlin"
Status: Astrologer
Born: May 11, 1602
Died: June 9, 1681
Era: English Civil War

William Lilly is considered one of the most influential astrological thinkers and writers of the 17th century.

William Lilly

The son of a Leicestershire farmer, his mother made sure he was well educated. He left the local grammer school with a secure grounding in the classics and a knowledge of Latin that would later serve him well, considering most astrology texts of the time were in that ancient language. Denied entry into Cambridge due to his father's increasing poverty, he went to London to act as secretary and general servant to a prosperous merchant ... and later married the man's widow.

Lilly now had time to pursue his interest in religion and, a short time later, he discovered astrology. He studied various authors, favoring Valentine Naibod's *Commentary* on Alcabitius. In 1647 he produced his own masterwork, the three-volume *Christian Astrology*. It is ranked as one of the classic texts for the study of medieval astrology, especially the horary discipline, which predicts future events and investigates the unknown qualities of current affairs. The book has never gone out of print and remains a popular reference today.

He also began to produce prophetical almanacs, and made a famous prediction of a great fire that would engulf London. It was such a vivid depiction, that when the Great London Fire occurred in 1666, he was suspected of starting it. In addition to 36 almanacs, Lilly produced at least two dozens books on astrology. These works gained the attention of many members of the Long Parliament, which sat for 20 years, encompassing the span of the Civil War, the execution of Charles I, and Cromwell's rule. Alas, when the English crown was restored with the coronation of Charles II, Lilly fell out of favor. He took his small fortune and bought a manor in Surrey ... where he relinquished astrology for the practice of medicine.

The publication of a facsimile of the original *Christian Astrology* by Regulus Publishing in 1985 played no small part in the revival of astrological scholarship that occurred in Europe and North America at that time. It also had a transformative effect on the techniques of contemporary astrology.

127

Biography

Name: William Frederick Allan
Status: Astrologer, author, publisher, Theosophist
Born: August 7, 1860; Westminster, London
Died: August 30, 1917; Bude, Cornwall
Era: Victorian

Alan Leo

Known as the "father of modern astrology" Leo was credited with reviving interest in the discipline in the West during the late 19th century after its popularity waned at the end of the 17th century.

He was responsible for the movement toward a more psychological analysis of the horoscope, factoring in trends of experience rather than simply predicting events.

In 1914, when Leo faced prosecution for "unlawfully telling fortunes," he realized the practice of astrology needed to be legitimized. He thus recommended that his brethren: "... part company with the fatalistic astrologer who prides himself on his predictions and who is ever seeking to convince the world that in the predictive side of Astrology alone shall we find its value. We need not argue the point as to its reality, but instead make a much-needed change in the word and call Astrology the science of tendencies."

In spite of this intent to change the nature of astrology, Leo was again charged in 1917, even though he was only describing "tendencies," and not telling fortunes. He stood trial and was convicted on July 16, was fined £5, and died several weeks later from a cerebral hemorrhage.

Among his contributions were many periodicals and natal charts and the founding of numerous institutions, including the Astrological Lodge of London, which still holds meetings. He hoped to simplify the processes of astrology and make its apparatus more accurate for students. He was also known for providing a theosophic slant to astrology. Theosophy deals with the nature of the soul based on mystical insight into God with the goal of spiritual emancipation. He traveled twice to India and also incorporated aspects of Vedic astrology such as karma and reincarnation into his work. His book *The Art of Synthesis*, where he gives the planets human qualities, likely inspired classical composer Gustav Holst's symphony, *The Planets*, which features orchestral movements such as "Mercury, the Winger Messenger" and "Mars, Bringer of War."

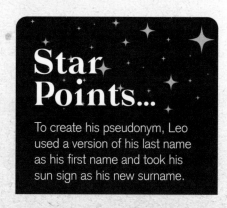

Star Points...

To create his pseudonym, Leo used a version of his last name as his first name and took his sun sign as his new surname.

Dane Rudhyar is often cited as the top astrologer of the 20th century. Influenced by the writings of psychologist Carl Jung he became instrumental in the formation of a psychology-based form of astrology. He was also a talented musician, composer, and transcendental artist.

Biography

Name: Daniel Chennevière
Status: Modernist composer, author, astrologer
Born: March 23, 1895; Paris, France
Died: September 13, 1985; San Francisco, California, US
Era: 20th century

Dane Rudhyar

Born in Paris, as a boy he was disabled by a severe illness and took refuge in music and intellectual pursuits. After graduating from the Sorbonne at age 16, he traveled widely, studied Japanese philosophy, and saw his polytonal work performed by the New York Metropolitan Opera. At age 25 he moved to California, where he supported the Theosophist movement—which predicted the onset of a New Age of enlightenment—with "an evangelical zeal." His conviction that existence was cyclical and his affinity for Nietzsche convinced him he was a "seed man" for such a cultural revolution.

In 1929 he met astrologer Mark Edmund Jones and began writing for *American Astrology* magazine. Rudhyar's astrology offered a fresh, person-centered approach that combined psychology with holistic and spiritual features and the metaphysical concepts of change, motion, space, and time. He believed that the stars, rather than causing effects on human life, detailed psychological forces working in an individual and did not override that person's freedom in choosing how to respond. He first called this harmonic astrology, then humanistic astrology; it became the basis for his mammoth 1936 book, *The Astrology of Personality*.

In 1969 Rudhyar founded the International Committee for Humanistic Astrology. This professional society would continue work on the development of his philosophy as Rudhyar himself began one of his most productive decades, publishing several books each year. His natural interest in the New Age movement also resulted in sophisticated volumes on planetary consciousness and New Age philosophy.

Although he was revered within the astrological community, few outsiders knew of him. But in the 1970s, with the increasing popularity of the New Age movement, publishers began to re-release his books and writings. These were particulary admired by the hippie community of San Francisco, where he lived and lectured until his death. Among Rudhyar's predictions was that the Age of Aquarius would begin in 2062.

Biography

Names: Lydia Emma Pinckert, Jeane Dixon
Status: Astrologer, psychic
Born: January 5, 1904; Medford, Wisconsin, US
Died: January 25, 1997; Washington, DC
Era: 20th century

Jeane Dixon

Most astrologers keep their heads out of the clouds when it comes to making predictions or casting birth charts. One notable exception was a woman named Jeane Dixon, who used what she claimed were her psychic powers along with her skill at astrology to guide celebrity clients.

She was without question the most prominent psychic/astrologer in the American pop culture that sprang up after World War II, in large part due to her widely read syndicated newspaper column. Dixon was one of 10 children born to German immigrant parents in Wisconsin, but she was raised in Missouri and California. As a child in California, she said a Gypsy gave her a crystal ball and read her palm, proclaiming that she would become famous as a seer for powerful people. In 1939 she married car dealership owner Jimmy Dixon, whose partner was film and TV producer Hal Roach. Jeane remained with Jimmy until his death and even served as president to their successful real estate business.

Advisor to Presidents

Dixon started out writing horoscopes and then turned to her crystal ball for making predictions. During World War II, President Roosevelt heard of her abilities and invited her to the White House. She informed him that the war would end around 1945. Dixon's most famous prediction, made in an interview in *Parade*, was that the winner of the 1960 presidential race, a Democrat, would later be assassinated. President John F. Kennedy indeed met that fate. Dixon also advised First Lady Nancy Reagan during Ronald Reagan's presidency. Her predictions were often wrong, however. Richard Nixon met with her in the Oval Office, called her "the soothsayer," and would put the military on alert if she predicted a terrorist attack ... but none ever occurred.

Dixon wrote seven books and a horoscope guide for dogs. Her life story, 1965's *The Gift of Prophecy* by Ruth Montgomery, showcased hundreds of correct predictions—including the massacre at the Munich Olympics and the career of Oprah Winfrey—and became a huge bestseller. This was in spite of the psychic's well-known reluctance to reveal details about her life. A devout Catholic, Dixon always insisted her visions came from God. This only added to her enormous fanbase.

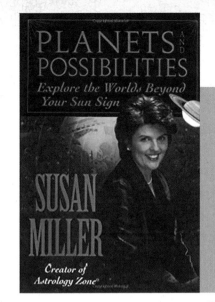

Popular astrologers often achieve celebrity status in the United States. First Lady Nancy Reagan made her personal astrologers, Jeane Dixon and Joan Quigley, household names in the 1980s. One of America's top celebrity astrologers today—and a mistress of social media with a worldwide following—is Susan Miller.

Susan Miller

Biography
Name: Susan Miller
Status: Astrologer
Born: Late 1950s
Era: 21st century

Miller has authored 11 bestselling books and, as of 2019, had 17 million readers on her website Astrologyzone.com and her mobile app. Her website alone had more than 300 million views. She is also a featured columnist in magazine outlets such as *Vogue* and *InStyle*.

Miller was born in the late 1950s and was homeschooled by her mother, who taught her astrology. After graduating with an MA in business from NYU, she worked as a photography agent. Her first horoscopes were written for Time Warner in the 1990s. Miller has suffered from chronic illness since she was 14; the condition still sometimes affects her ability to meet forecast deadlines.

Miller's website is free but her famously lengthy personal horoscopes require a subscription. The majority of her subscribers are young millennials, although she has also worked with stars like Cameron Diaz, Pharrell Williams, Katy Perry, and Alexa Chung and fashion-industry notables Cynthia Rowley, Gloria Vanderbuilt, and Glenn O'Brien. She focuses on personal horoscopes, but has taken aim at a few national events. She was spot on about Barack Obama's re-election, but missed the mark when she said Hillary Clinton's email problems wouldn't keep her from besting Donald Trump.

The astrologer is particularly popular in England. Of her success with millenials there, the *Guardian* wrote: "... she is the queen of fortune telling, single-handedly responsible for fuelling their obsession with all things celestial. Somehow she has managed to turn the mystical, ancient pseudo-science of astrology into a world-wide phenomenon."

Miller's official take on astrology is that it is able to give her insight into the circumstances of the future, but not necessarily predict the outcome. She tends to be more optimistic than some of her competitors, advising followers that no matter what occurs, they are going to be fine, and if they are not, she offers several ways they can cope.

Chapter Four

The Modern Western Zodiac

An Astrological Reawakening | Introducing the Sun Signs: Aries through Pisces | Feature: Influence Over Body Parts | Rising Signs | Moon Signs | Mercury, Mars, and Venus | Houses of the Zodiac | Dignities, Debilities, and Aspects | Zodiac Love Connections | Consulting an Astrologer

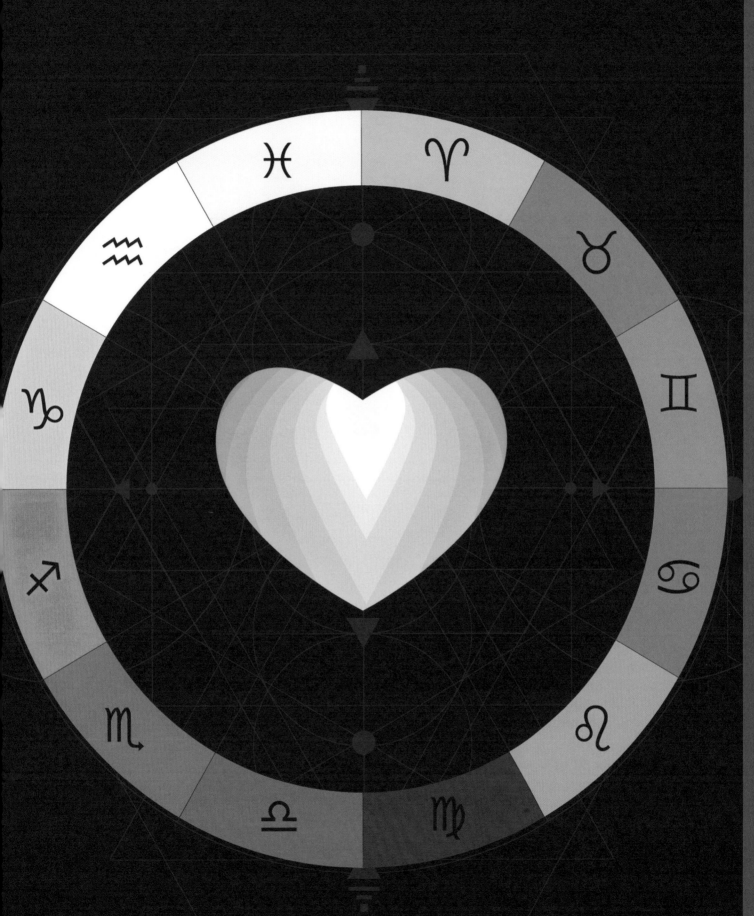

An Astrological Reawakening

While astrology enjoyed a heyday during the Renaissance, interest in the discipline waned with the onset of the European Enlightenment, or Age of Reason (1685–1815). During this period a belief in the critical process—and the declaration that all things could be demystified and catalogued—began replacing superstition and seasonal rituals, even religion to some extent.

This trend combined a questioning of traditional authority with the concept that humanity could be improved by the use of rational thinking. This doctrine ended up affecting politics, philosophy, science, and communications as well as inspiring numerous books, essays, inventions, discoveries, and laws . . . and resulted in the American, French, and Haitian revolutions. When the Enlightenment eventually declined it was replaced by the emotive climate of European Romanticism, and astrology again made a popular comeback, this time as part of a general revival of spiritualism and curiosity about the occult.

Romanticism was an artistic and intellectual movement characterized by its focus on imagination and individualism as well as worship of nature and the past. It emphasized intense emotion as a genuine source of aesthetic experience and placed new import on extreme feelings such as apprehension, horror, terror, and awe. Witness the 19th-century rise of the Gothic novel. It further sought to honor the common man, in part by emulating more "idyllic" times and elevating the humble life into something noble. It should be no surprise that such a movement found the mysteries and ancient rituals of astrology of great appeal. This receptivity was further encouraged by the Arts and Crafts movement, an artistic and literary protest

Project Hindsight

This project, begun in 1993 by Robert Schmidt, Ellen Black, Robert Zoller, and Robert Hand, was intended to create modern English translations of primary source Greek astrology texts. These texts were the basis for the Hellenic astrology developed in Egypt and the Mediterranean after the Alexandrian conquests and which continued through the Roman period. This same Hellenic astrology went on to become the foundation of Western astrological thought. The project sparked an interest in the discipline in many locations, including New Zealand.

against the impersonality of the Industrial Age.

New Advocates

During the late Victorian period the interest in astrology and spiritualism really soared. Seances, horoscope readings, and investigations of the occult were all the fashion, especially among the wealthy. It soon became the custom to hire fortunetellers or astrologers to entertain guests at social gatherings. Meanwhile, the English secret society, the Hermitic Order of the Golden Dawn, heralded a rebirth of Renaissance hermeticism, the

study of astrology, alchemy, and other occult pursuits based on the writings of the mythic Hermes Trismegistus.

Astrology retained much of its popularity into the early 20th century, but then waned again as major wars, a flu pandemic, and a financial Depression struck the globe, these upheavals lasting at least until the middle of the century. Then, during the years following World War II, countries were too busy rebuilding or sorting out new boundaries—or staving off nuclear annihilation—to have time for the intuitive arts.

Then in the 1970s the

pendulum of astrology swung upward, *way* upward. This was due to the emergence of the youth counterculture along with a New Age philosophy that encouraged people to seek an enlightened consciousness that incorporated mind, body, and spirit. Linda Goodman's Sun Sign books became bestsellers in America, and horoscopic astrology was again embraced by millions around the world. The astrology trend was quickly taken up by mass media— books, newspapers, magazines, and, more recently, the internet, all generating horoscopic advice for a seemingly insatiable audience.

Introducing the Sun Signs

In the Western zodiac, birth signs are often referred to as sun signs. This is because a person's astrological sign is based on which constellation the sun was "in" on their day of birth. (Each constellation extends 30 degrees across the ecliptic, and the sun remains in each sign for approximately 30 days.) The name is also used because the sun symbolically represents light, hope, vitality, and love. Sun sign can be used interchangeably with zodiac sign or star sign. Originally the 12 signs of the zodiac were conceived by the Babylonians in the first half of the 1st millennium BC. Even though ancient astronomers believed the sun was merely one of the celestial bodies that orbited around the earth, they understood its crucial role as the provider of light and warmth.

The Birth of Sun Signs

It is likely 17th-century Englishman William Lilly was the first newspaper astrologer, but the publication of daily or monthly horoscopes truly began in England in 1930. This was when the *Sunday Express* asked noted astrologer R.H. Naylor to write a horoscope for newborn Princess Margaret, younger sister to the future Queen Elizabeth II. The thrust of his prediction was that her life would be "eventful," pretty much a given. When the horoscope generated a positive public response he was assigned a column, "What the Stars Foretell," an idea soon being appropriated around the globe . . . and thus horoscopic astrology found its seemingly permanent niche with the public.

Naylor decided he needed a simplified version of Western astrology that would be suitable to a newspaper column. Sun signs was what he came up with, a system that takes into account only the position of the sun in a given zodiac constellation at the time of a person's birth.

He created a basic guide that named each sun sign, showed its symbol, and provided its English name, its element, its modality, its polarity—features that most followers of horoscopes are familiar with—but he further listed an approximate span of time showcasing the seasonal phenomena that accompanied each sign. This is significant because it harks back to one of the original uses of astrology: the prediction of agricultural markers.

Predicting Agricultural Markers

Aries	**Vernal Equinox** (Mar 21 to day before Corn Rain)
Taurus	**Corn Rain** (April 20 to day before Corn Forms)
Gemini	**Corn Forms** (May 21 to day before Summer Solstice)
Cancer	**Summer Solstice** (June 21 to day before Great Heat)
Leo	**Great Heat** (July 24 to day before End of Heat)
Virgo	**End of Heat** (Aug 23 to day before Autumnal Equinox)
Libra	**Autumnal Equinox** (Sept 23 to day before First Frost)
Scorpio	**First Frost** (Oct 23 to day before Light Snow)
Sagittarius	**Light Snow** (Nov 23 to day before Winter Solstice)
Capricorn	**Winter Solstice** (Dec 22 to day before Great Cold)
Aquarius	**Great Cold** (Jan 20 to day before Vernal Showers)
Pisces	**Vernal Showers** (Feb 19 to day before Vernal Equinox)

Star Points

The term "horoscope" comes from the Greek hõra (time or hour) and scopos (observer). Ideally, horoscopes are based not just on a birthdate and time, but also on a location, since these data points are needed to determine the precise alignment of planets and stars.

Sun Sign Affiliates

Each sun sign is associated with and affected by one of four elements, one of three modalities, one of two polarities, and one or more planets. The four elements assigned to the sun signs can briefly be described thus: air signs thrive on ideas and information; fire signs are aflame with passion and power; water sign plunge into emotions and memories; and earth signs are generally grounded, practical, and stable. But there are also affiliated or "lucky" symbols such as birthstones, colors, and plants that each zodiac sign has acquired over time.

Stones of Power

The concept of birthstones goes back to the book of Exodus, when 12 stones representing the 12 tribes of Israel were worn on the breastplates of Jewish high priests. It became the tradition for observant Jews to wear all 12 of these stones, then, eventually rotating them one month at a time, depending on when each one seemed to have the most power. Each zodiac sign may have several lucky gemstones associated with it, but there is typically one that is considered the birthstone.

Aries

March 21 to April 19

AFFILIATES
Element: **Fire**
Modalit: **Cardinal**
Polarity: **Positive**
Planet: **Mars**
Gems: **Bloodstone for action and vitality;** diamond, ruby, emerald, amethyst
Colors: **All shades of red**
Plants: **Poppy, thistle, fern, wild olive, dogwood, pomegranate, blackthorn, willow**

Overview: Aries is the baby of the zodiac, the first sign in the wheel, originally positioned at 0 degrees of the ecliptic band. Like most babies, its energies, attributes, and liabilities are softened somewhat. As a fire sign, it can seem like more of an ember than an outright conflagration. Still, there is impulsivity in good measure, and a brash eagerness to start projects. Finishing, however, is another matter.

The sun, which represents life force and essence, is exalted in Aries. When a planet or luminary is exalted in a sign, that means it has the greatest power to achieve its potential.

Positive traits: This sign combines the courage of Mars the Warrior with creativity, spontaneity with confrontation. They are the perfect choice to dive into a situation while keeping their eyes on the goal. If a project needs a forceful, can-do achiever who will fight for a cause or a dynamic leader who loves a challenge, look no further. Stylistically they want to start trends, raise eyebrows, or be the first through the door at all the new hot spots.

Questionable traits: Like its namesake, a Ram can be brusque and aggressive, with a manner that often lacks subtlety or finesse. Expect a certain impatience and even the infant's "I want it now!" attitude. They may overlook or ignore the consequences for their hair-trigger or hot-headed reactions but others probably won't.

Love trends: When an Aries falls in love, acting like a passionate fool is not out of the question. Whirlwind courtships are also quite common as is some measure of promiscuity and bad choices ... yet once an Aries gives his or her heart away in a grounded and mature relationship, the connection is often for life.

Best matches: Rams blend well with companion fire signs Sagittarius, Leo, and other Aries. Yet the complimentary air signs of Gemini, Libra, and Aquarius have a history of providing the best long-term love matches. The signs that might lead to romantic woes are Taurus, Cancer, Capricorn, and sometimes other Aries.

Career signposts: On the job, Aries can work and think independently and are decisive, confident, and results-oriented. During a crisis, they are quick to respond, and bring their A-game when facing a tough deadline. Careers choices for the Ram include public relations specialist, communications manager, retail store manager, magazine editor, real estate agent, hair stylist, sales representative, holistic healthcare practitioner, registered nurse, or defense attorney.

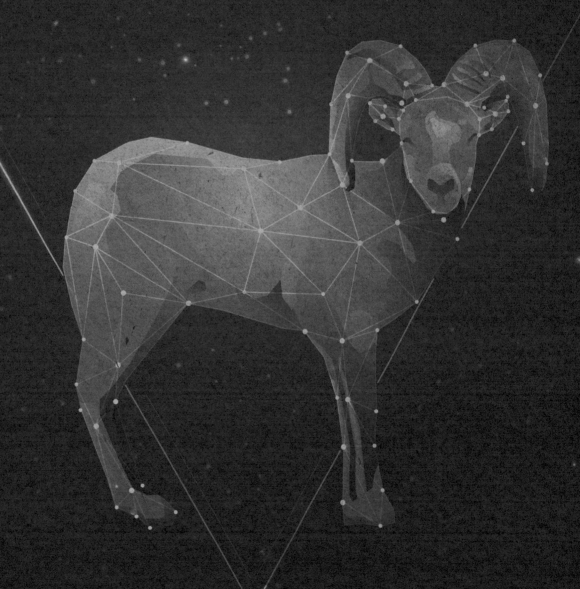

Aries the Ram

Taurus

April 20 to May 20

AFFILIATES:
Element: **Earth**
Modality: **Fixed**
Polarity: **Negative**
Planet: **Venus**
Gems: **Sapphire for self expression and truth;** rose quartz, emerald, lapis lazuli
Colors: **All shades of blue, deep green**
Plants: **Daisy, dandelion, lily, blackthorn, willow, hawthorn**

Overview: Taurus arrives directly after "baby" Aries, and as a result Taureans can sometimes act like the least mature of the three earth signs. This fixed sign craves comfort and wants to be surrounded by beautiful things ... and is willing to focus its earthly energies to ensure such pleasures. The moon is exalted in Taurus, meaning its power to inspire the imagination and creativity is at its peak.

Positive traits: These goal-oriented lovers of possessions are like all earth signs in that they value tangibles. Naturally sensuous and patient, the Taurean may take its sweet time to accomplish a task, yet it can be a skilled artisan or builder. Many Taureans have a resonant voice and enjoy singing or public speaking.

Questionable traits: The Bull is frequently stubborn and resists change. Although it can be stingy or childishly selfish, this sign is usually generous with those it holds dear. The notion of giving things away has to be purposely cultivated, however. Weight gain may become a problem if the Taurean diet is not monitored closely.

Love trends: The Venus-ruled Taurean in love is sensual and loyal, willing to share some of the luxuries it craves with its special person. With their sweet natures and generous inclinations toward lovers, Taureans make some of the best romantic catches in the zodiac. They want the best not only for themselves but also for their cherished ones. On the other hand, partners of certain Taureans may have to avoid becoming a carefully guarded "possession" or being . . . smothered by their constant physical and emotional attention and need for hugs and kisses.

Best matches: The Bull insists on loyalty, stability, intimacy, and commitment in his or her relationships and will only get along with a few other sun signs. The best bets are the earth signs Virgo and Capricorn, as well as other Taureans, and two water signs, Cancer and Pisces. Scorpio is also a water sign, but opposite Taurus on the zodiac wheel, which if matched with this sign can lead to clashes.

Career signposts: Taureans bring excellent qualities to a job. They are methodical and practical as well as professional and grounded, and have proven to be skilled planners and organizers. They don't mince words on the status of an assignment and are able to visualize projects still in the early stages. Some careers that goal-oriented Taureans might excel at include retail banker, project manager, landscape photographer, art director, interior designer, chef, restaurant manager, entertainer/performer, makeup artist, and museum curator.

Taurus the Bull

Gemini

May 21–June 20

AFFILIATES:
Element: **Air**
Modality: **Mutable**
Polarity: **Positive**
Planet: **Mercury**
Gems: **Agate for balance and stability; citrine, amber, tourmaline**
Colors: **Yellow, light green**
Plants: **Tansy, yarrow, privet, hawthorn, heather, cedar, linden, oak**

Overview: The first of the air signs, Gemini earns its affiliation with its ruling planet Mercury, as those born under the sign can be quite mercurial—as in changeable, many-sided, switchable. With this duality in mind, a person's positive traits may sometimes be perceived as negatives: their versatility can read as shallowness, their ambition as ruthlessness, their youthfulness as immaturity, and their speed at performing tasks as impatience.

Positive traits: These are the quick-witted intellectuals, the curious seekers of novelty, the identifiers of trends, in short, people who are adaptable, friendly, and fun. Because they are outgoing, enthusiastic, and intelligent, they are often a joy to be around, especially at social gatherings.

Questionable traits: This Twins sign can include some capricious flip-flopping and even trickster behavior. Geminis might be drama queens or party boys who may lack the motivation or appropriate focus for really important projects. But they also like to learn and absorb new information swiftly. Yes, there are times they can be two-faced, but many non-Geminis also "code-switch" ... putting on professional voices on the phone, watching their language around elderly relatives, and offering polite untruths to acquaintances.

Love trends: This creative, dynamic sign can be very easy to love. A Gemini who is looking for romance is playful and fun, flirting with the opposite sex and thrilled by meeting new people. Yet they can also be slow to give their hearts—their protective instincts insist they take time to know potential partners before making any emotional commitment. Sometimes love actually takes them by surprise.

Best matches: The strongest matches for Geminis are Aries, Leo, Libra, and Aquarius. The least compatible sign is Virgo and Pisces. Statistically Gemini women are most likely to marry Gemini men (there's that duality again), and also least likely to part with them, but will divorce Scorpio, Sagittarius, and Aquarius men at a higher rate. Men are also most likely to marry other Geminis, and have a higher-than-average divorce rate with Capricorn women, but are least likely to part from Taurus, Gemini, and Scorpios.

Career signposts: On the job, Geminis display strong communication skills. They are logical thinkers who love doing research and flexible performers who find multitasking a breeze. Witty and clever, they make ideal seminar leaders, fundraisers, or blog hosts. Careers Geminis might excel at include news reporter, event DJ, equity trader, dance instructor, director of photography, web analytics developer, patent agent, interpreter, or content writer.

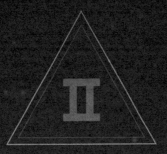

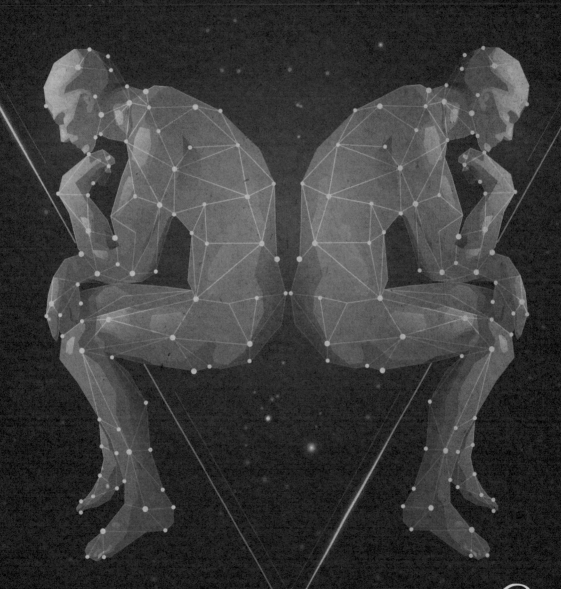

Gemini the Twins

Cancer

June 21–July 22

AFFILIATES:
Element: **Water**
Modality: **Cardinal**
Polarity: **Negative**
Planet: **Moon**
Gems: **Emerald for love and kindness;** pearl, peridot, moonstone
Colors: **Pale colors, cream, white**
Plants: **Water lilies, rushes, heather, cedar, linden, oak, holly**

Overview: Cancer is a cardinal sign that falls at the beginning of summer. As the first elemental water sign, Cancer may tend toward shallow depths, but it is brimming with life. Cancerians are ruled by the moon, which heightens maternal or paternal instincts and often makes them into caregivers, nest builders, and home lovers.

Positive traits: Cancers are all about emotion, frequently— and a little selfishly—their own. They become absorbed in their moods and this can make them cautious around new people. Yet the very sensitivity that restricts them at times also gifts them with intuition, creativity, and a great capacity to care . . . for people, animals, and causes. They are wise, empathetic, keepers of family lore, and storehouses of surprising hidden strength. Watch a weepy Cancer take charge in an emergency and be amazed. They can also sense undercurrents and read between

the lines, making them excellent BS detectors.

Questionable traits: The moody Crab can be an irritable crybaby and may throw temper tantrums out of frustration or from suspecting that their words were misunderstood. They are also emotionally clingy and may restrict the free movement of others in their family circle.

Love trends: The Cancer in love is self-protective, yet Moon Children are also known to fall very quickly and so may rush into relationships. This is a highly sensitive and nurturing sign, which often means Cancers are tender lovers who express their caring in ways that might never occur to other signs. They are unlikely to bail at the first hint of trouble, but prefer to dig in and try to work things out. Some Cancerians can be intrusive "helicopter" parents who smother their offspring with worry; these moms and dads

need to work extra hard to open those crab claws and let go.

Best matches: The best love matches for Cancer are Taurus, Virgo, Scorpio, and Pisces; the least promising signs are Aries and Libra. Two Cancers can easily overdo it in the sweet romance department, which can lead to anxiety . . . and sugar shock.

Career signposts: Cancers are among the most loyal workers. Add to that their creativity, concern for coworkers, and ability to bring a team or family spirit to projects . . . and their worth escalates. They are also skilled financial managers and extremely intuitive when it comes to anticipating problems or finding solutions. Ideal positions for them include chief executive officer, childcare worker, content editor, attorney, physical therapist, regional planner, interior designer, computer systems analyst, and art gallery manager.

Cancer the Crab

Leo

July 23–August 22

AFFILIATES:
Element: **Fire**
Modality: **Fixed**
Polarity: **Positive**
Planet: **Sun**
Gems: **Onyx for strength and calm;** yellow topaz, tiger's eye, ruby, milky yellow amber
Colors: **Ocher, golden hues**
Plants: **Sunflowers, chamomile, lavender, holly, hazel, almond, apple**

Overview: As a fire sign, the spirited Leo usually understands its own power enough to control it. That's a good thing, because their larger-than-life personalities and conceit often need to be tamed . . . or at least toned down. It should also be noted that no one can fault them for dreaming big and that their intentions are almost always good.

Positive traits: It is no wonder the classic Leo—vivacious, theatrical, driven, and intense— seeks the spotlight. Even in a less-visible setting they remain proud, glamorous, and regal. At home among family they are big-hearted and expressive, on the job ambitious and unafraid of challenges. They crave adventure and have no problem facing risks.

Questionable traits: Lions always compete to win. They can be be egomaniacs who steal the show, pompous asses acting like they are better than everyone, vengeful children, or bossy control freaks. They may challenge the wrong person who will quickly put them in their place—even lions have to give way to other animals on occasion. They can also manifest a false confidence that comes across as prideful. Finally, they resist change and are reluctant to take advice.

Love trends: Leo is the sign that rules the human heart, so its not surprising that as lovers they are passionate and demonstrative . . . once they let down their guard. It is said they know they are in love when they finally put the needs of their partner before their own. On the downside, Leos can be jealous and possessive, requiring a patient paramour to calmly reassure them. They are also known to stray and can even end up as promiscuous alley cats.

Best matches: The Lion matches up well with all three air signs—Libra, Gemini, and Aquarius. When Leos are paired with other Leos, or other fire signs for that matter, the couple might generate too much scorching energy, resulting in struggles for dominance. If there is mutual respect, however, Leos and fire sign Sagittarians have a history of finding enduring love.

Career Signposts: These powerful natural leaders may rise to advanced positions in many fields. Their take-charge attitude, dynamism, and fearlessness make them ideal military or law enforcement officers, teachers, stockbrokers, politicians, researchers, and sportsmen and women. Their histrionic side often situates them in the arts. Career paths might include advertising executive, broadcaster, actor, standup comedian, events planner, special education teacher, fashion designer, graphic or production artist, personal trainer, dog trainer, and business coach.

Leo the Lion

Virgo

August 23–September 22

AFFILIATES:
Element: **Earth**
Modality: **Mutable**
Polarity: **Negative**
Planet: **Mercury**
Gems: **Carnelian for confidence and passion;** amethyst, pyrite
Colors: **Silver, indigo, dark violet**
Plants: **Wintergreen, sage, privet, hazel, almond, apple, grapevine, blackberry, white poplar, aspen**

Overview: Compared to the fiery lions that precede them, logical, practical Virgos might seem to suffer by comparison. But they bring much to the table in terms of positive qualities and are less wearing to be around than those demanding Lions. Their constellation, a long-haired maiden bearing a sheaf of wheat, symbolizes the bounty that Virgo can provide. As an earth sign, Virgos are sensual; being ruled by Mercery makes them quick-witted and articulate, with a fine sense of humor, in other words good communicators.

Positive traits: Virgos understand the value of hard work and are conscientious on the job. They seek a level of precision and purity in all things and feel safest following a routine. Like Mercury the Messenger, the Virgo hurries from place to place, busy organizing, planning, implementing. This independent sign is convinced it can accomplish anything . . . and it is often right. Yet in spite of their achievements, Virgos also know how to remain humble and kind. There is also a traditional belief that Virgo produces more attractive people than any other sign.

Questionable traits: The fastidious Virgo can be a relentless critic, of themselves and others. While they are quite observant, Virgo vigilance may devolve into anxiety. They can also seem square, uptight, and hesitant to try new ideas. Caution is their watchword, and they back it up with a stubborn streak.

Love trends: Virgos are sincere but discriminating when it comes to romance, seeking the kind of love where souls, minds, and bodies blend effortlessly. Virgos might be guarded about their inner feelings at first, but that is to protect themselves until trust develops. Once that barrier is down, Virgos focus intently on their partners.

Best Matches: Virgo's best matches are Taurus, Cancer, Scorpio, and Capricorn. The least compatible signs are Gemini and Sagittarius. Two Virgos together can be lackluster: they tend to let their conservative side prevail, putting a damper on passion.

Career Signposts: Virgos are planning and organizing champs, with strong verbal skills. They also know how to sit and listen, a rarity in the business world. Marvels at solving problems and handling crises, they make supportive team leaders. Promising career options include veterinarian, laboratory technician, environmentalist, biologist, accounting analyst, registered nurse, nutritionist, life skills coach, or social worker.

Virgo the Virgin

Libra

September 23–October 22

AFFILIATES:
Element: **Air**
Modality: **Cardinal**
Polarity: **Positive**
Planet: **Venus**
Gems: **Peridot for radiance and purpose;** opal, jade
Colors: **Primary colors, shocking pink, night blue**
Plants: **Pansy, primrose, violet, strawberry, white poplar, aspen, grapevine, blackberry, ivy**

Overview: Those born to this air sign are often the aesthetes of the zodiac—cultured, refined, intellectual, sensitive, and attracted to the glories of art or nature. These connoisseurs of life are ruled by Venus, the planet that oversees love, beauty, and money, but they are not profligate in their pursuits of same. No, their psyche is more rational—they need to create equilibrium in all aspects of their life.

Positive traits: Few are more stylish or sophisticated than Libras, with their love of art and fashion. This chatty, charming sign enjoys being around others and is known for being open-minded and willing to compromise. They make interesting, clever friends who are always up for group activities. They also act as peacemakers when there is family discord.

Questionable traits: The Scales, signifying the ability to keep things in balance, may also indicate someone evading confrontation. Maintaining the peace doesn't work when strong feelings need a healthy outlet. Libras also analyze everything to death, constantly weighing the pros and cons of an issue. This comes from a need to please everyone—often an impossible task. When things go awry, Libras feel like the whole world is against them. With their need to connect with everyone, they may seem shallow, but they normally don't lack depth. They can also seem unreliable and even flighty at times.

Love trends: It is said that Libras are "in love with love." While this sounds romantic and thrilling, their desire for excitement also means they are prone to getting "love drunk" and losing good judgement. They are happy to engage in lighthearted flings with a series of partners, but they are quite choosy if and when they desire to settle down. And once they are truly in love, they take commitment very seriously.

Best matches: Libras click with Gemini, Leo, Sagittarius, and Aquarius partners and are least compatible with Cancer and Capricorn. A match of two engaging Libras would have great potential.

Career Signposts: Natural leaders, Libras do best when left alone to generate ideas. Still, they might help them with follow-through, not always a Libra strong point. With their sense of design and balance, they often gravitate to the arts. Careers ideas for Libras include interior decorator, journalist, municipal court judge, mediator, public relations specialist, teacher, customer service representative, graphic artist, web designer, or brand marketing consultant.

Libra the Scales

Influence Over Body Parts

The influence of the zodiac on humans is not limited to character traits or future events.

Many astrologers also believe that the constellations rule different parts of the human body, from Aries at the top of the head to Pisces at the feet and toes. There is some debate, however, as to just how these influences manifest. Many astrologers view these body parts as "points of influence or trigger points," rather than being targeted for illness. For those couples in courtship mode, it helps to know that the other person's birth sign likely indicates touch-sensitive body parts or their most receptive erogenous zones.

Aries

Head, Face, Brain, Eyes

Aries rules the head, except the nose. In the Middle Ages doctor/astrologers would never treat a head ailment if the moon were in Aries. Today it is believed that Aries people are robust and rarely suffer chronic illnesses. They can get stress headaches, however, but a gentle head massage from a loved one can work wonders.

Taurus

Throat, neck, vocal chords, tonsils, thyroid

Ailments or injuries in earth signs like Taurus can take time to heal. Taurean tends to be constant communicators, good singers, and frequent noisemakers, leading to possible sore throats or laryngitis. Loving partners should brew them tea with lemon and run a warm bath.

Gemini

Arms, lungs, hands, shoulders

This sign of the twins rules body parts that come in pairs. Gemini's desire to communicate often engages the lungs, arms, and hands; bear in mind they also enjoy giving and receiving flirty hugs.

Cancer

Chest, breasts, stomach, diaphragm

Both chest and breast indicate nurturing tendencies such as preparing and serving food to family and friends. Cancerian mothers are often naturals at breastfeeding. For courting Cancerians, consider the allure of oysters or strawberries, champagne, and chocolate.

Leo

Heart, spine, spinal column, upper back

The powerful leonine sun sign rules the human seats of strength and feelings—the back and spine support the body, while the heart provides both physical and emotional life. To help a stressed Leos rise to meet their challenges, offer a backrub.

Virgo

Abdomen, digestive system, spleen

When Virgos worry—which they do a lot—their stomachs and intestines suffer. The best solution to combat this is good nutrition—camomile or ginger tea, steamed vegetables, brown rice, fresh fruit. Keep in mind the Virgo belly can be a very erogenous zone.

Libra

Kidneys, skin, lower back, buttocks

Libras, both men and women, are noted for their sleek, toned backsides and clear, bright facial skin. The goddess Venus rules their romantic side, but they should go cautiously or they might fall too hard too fast.

Scorpio

Reproductive system, sexual organs, nose, blood, bowels

Not surprisingly, many people associate this sign with sex, but Scorpios more closely represent creation and transformation. Still, they "love" to love and so showing passion is a sure way to gain their attention.

Sagittarius

Hips, thighs, liver, sciatic nerve

Archers love travel and adventure, but might then be prone to injuries of the hips or thighs or flare ups of the sciatic nerve. Help them discover the sensual pleasure of both the hips and thighs.

Capricorn

Knees, joints, skeletal system, teeth

How fitting that these supportive body parts are ruled by the sun sign that values structure. Caps love to laugh during dating and courtship and find the backs of the knees very tantalizing.

Aquarius

Calves, ankles, shins, circulatory system

Aquarians are about connections, just like the ankle connecting the leg to the foot. Yet they are delicate and need special care . . . partners could focus on therapeutic reflexology of the lower legs and ankles.

Pisces

Feet, toes, lymphatic system

This sign is said to absorb the lessons of the other zodiac signs . . . good thing their feet and toes give them stability. They also like to put their feet to good use traveling. An attentive partner might end a day of shopping or sightseeing by preparing a soothing bubble bath.

153

Scorpio

October 23–November 21

AFFILIATES:
Element: **Water**
Modality: **Fixed**
Polarity: **Negative**
Planet: **Mars/Pluto**
Gems: **Topaz for strength and intelligence;** ruby, **Garnet, Carnelian, Black Pearl**
Colors: **Black, blood red, charcoal gray**
Plants: **Root vegetables, black poppy, hemlock, ivy, reed**

Overview: Scorpios tend to be intense and brooding but also very magnetic. Like fellow water signs Cancer and Pisces, they are intuitive and insightful, but also secretive. Ruled by the warlike planet Mars, this sign engineers its attacks with precision. Slow-moving Pluto also manifests influence here—it sat in Scorpio from 1983 to 1995, so most Millennials have Pluto in Scorpio, meaning they are tough, resilient, and up to the challenges of a changing world.

Positive traits: Admirers find Scorpios soulful and profound, truth seekers who are rarely cowed. Skilled healers, they may be drawn to the occult, hidden processes of the world. Yet they can be brave and honest, able to succeed in a number of arenas. Their loyalty to friends knows no bounds.

Questionable traits: Scorpios can be tough-minded, aggressive, and quick to respond to provocation— they may sting if threatened. Frequently ambitious, they can turn resentful, even vengeful, if slighted or demeaned. They have a hard time trusting others or getting others to trust them. Love trends: Even in love, Scorpios can be guarded. These barriers make them extremely beguiling to the opposite sex. Scorpios enjoy being in control and are capable of drawing potential lovers into their orbit. But don't pity their "victims"— Scorpios are reputedly the most intimate, passionate, and creative lovers in the zodiac. On the other hand, they are often possessive.

Best matches: Scorpio partners should be independent, loyal, and understanding. This sign is most compatible with water signs Cancer and Pisces, and earth signs Capricorn and Virgo. Less favorable are Sagittarius, Gemini, and Libra. Two Scorpios may light up the bedroom sexually, but for a lasting connection they need to turn down the intensity and open up emotionally.

Career signposts: At work, the Scorpion uses its sharp focus and strong observation skills to keep on top of developing situations and intervene if needed. Scorpios offer enduring loyalty and as managers will quickly flex their power. Career options include psychologist/psychiatrist, surgeon, medical examiner, pharmacist, engineer, litigation attorney, musician, appraiser, massage therapist, realtor, mortgage banker, or financial analyst.

Scorpio the Scorpion

Three Stages of Scorpio

Many astrologers believe Scorpios are able to evolve through three stages, each subsequent stage representing emotional growth and increased insight.

Stage One is symbolized by the Scorpion, which exercises power through emotion and instinct; this can sometimes result in destructive or competitive behavior.

Stage Two is represented by the Golden Eagle; it exercises power through the intellect. This means they now have the ability to see what is hidden from others and discover the deeper truths of life.

Stage Three is symbolized by the Phoenix of Love and the Dove of Peace. This is Scorpio on a higher plane—transformed and reaching inside to commune with the mystical qualities of the soul rather than embracing the ego. The obsession with power has faded, replaced by compassion and the desire to find a spiritual purpose.

Sagittarius

November 22–December 21

AFFILIATES:
Element: **Fire**
Modality: **Mutable**
Polarity: **Positive**
Planet: **Jupiter**
Gems: **Turquoise for health and good fortune;** amethyst, citrine
Colors: **Denim blue, beige, bronze**
Plants: **Asparagus, chestnuts, soybeans, reed, elder, yew**

Overview: Sagittarius is the third and final fire sign—if Aries is the struck match and Leo the glowing campfire, Sagittarius is the roaring bonfire. It is also a mutable sign, dealing with adaptability and flexibility, the perfect compliment to the Sagittarian penchant for change. Ruled by Jupiter, the planet of expansion, this energetic sign is always looking for novel places to travel, new languages to learn, and fresh ideas to try out, typically with a total lack of inhibition. Still, who doesn't adore a shooting star who has no selfishness or greed.

Positive traits: These eternal optimists just gush with enthusiasm . . . and why shouldn't they? They are rare among humans in that they are able to transform their thoughts and dreams into real actions. Archers also love to collect people, hosting parties, organizing road trips, showing up with an entourage at movie premieres or book signings. Any holiday gatherings become an art form . . . think Auntie Mame on speed. They are noted for their generosity, idealism, and great senses of humor as well as endless curiosity and open minds.

Questionable traits: Archers are not known for their patience or diplomacy, and their critical arrows often hit the mark. Their judgements can be frank, to the point of hurting people's feelings. They often promise more than they can deliver, leading to disappointment and frustration in their friends and family members. Their desire for never-ending personal growth can make them seem flighty, fickle, or even unstable.

Love trends: Sagittarians value freedom almost more than anything else. But this passionate sign also enjoys having fun with romantic partners and places a premium on those who tend to be more sexually adventurous. Archers in love are loyal and dedicated, especially with partners who are intelligent, expressive, and sensitive.

Best matches: Sagittarius matches up well with the other two fire signs—Aries and Leo, as well as with Libra and Aquarius.

Career signposts: Slotting well into positions of leadership or authority, Sagittarians are big-picture thinkers and fearless risk takers. Their people skills make them popular, and their super-charged personalities draw staff together into effective teams. Yet even working alone, they bring that trademark enthusiasm and flexibility to any project. Career paths might include those of architect, teacher, hospitality manager, entrepreneur, publishing manager, Uber driver, environmental engineer, freelance writer, travel consultant, global project manager, sports coach, or personal trainer.

Capricorn

December 22–January 19

AFFILIATES:
Element: **Earth**
Modality: **Cardinal**
Polarity: **Negative**
Planet: **Saturn**
Gems: **Ruby for protection and vitality;** diamond, falcon's eye, white sapphire
Colors: **All shades of brown, orange, black**
Plants: **Hemlock, black poppy, burdock root, yew, elder, birch**

Overview: The symbol of the final earth sign is the "sea goat," a mythical creature with the head and forelegs of a goat and the tail of a fish. Like the stubborn goat, that forcefully goes where it wishes, the Capricorn uses all its means to forge ahead toward a goal and rarely lets anything stand in its way. Urgency underlies much of its actions—there is no faith in second chances. They are born managers and tend to be traditionalists. The influence of ruling planet Saturn represents structure and discipline, making Capricorns practical and responsible, but also emotionally aloof, even cold.

Positive traits: Resourceful, hard-working Capricorns are often considered pillars of society. They crave acceptance in the established order and need to believe they have left a legacy behind them. They value tangible results and are willing to strategize and exert control in order to achieve them. Capricorns are typically independent, but at home they relish time spent with family. Their emotional connections to childhood memories are ever-present. They make loyal, reliable, and lasting friends, providing those in their circle understand boundaries and don't probe too deeply.

Questionable traits: Capricorns often come across as know-it-alls and can be annoyingly pessimistic, always fearing the worst. If crossed or challenged, they can also carry a grudge and withhold forgiveness. Many of them maintain a long list of things and people they don't like.

Love trends: The Capricorn in love can be earthy, but remains status-minded. Their walls are high and hard to breach, but once they are won over, they stay committed. Even then, though, their demeanor can be confusingly remote or lacking in compassion. But their track record as devoted partners and providers is stellar.

Best matches: Capricorns tend to be ambitious and persistent, even while dating. Men want a woman who fits into their lives seamlessly; women, however, want a man who makes them smile. The romantic matches with the most potential are Taurus, Virgo, Scorpio, and Pisces. Signs to be wary of are Aries and Libra.

Career signposts: Capricorns set high standards for themselves and expect others around them to do likewise. This makes them excellent, if demanding, managers or supervisors. Loyalty and a strong work ethic are often valued morethan skill or intellect. They set long-term goals and have the stamina to stay the course and meet them. Careers that suit this sign include chief executive officer, human resources manager, business analyst, financial planner, architect, copywriter, foreign affairs specialist, intelligence analyst, and commissioner.

Capricorn the Goat

Aquarius

January 20 – February 18

AFFILIATES:
Element: **Air**
Modality: **Fixed**
Polarity: **Positive**
Planet: **Saturn**
Gems: **Garnet for vitality and passion;** amazonite, aquamarine, hematite, amber
Colors: **Electric blue, silver gray, fluorescent colors**
Plants: **Dandelions, resins, frankincense, myrrh, birch, rowan, mountain ash, ash**

Overview: The water bearer, the third air sign, can be much more fanciful or cerebral than its two predecessors. As a fixed sign, it is resistant to outside influences. Aquarians can be quiet and shy, even come across as eccentric. They have a need to help others and stand up for causes they believe in. Uranus, their ruling planet, bestows a timid, abrupt, or even pugnacious nature, but it also endows them with vision and a clear sense of the future. They see a world teeming with possibilities as they focus on the big picture.

Positive traits: Aquarians may the ones you watch ambling down the street, styled in scarves, boots, ethnic jackets, slouchy hats . . . the tuned-in visionary. They are open-minded, quirky, and friendly in a vaguely distant way. Yet they are also keen thinkers who relish a mental challenge. They enjoy company and work to establish a community. Because they can view conflicting issues from both sides, they make skilled problem solvers.

Questionable traits: When lost in their dream world, Aquarians may run from emotional demands. A love of theorizing can blind them to the realities of daily life, impacting their ability to connect with people. They can also be uncompromising and temperamental.

Love trends: An Aquarian in love can be unconventional. Their natural tendency is to cherish their freedom. This means it can take time for them to achieve intimacy. For this transformation to occur, they must consciously work at expressing their emotions. Yet they make loyal and committed lovers who consider their partners their equals.

Best Matches: This sign does well romantically with Gemini, Libra, and Sagittarius. A match of two Aquarians can be exciting and liberating, but one or both partners may not understand traditional sexual taboos. Less-promising signs for love are Taurus, Cancer, Scorpio, and Capricorn.

Career signposts: Aquarians won't thrive in jobs that squelch their dreamy natures. They need positions that encourage their assets: out-of-the-box thinking, fair mindedness, and a spirit of community. Career options include teacher, research scientist, social worker, industrial engineer, mechanical designer, computer programmer, software developer, astronomy or physics professor, fiction writer, or personal stylist.

Aquarius the Water Bearer

An Aquarian Age

Heralded by a song in the Broadway musical *Hair*, the "Age of Aquarius" connotes a time of "harmony and understanding, sympathy and trust abounding, no more falsehood or derisions, golden living dreams of visions." In 2004's *The Book of World Horoscopes*, Nicholas Campion suggests that the Age of Aquarius ranges from AD 1447 to AD 3597; others astrologers say it started as recently as March 20, 2021. It is meant to be a time when humanity takes control of the earth and its own destiny, which involves the revelation of truth, respect for individual thought, an increase in innovation, and the expansion of consciousness. Each astrological "age" lasts roughly 2,160 years, the time it takes for the vernal equinox to move from one zodiac constellation to the next.

Pisces

February 19–March 20

AFFILIATES:
Element: **Water**
Modality: **Mutable**
Polarity: **Negative**
Planet: **Neptune**, formerly **Jupiter**
Gems: **Amethyst for calm and healing;** white opal, jade, pearl
Colors: **Mauve, purple, aquamarine**
Plants: **Mosses, ferns, seaweed, ash, alder, pomegranate, dogwood, furze, gorse, wild olive**

Overview: Pisces is the last water sign and the final sign of the zodiac. It is believed that in this position it has absorbed every practical guideline and emotional lesson from the previous 11 signs. This might account for Pisces being the most perceptive, empathetic, and intuitive sign, those born to it navigating like their fish namesakes through the labyrinths of the human psyche. The distant planet Neptune gives them mystical qualities, while former sign, majestic Jupiter, may still offer remnants of luck and spiritual growth. As a mutable sign, it is ready to adapt to new ideas or trends, which it welcomes and accepts.

Positive traits: These generous, caring souls are loyal, devoted family members who also provide selfless friendship. They can be artistic as well as musical and enjoy any type of visual media. Sublime thoughts and spiritual musings attract them. Not surprisingly, Pisces like swimming and other water sports. Most people find them enchanting, even if they are frequently caught daydreaming.

Questionable traits: Pisceans often feel at risk—like lost children—and tend to play the victim. As dreamers they can seem out of touch with reality, even unreachable. They like to be alone, an odd preference for such a giving sign. They do not like criticism, cruelty, or past mistakes being dredged up,

Love trends: When Pisces fall in love, they become hopelessly smitten. They are not flirts or players, but rather gentle, passionate lovers who require a real connection with a partner. They know how to express their feelings, but they can also be blindly loyal.

Best matches: Pisces may find lasting love with Taurus, fellow water signs Cancer and Scorpio, and Capricorn. Success is less likely with Gemini and Sagittarius. A Pisces-Pisces match can seem like a fairytale coupling between two dreamers, but their "soft" personalities may cause difficulty as they shift from friends to lovers. If romance blooms, however, their understanding of each other's needs can make them extremely compatible in bed.

Career signposts: Pisces tend to be imaginative and creative on the job, as well as hard-working, reliable, and compassionate. Not aggressive go-getters, they use their empathetic people skills to inspire and motivate others. They go beyond the 9-to-5 bounds to complete assignments and are great at problem solving. Career paths include attorney, architect, filmmaker, veterinarian, psychologist, physical therapist, musician, librarian, wedding/ events photographer, social worker, human resources coordinator, or game designer.

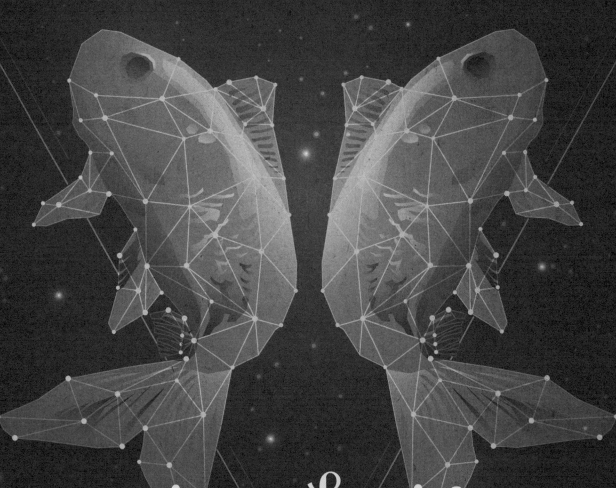

Pisces the Fish

Rising Signs

In the language of astrology, there are a number of key indicators that may appear on a birth chart. In addition to the 12 sun signs, which are almost universally known in the West, there are also 12 rising signs and 12 moon signs.

Rising, or ascendent, signs are determined by which zodiac constellation was rising on the eastern horizon at the time of a person's birth. These make up one of the "three legs" of a horoscope, which are the sun sign, rising sign, and moon sign (reflecting the inner self). These three main planetary points indicate a person's everyday personality . . . and can suggest the optimum times to book a workout or spa treatment, make a career move, visit a family member, or do any of the dozens of activities that require some forethought. On a larger scale, these guideposts can also help people discover their life purpose, improve their relationships, and maybe even find their soulmate.

The rising sign is meant to indicate the social personality or how one appears to others. It represents the physical body and individual style. It has been said that when a person meets a stranger, it is often his or her rising sign that the stranger first perceives and that makes an impression, more so than the traits of their sun sign or moon sign.

The following are some characteristics of the different rising signs that may additionally influence a horoscope:

Aries

Strengths: hopeful, active, energetic, honest, adaptable, brave, adventurous, passionate, generous, cheerful, curious, warm, dynamic
Weaknesses: impulsive, naive, self-willed, quarrelsome.

Taurus

Strengths: romantic, decisive, logical, hard-working, passionate, patient, artistic, perseverant, kind, practical, calm,
Weaknesses: prejudiced, needy, stubborn, hedonistic

Gemini

Strengths: insightful, smart, cheerful, quick-witted, warm, charming
Weaknesses: fickle, gossipy

Cancer

Strengths: strong sixth sense, gentle, imaginative, careful, dedicated, perseverant, kind, caring
Weaknesses: greedy, possessive, sensitive, prudish

Leo

Strengths: proud, charitable, reflective, loyal and enthusiastic
Weaknesses: arrogant,

conceited, indulgent, wasteful, willful

Virgo

Strengths: precise, intelligent, helping, elegant, perfectionist, modest, practical, perceptive
Weaknesses: fussy, nosey, tortuous, limiting

Libra

Strengths: idealistic, reasonable, just, strong social skills, charming, artistic, kind-hearted
Weaknesses: hesitant, egotistic, lazy, careless, freewheeling

Scorpio

Strengths: mysterious, rational, intelligent, independent, intuitive, devoted, insightful, sensible
Weaknesses: suspicious, obsessive, complicated, possessive, arrogant, self-willed

Sagittarius

Strengths: adventurous, outspoken, upbeat, insightful, rational, brave, lively, optimistic

Weaknesses: forgetful, unthinking, rash

Capricorn

Strengths: intelligent, practical, reliable, perseverant, generous, optimistic, endearing, persistent
Weaknesses: stubborn, solitary, and suspicious

Aquarius

Strengths: unique, tolerant, calm, sociable, charitable, independent, smart, practical
Weaknesses: changeful, disobedient, hasty, rebel

Pisces

Strengths: conscious, friendly, dedicated, kind, good tempered
Weaknesses: retreating, sentimental, indecisive, unrealistic

Moon Signs

In addition to sun signs and rising signs, astrologers may also look for a person's moon sign when plotting their chart. Some astrologers feel that moon signs are nearly as important as sun signs. Others believe they hold even greater importance, and that approaching life through one's moon sign can increase clarity of purpose and attract good fortune.

Whereas sun signs influence personality and sense of identity, moon signs reflect a person's inner self, their instincts and intuition, and guide their emotions and influence their soul. They affect the subconscious, where deep feelings lie, and can help an individual gain faith in their life decisions and offer a sense of security. Moon signs may also alter the ways a person's sun sign is expressed—a fiery or passionate sun sign might be tempered by a mellow or easy-going moon sign. Conversely, a home loving or peacemaking sun sign might experience unexpected emotional heat based on a more tempestuous or reactive moon sign. It's also significant if the sun sign and moon sign share the same elements: having two water, air, earth, or fire signs could increase the effect of each element. Compatibility can also be influenced by moon signs. Certain happy couples with incompatible sun signs are not surprised to discover their moon signs are quite compatible. Some astrologers believe that two moon signs that share the same element are the best indicators of whether or not a couple will have a successful relationship.

The moon sign is calculated based on its position in the zodiac at the time of birth. There are charts available online that allow people to go back as many years as needed to see where their birth moon was located. Because the moon moves into a different sign every two to three days, the moon signs can be different, say, for a Pisces born on March 4 and one born on March 8.

Characteristics

Aries Moon
This sign requires autonomy, action, novelty, and to be "first." The Aries moon needs to feel alive and turned on and can demand extra attention. While a challenge is always welcome, it often wants to be coddled and be the center of attention.

Taurus Moon
The Taurus moon needs stability, creature comforts, affection, and beauty. They have to feel that they're working on something worthwhile and expect a return on their emotional investment. They can become obsessed with security.

Gemini Moon
This sign enjoys constant communication, new ideas, and stimulating dialogue. It is attracted to kindred spirits, those who can mirror or reflect ideas back to them.

Cancer Moon
This sign requires nurturing, safety, family, and material comforts. It can have abandonment issues and might need a lot of reassurance to feel secure.

Leo Moon

This high-maintenance moon looks for attention, glamour, affection, constant entertainment, and playfulness. It craves excitement and seeks a partner with whom to celebrate life. Its leonine sense of leadership also needs to be expressed

Virgo Moon

This moon sign needs structure, to feel helpful, and mental challenges. It enjoys problem solving and analyzing data, but can also be anxious or fretful.

Libra Moon

This signs looks for harmony, beauty, companionship, and equality. It does not seek conflict and would rather savor a peaceful and visually pleasing environment with stylish clothing and fine art. It also has a strong sense of justice.

Scorpio Moon

This moon sign needs privacy, intensity, and soul bonding. It requires strong sexual chemistry but has a hard time opening up—yet those who win a Scorpio moon's confidence will be rewarded with enduring loyalty.

Sagittarius Moon

This sign seeks adventure, conquests, wisdom, and variety. It desires contact with worldly and open-minded people from all walks and loves travel and new experiences. Life should be a constant carnival keeping boredom at bay.

Capricorn Moon

This moon needs to feel worthwhile, to create something lasting. Power can become too alluring, so the best partner is one with boundaries and ambitions of their own. Can be emotionally distant, and also seeks solitude when depressed or melancholy.

Aquarius Moon

Give this sign friendship, collaboration, and a common cause. Yet this rebellious moon can also challenge the powers that be. Independence can lapse into people pleasing, and even when settled down, this sign needs a lot of freedom.

Pisces Moon

This dreamy moon craves fantasy, understanding, escape, creative outlets, and security. Can be emotionally hard to pin down; most are not even sure how to explain or navigate their own deep feelings. These powerful healers are drawn to artistic, sensual, and spiritual pursuits.

Mercury, Mars, and Venus

Most astrologers agree that major placements on a birth chart start with the sun, moon, and rising signs. But there are another three key signs that they also focus on to gain a more thorough picture—Mercury, Mars, and Venus. Together these are known as the "Big 6" of astrological placement.

To briefly recap, one's sun sign governs ego, basic personality, and identity. The moon sign represents who a person is when they are alone and governs their inner thoughts. The rising sign is the outer, physical person, the face presented to, and perceived by, the world.

The Mercury Sign

Mercury is the planet of communication, so the sign describes how people expresses themselves in conversation and writing, how they absorb information, and how their decision-making and thought processes work. This sign provides insights on how someone learns and how they approach conflict. Understanding this sign may be more useful than analyzing the sun sign. It can impact all aspects of life, from the office to the bedroom—anywhere successful communication is critical. Because Mercury is closest to the sun, its sign will always appear in the person's Sun sign, or the sign before or after. (For instance, for an Aries, the Mercury sign will be in Aries, Taurus, or Pisces.)

Mercury in:	Traits:	Mercury in:	Traits:
Aries	On the lookout for spontaneous adventure, road trips	Libra	Social butterfly who likes to listen and create harmony
Taurus	Sensual but possessive, predictable and loyal	Scorpio	Deep thinker, explorer of hidden realms
Gemini	Youthfully energetic, perpetually curious	Sagittarius	Adaptable, far-reaching mental powers, fiery enthusiasm
Cancer	Capable, adaptable, favored with unexpected gifts	Capricorn	Businesslike mindset; willing to sacrifice for career growth
Leo	Fiery and creative; sometimes petty and petulant	Aquarius	Open-minded, philosophical, eases barriers down
Virgo	Detail-oriented, making things run efficiently	Pisces	Deeply emotional, social nature, creates meaningful connections

The Mars Sign

Mars is the planet of aggression and passion. It represents the human will, sexual energy, and how people assert themselves. It provides the impetus to get up each day, propels ambition, and provides direction. Mars reflects how people handle anger and frustration, especially when independence is at risk. It also impacts most relationships . . . it has been said that the Venus sign decides who an individual desires, but it is the Mars sign that pursues them. It's up to each person whether they control it or "work" it. The Mars sign can be determined by an online calculator or an astrologer.

Mars in:	Traits:	Mars in:	Traits:
Aries	Direct and impulsive; don't let Mars gain control	Libra	People pleaser and peacekeeper; indecisive at times
Taurus	Strong, stable; just keep the raging Bull in the barn	Scorpio	Craves challenge; needs to make time for sex life and exercise
Gemini	Restless chameleon; try not to use words as weapons	Sagittarius	Terrific sense of adventure; very little patience
Cancer	Protective and nurturing; could be passive-aggressive	Capricorn	Ultimate placement for Mars: focused, ambitious, clear-headed
Leo	Powerful, ambitious, sexual; hold that temper in check	Aquarius	Intellectual with original viewpoint; headstrong, remote during sex
Virgo	Super heroic multitasker; chill out during romantic encounters	Pisces	Easy-going, compassionate; tends to be passive

The Venus Sign

The planet of love can help a person understand who they are attracted to and why, how they connect and experience lovemaking, and what kind of partner they can become. Venus also oversees pleasure and determines what indulgences individuals crave. More importantly, Venus governs value, one's relationship to money, and their sense of aesthetics. The Venus sign can be calculated based on date of birth, unless it was a day that Venus switched signs, which requires time and location of birth.

Venus in:	Trait:	Venus in:	Trait:
Aries	Bold, impulsive, dominant; can be egotistical	Libra	Venus rules here: seeks harmony, hates conflict
Taurus	Sensual, physically affectionate, wants to be spoiled	Scorpio	Focused, intensely intimate; once committed, no turning back
Gemini	Affectionate, loyal, communicative; may struggle to commit	Sagittarius	Adventurous, free-spirited, romantic; needs spontaneous partner
Cancer	Seeks love, comfort, and commitment; must build trust	Capricorn	Calculates romance, wants to build foundation for the future
Leo	Celebrates love, sentimental; needs doting partner	Aquarius	Aloof, distant at start, but ready to commit when swept away
Virgo	Wants love to be logical; tends to try to "fix" relationships	Pisces	Dreamy and poetic; loves fantasies, needs some grounding

Houses of the Zodiac

The song "Aquarius" from the Broadway musical *Hair* famously starts out with the line, "When the moon is in the seventh house and Jupiter aligns with Mars, then peace will guide the planets, and love will steer the stars." It all sounds very mystical and hopeful, like the era of great accord that humans have been awaiting. But what exactly does the term "house" mean in astrological terms?

As has previously been established there are 12 birth signs, and 10 "planets" that affect a horoscope. In the same way that birth signs and planets have specific meanings, the 12 houses on a natal chart rule over separate areas of a person's life, representing the totality of their experiences. Houses one through six are known as the "personal or subjective houses," revolving around matters of self, while seven through 12 are "interpersonal or objective houses," relating to an individual's connection to the world around them.

Each of the houses also has its own *natural* zodiac sign and planetary ruler that will likely differ from the personal ones shown on a natal chart. For instance, the first house of the zodiac is *naturally* ruled by the sign Aries and is associated with the planet Mars. But on one's *personal* chart, the sign could be Libra, which is ruled by the planets Mercury and Jupiter. Or Cancer, which is overseen by the Moon.

Houses are determined by where they fall on the natal chart: If, for instance, Gemini is positioned at 9 o'clock on the chart, it falls into the first house. It is also the querent's rising sign. Cancer then falls into the second house, Leo, the third, and so on. Planets are also affected by their positioning in a certain house—near the cusp, near the center of the arc. It is clear to see why the addition of houses to a horoscope contributes a deeper understanding and more possibilities for interpretation. So how did houses evolve? In most horoscopic traditions from around the world, houses are divisions—typically 12—of the ecliptic plane at the time and place of the horoscope in question. (Remember, the ecliptic plane is the projected circle containing the sun's "orbit" as seen from the earth.) The position of the houses is dependent on time and location, not date. In Vedic astrology, these divisions are called Bhavas. On the circular natal chart, the houses are numbered counter-clockwise from the cusp of the first house. Commonly, houses one through six are below the horizon and houses seven through twelve are above the horizon, but some systems may not entirely follow that division.

Each house of the horoscope represents a different area of experience, where the energies

Left: Each of the 12 houses has a "natural" zodiac sign, starting with Aries at 9 o'clock and flowing counterclockwise. On a natal chart, different signs may fall into the 12 houses, depending on date of birth.

of the signs and planets manifest. They relate to physical surrounding and personal life experiences. Yet different astrologers used different methods to calculate houses and these variations stem from disagreement over what they mean mathematically in terms of space and time. Even though all Western astrology uses 12-houses projected on the ecliptic, the discord arises over which fundamental plane is the object of the division and whether the division represents units of time or degrees of distance.

If *space* is the basis for the divisions, then the chosen plane is divided into arcs of 30 degrees. Sometimes these divisions are made directly on the ecliptic, sometimes they are calculated on the celestial equator before being projected onto the ecliptic. If *time* is being used for the divisions, there are two main options: houses are based on *equal hours*, representing two hours of the sun's movement each day; or they are based on *temporal hours*, where daytime and night-time are divided into six equal parts, meaning these lengths will vary according to season and latitude.

Different methods

notwithstanding, house divisions in Western astrology share a number of factors. The cusps of the 12 houses are always projected on the ecliptic; the cusp of the first house is placed near the eastern horizon; and every cusp for each house will be 180 degrees of longitude from the sixth following house,

that is, the first is opposite the seventh, the second is opposite the eighth, etc.

When a planet or multiple planets are in any of these houses, their functions are altered accordingly. If Venus, the planet of love, is in the Eighth House, the House of Transformation, it could mean a person reinvents themselves each time they start a new relationship or that they like romantic role-playing. If the querent looks at their natal chart and sees multiple planets in a given house, this means the universe is telling them to pay attention to this critical area of their life. If there are no planets in a house, however, that does not mean that sector of their life is barren, only that there are fewer powers influencing it.

The Significance of Houses

Astrologers interpret the effects of the different houses in a number of ways. In the following list one interpretation/explanation of their intent is presented. The houses are numbered from the eastern horizon downward, the way they would appear on a circular natal chart.

First House

Natural rulers: **Aries and Mars**
Latin motto: *Vita*
Translation: **Life**
Modern name: **House of Self**
Interpretation: **Physical appearance, traits and characteristics, resourcefulness, outlook and impressions, ego, beginnings and initiatives**

Explanation: This house represents the querent in simple terms, governing the self-image that he or she projects . . . It rules physical appearance, first impressions, new beginnings, and the initiative to take on new tasks. Any planets located in the first house carry additional weight when it comes to shaping personality.

Second House

Natural rulers: **Taurus and Venus**
Latin motto: *Lucrum*
Translation: **Gain**
Modern name: **House of Value**
Interpretation: **Material and immaterial things of certain value; money, possessions and acquisitions; cultivation, substance, self-worth**

Explanation: This house rules tangible things, including the five senses and other sensory experiences. It's about money, wealth and material possessions, but also the person's attitude toward them, how a person values things and him- or herself. Could also indicate greed or financial hardship.

Third House

Natural rulers: **Gemini and Mercury**
Latin motto: *Fratres*
Translation: **Order**
Modern name: **House of Sharing**
Interpretation: **Communication; distribution/generosity; intelligence/development; siblings; locomotion and transportation; ephemera**

Explanation: Here, people begin to move outside themselves slightly and interact with the people and things around them. This house rules self-expression through words (including virtual communication), basic daily activities, thinking, logic, and simple relationships. Due to chatty overseers Gemini and Mercury, it also rules small talk and gossip.

Fourth House

Natural rulers: **Cancer and Moon**
Latin motto: *Genitor*
Translation: **Parent**
Modern name: **House of Home and Family**
Interpretation: **Ancestry, heritage, roots; foundation and environment; mother or caretaker; housing and the household; neighborhood matters; comfort, security; tidiness; pets**

Explanation: The sign at the bottom of the zodiac wheel represents foundation and covers matters of security—literal and emotional. It relates to the sense of home, both the physical haven and those who bring comfort. Planets in this house may signify large amounts of family-based energy.

Fifth House

Natural rulers: **Leo and Sun**
Latin motto: *Nati*
Translation: **Children**
Modern name: **House of Pleasure and Creativity**
Interpretation: **Recreational and leisure activities; things which make for enjoyment and entertainment. games/gambling/risk; romance and limerence; children/fertility; creative self-expression**

Explanation: This is the place to channel creative energy and express pleasure. It includes hobbies and recreational activities, as well as all things related to romance. It also rules over children. This is the house of "luck," so any planets here may determine one's success in games of chance. As the house of the heart and creativity, any planetary placements and signs here can reveal how a person deals with these matters.

Sixth House

Natural rulers: **Virgo and Mercury**
Latin motto: *Valetudo*
Translation: **Health**
Modern name: **House of Health**
Interpretation: **Routine tasks and duties. Skills or training acquired; employment (job); service performed for others; strength, vitality; wellness and healthcare; courage**

Explanation: This house relates to the service a person puts in during their life—their work ethic, how they help others, and the mundane tasks they perform each day. Less about career, it is more focused on the dedication shown during work. This house also rules wellness (thus, the capability to do work). It relates to healthy lifestyles, diet and nutrition, exercise, and self-improvement.

Seventh House

Natural rulers: **Libra and Venus**
Latin motto: *Uxor*
Translation: **Spouse**
Modern name: **House of Balance**
Interpretation: **Partnerships; marriage and business matters; diplomacy; agreements, contracts and all things official; equilibrium**

Explanation: Sitting opposite the House of Self, this house changes the focus from self to connections to others. It rules relationships, partnerships, anything that brings people together. It also rules over negative connections: competitors, enemies, divorce, lawsuits. Planetary indicators can help the querent steer clear of bad contracts.

Eighth House

Natural rulers: **Scorpio and Pluto**
Latin motto: *Mors*
Translation: **Death**
Modern name: **House of Transformation**
Interpretation: **Cycles of deaths and rebirth; sexual relationships and commitments of all kinds; joint funds, finances; other person's resource; karma and debt (judgment); regeneration; self-transformation**

Explanation: This house can be mysterious, hard to define, even dark. It rules death, regeneration, taxes, legacies, sex, sacrifices . . . anything to do with transformation and transfer of energy. It is as much about beginnings as endings. Mainly, though, it relates to personal growth.

Ninth House

Natural rulers: **Sagittarius and Jupiter**
Latin motto: *Iter*
Translation: **Passage**
Modern name: **House of Purpose**
Interpretation: **Travel and foreign affairs; culture; expansion; law and ethics; education/learning/ knowledge; philosophical interests, belief systems; experience through exploration; long-term issues**

Explanation: This philosophical house deals with core belief systems, higher learning, religion, and the acquisition of knowledge. The third house pertains to basic thoughts, but its opposite house rules more complex thought. Sagittarius helps it engender a sense of adventure, including travel, long journeys, spiritual quests, and exploring different cultures. This house is where life's deeper meaning might be found.

Star Points:

In astrology a cusp is the imaginary line that separates two consecutive signs of the zodiac or houses in a horoscope. When someone's birthdate is "on the cusp," meaning two or three days before or after the sign change, they will often possess characteristic energies drawn from both signs.

Tenth House

Natural rulers: **Capricorn and Saturn**
Latin motto: *Regnum*
Translation: **Kingdom**
Modern name: **House of Enterprise**
Interpretation: **Ambitions; motivations; career, achievements; society and government; father or authority; notoriety; advantage**

Explanation: The cusp of this house is located at the top of the natal chart, so it is also known as the "midheaven" or MC (Medium Coeli). The house pertains to one's overall life path and career and governs the public-facing image, reputation, professional life, social status, and moments in the spotlight. It also represents authority—often a "father figure"—in an individual's life. Placements in this house should shed light on possible career paths.

Eleventh House

Natural rulers: **Aquarius and Uranus**
Latin motto: *Benefacto*
Translation: **Support**
Modern name: **House of Blessings**
Interpretation: **Benefits from effort; friends and acquaintances of like-minded attitudes; belonging; groups, communities, and associations; charity; connectedness/ networking; love; wish fulfillment; wealth**

Explanation: Unlike the house of partnerships, which focuses on contractual or one-to-one relations, this house focuses more on community, memberships, organized groups, and working together. It is the ruler of friendship, teamwork, networking, and social justice. It also instills a very Aquarian desire to shake up the status quo. It represents a person's collective or lifelong goals—as well as their wishes for humanity—and indicates what they can do to make those goals a reality.

Twelfth House

Natural rulers: **Pisces and Neptune**
Latin motto: *Carcer*
Translation: **Rehabilitation**
Modern name: **House of Sacrifice**
Interpretation: **Privacy, refuge; seclusion and retreating; clandestine revelation; intuition; extremities/abundance, but also addictions; luck, miracles; releasing/relinquishing, healing, forgiveness, and peacefulness; finality/completion/conclusion**

Explanation: The mystical and mysterious 12th house, the last house in the zodiac, represents endings as well as the deepest evolution of the soul. It rules the unconscious, secrets, dreams, and sleep, as well as karma and past life trauma, the shadow self, surrendering, the occult and paranormal energies, and both physical and metaphorical imprisonment. This house oversees the parts of themselves that people flee from or don't even know exist. Placements in the twelfth house can help unlock the inner-workings of who a person truly is; the revelation and healing of deep, hidden wounds can prevent emotional darkness from manifesting in other confusing ways.

Dignities, Debilities, and Aspects

People whose sole acquaintance with astrology has been horoscopes based on sun signs would likely be shocked by the number of other factors that can be instrumental in assessing a comprehensive birth chart. Some of these indicators are employed regularly by astrologers and amateurs alike, while others are a bit more arcane, though no less telling.

Essential Dignities

A number of traditional astrological influencers seem to have fallen out of favor in modern-day birth charting. One classic influencer that is not always included is the Five Essential Dignities. These dignities—rulership, exaltation, triplicity, term, and face— indicate how comfortable a planet is residing in a sign and a degree on the zodiac wheel. If there is a lot of essential dignity, the planet will properly influence those signs where it appears. If there is no essential dignity, the planet will need to find other means for fulfilling its function.

Rulership

Planetary rulership is the first and strongest level of essential dignity. Originally there were seven ruling "planets," including the sun and moon, but now there are ten if the three trans-Saturnian planets—Neptune, Uranus, and Pluto (still astrologically a planet)—are included. (*See* Ruling Planets in Chapter One.) Planets and signs are also classified into sects, or day and night. Air and fire birth signs belong to the day; earth and water signs to the night.

The sects of the original seven planets break down as:

The sun, Jupiter, and Saturn belong to the day

The moon, Venus, and Mars belong to the night

Mercury belongs to both

Planetary signs are further categorized into Day Houses and Night Houses. Planets are stronger when found in a zodiac sign that matches their sect. Even though Venus rules both Taurus and Libra, her influence is considered stronger in Taurus, a fellow night sect. The planets ruled by luminaries have only one sign: Leo, ruled by the sun, belongs to the day and Cancer, ruled by the moon, to the night.

Planet (sect)	Day house	Night house
Mercury (day/night)	Gemini	Virgo
Venus (night)	Libra	Taurus
Mars (night)	Aries	Scorpio
Jupiter (day)	Sagittarius	Pisces
Saturn (day)	Aquarius	Capricorn

Exaltations

A number of planets or luminaries are "exalted" when they appear in certain signs on a birth chart. They do not govern the sign as a ruling planet does, rather their presence there is like a VIP visit. The sun, for example, is exalted when found in Aries. This means it has the greatest power to achieve its potential in that sign. Whatever benefits the sun brings, for those with an Aries birth sign it will be magnified.

Not every sign has an exaltation, and there is debate among astrologers whether signs with more recently discovered planets—Neptune, Uranus, and Pluto—are truly influential.

Noted astrologers of the past, Claudius Ptolemy and William Lilly, assigned exaltation to one specific degree of a sign; most astrologers reject this limitation as unrealistic and use the entire sign.

Aries: The sun is exalted here, representing primary essence, life energy, which further spurs on the already self-directed and driven Aries' nature. Pluto is also exalted according to some astrologers, representing leadership qualities, personal power, and charisma.

Taurus: The moon is exalted in this sign, representing emotions, self-care, comfort, and a striving for beauty and harmony along with a desire for physical pleasure.

Cancer: Jupiter is exalted in this sign, juxtaposing the powerful, adventurous planet with the most home loving sign. Here, Cancer attempts to acquire the wisdom, knowledge, and truth of Jupiter without having to leave its comfort zone.

Leo: Some astrologers maintain that Neptune is exalted in Leo, but the notion is controversial. In Leo, Neptune brings creative vision, inspiration, and love to an already top-loaded sign. Neptune, however, allows Leo to contribute in a way that is grounded and reaches out to all.

Virgo: Mercury is exalted in Virgo (and is also its ruling planet), representing precision, attention to details, organization, and structure.

Libra: Saturn is exalted here, signifying laws, authority, and structure. When Saturn appears in Libra, the sign of balance, it emphasizes fairness and justice and is able to create boundaries and establish inclusive rules that meet all needs.

Scorpio: Uranus may be exalted here, according to some skywatchers . . . increasing the sign's ability to enact change and transformation.

Capricorn: Mars is exalted here, representing ambition, and the achieving of goals by showing people what it is that motivates them. Mars is not impulsive or belligerent in this sign, it is focused and driven.

Pisces: Venus is exalted in Pisces, indicating this already compassionate and empathetic sign echoes Venus in its quest for harmony and balance in life and relationships.

Triplicity

Triplicity rulers are the third level of essential dignity. Somewhat like a board of directors, they have a voice in the character of a sign but do not act independently. How they are factored into a horoscope is complex and confusing and detailed . . . and may explain why they are often absent from charts. Dorotheus of Sidon established that each element has three triplicity rulers: day, night, and participating. The birth chart determines the first two rulers: if the sun is above the horizon, it is a day chart, below the horizon, it is a night chart.

Fire signs Aries, Leo, Sagittarius: Sun (day), Jupiter (night), Saturn (participating)

Earth signs Taurus, Virgo, Capricorn: Venus, (day), Moon (night), Mars (participating)

Air signs Gemini, Libra, Aquarius: Saturn (day), Mercury (night), Jupiter (participating)

Water signs Cancer, Scorpio, Pisces: Venus (day), Mars (night), Moon (participating)

Noted Renaissance astrologer William Lilly created his own, more concise triplicity rulership:

Fire: Sun (day), Jupiter (night)

Earth: Venus (day), Moon (night)

Air: Saturn (day), Mercury (night)

Water: Mars (day and night)

Term

Also referred to as bounds, this level of essential dignity consists of specific degrees in each sign that are ruled by non-luminary planets. This rulership is akin to a low level of supervision. These triplicities were recorded by early astrologer Ptolemy in both Egyptian and Chaldean.

Face

Face is also called *decante*. It is not to be confused with the decante used by modern astrologers. These classical/traditional decantes are somewhat different, each governing one third of a sign, in the role of mentor or advisor.

Face, or Decante

	0-10	10-20	20-30
♈	♂	☉	♀
♉	☿	☽	♄
♊	♃	♂	☉
♋	♀	☿	☽
♌	♄	♃	♂
♍	☉	♀	☿
♎	☽	♄	♃
♏	♂	☉	♀
♐	☿	☽	♄
♑	♃	♂	☉
♒	♀	☿	☽
♓	♄	♃	♂

Essential Debilities

In contrast to the Five Essential Dignities are the Essential Debilities. These indicate how uncomfortable a planet is within a certain sign. Such a planet might have difficulty functioning as it ought to or—if it is a signifier of something— that thing will likely go badly. If a chart shows both dignities and debilities in a degree of a sign, some astrologers believe they cancel each other out. Others give each planet due consideration and try to figure out how they would impact "each other."

Peregrine

When a planet in a sign does not possess even one of the Five Essential Dignities, it is said to be peregrine. Think of a lost traveler in a foreign land . . . with no authority or power. Peregrine planets need to do something creative to meet their assigned goals.

Detriment

When a planet is in a sign that is directly opposite where it resides on the zodiac wheel, the Cancer moon in Capricorn, say, it is said to be in detriment. This is similar to a soldier who has crossed over into enemy territory. The situation is even more dire if the planet is peregrine and has no dignities. At least a planet with a dignity or two has a fighting chance to accomplish something. The luminaries each have only one sign of detriment, the sun in Aquarius and the moon in Capricorn. The non-luminary planets rule two signs and so are in detriment in two signs, one day sign and one night sign. Their detriment is milder if they are in the sect that matches their own—for instance, a night planet in a night sign..

Fall

When a planet is positioned opposite its sign of exaltation on the zodiac wheel, it is in fall. This indicates shame or inferiority. If a planet is in fall with dignity, that is less severe than a fall in peregrine. The planetary falls are as follows:

Sun in Libra

Moon in Scorpio

Mercury in Pisces
(also in detriment in Pisces)

Venus in Virgo

Mars in Cancer

Jupiter in Capricorn

Saturn in Aries

Planets in Detriment

Planet (sect)	Day	Night
Mercury (day/night)	**Sagittarius**	**Pisces**
Venus (night)	**Aries**	**Scorpio**
Mars (night)	**Libra**	**Taurus**
Jupiter (day)	**Gemini**	**Virgo**
Saturn (day)	**Leo**	**Cancer**

Planetary Placement

Sun
Home (home base) **Leo**
Detriment (opposite home; difficult time) **Aquarius**
Exaltation (comfortable spot) **Aries**
Fall (opposite exaltation; debilitated) **Libra**

Moon
Home (home base) **Cancer**
Detriment (opposite home; difficult time) **Capricorn**
Exaltation (comfortable spot) **Taurus**
Fall (opposite exaltation; debilitated) **Scorpio**

Mercury
Home (home base) **Gemini and Virgo**
Detriment (opposite home) **Sagittarius and Pisces**
Exaltation (comfortable spot) **Virgo**
Fall (opposite exaltation; debilitated) **Pisces**

Venus
Home (home base) **Taurus and Libra**
Detriment (opposite home) **Scorpio and Aries**
Exaltation (comfortable spot) **Pisces**
Fall (opposite exaltation; debilitated) **Virgo**

Mars
Home (home base) **Aries**
Detriment (opposite home; difficult time) **Libra**
Exaltation (comfortable spot) **Capricorn**
Fall (opposite exaltation; debilitated) **Cancer**

Jupiter
Home (home base) **Sagittarius**
Detriment (opposite home; difficult time) **Gemini**
Exaltation (comfortable spot) **Cancer**
Fall (opposite exaltation; debilitated) **Capricorn**

Saturn
Home (home base) **Capricorn**
Detriment (opposite home; difficult time) **Cancer**
Exaltation (comfortable spot) **Libra**
Fall (opposite exaltation; debilitated) **Aries**

Uranus
Home (home base) **Aquarius**
Detriment (opposite home; difficult time) **Leo**
Exaltation (comfortable spot) **Scorpio**
Fall (opposite exaltation; debilitated) **Taurus**

Neptune
Home (home base) **Pisces**
Detriment (opposite home; difficult time) **Virgo**
Exaltation (comfortable spot) **Aquarius**
Fall (opposite exaltation; debilitated) **Libra**

Pluto
Home (home base) **Scorpio**
Detriment (opposite home; difficult time) **Taurus**
Exaltation (comfortable spot) **Leo**
Fall (opposite exaltation; debilitated) **Aquarius**

Aspects

When it deals with aspects, astrology puts on its math hat. Aspects are the angular relationships between the planets and the points (the ascendent, midheaven, etc.) found on birth chart. Aspects are represented by the lines in the center of the chart. They reflect the number of degrees between the planets and describe how various parts of the psyche relate to one another. The closer the aspect is to exact, the more powerful it is.

The majority of astrologers are familiar with the classic Ptolemaic aspects—conjunction, sextile, square, trine, opposition, and some of the new ones— semi-sextile and quincunx. All these aspects are based on the division of the zodiac circle into multiples of two (hard aspects, marked in red) and multiples of three (soft aspects, marked in blue). These are all popular and easy to locate using the 1–30 degree-per-sign labeling system common to birth charts. More difficult are the aspects that result from dividing the wheel into 5ths, 7ths, 11ths, and 13ths, which are referred to as "harmonics." This terms comes from John Addey's work on harmonic charts in the 1970s, which increased the usage of these aspects. The importance of harmonics is still debated, but some astrologers advise their usage based on their experiences of casting successful charts.

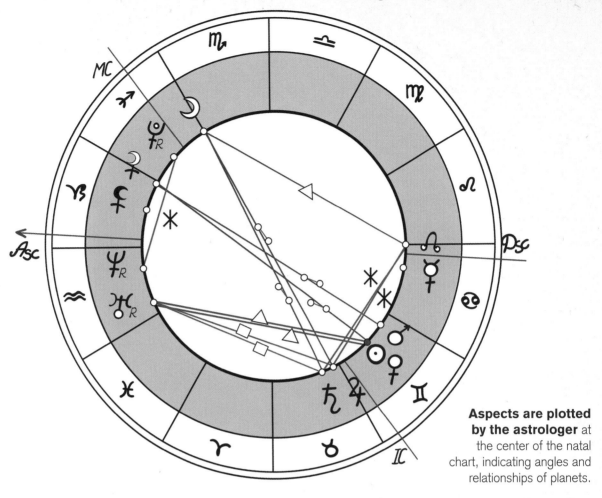

Aspects are plotted by the astrologer at the center of the natal chart, indicating angles and relationships of planets.

The Five Classic Aspects

1. The Conjunction: Planets are 0 degrees apart. Planets link up together in the same sign, blending their effects and amplifying their energies.

2. The Sextile (soft): Planets are 60 degrees apart. Planets in sextile work well together; they evoke creativity and vision.

3. The Trine (soft): Planets are 120 degrees apart, sharing the same element. These relaxed planets don't try to influence each other; they support the querent.

4. The Square (hard): Planets are 90 degrees apart. They experience tension, competing for dominance; they may create internal dilemmas for the querent.

5. The Opposition (hard): Planets are 180 degrees apart. Even though they share modality, these planets struggle to work together. There is a push-pull dynamic to their energies . . . if these polar ends become overemphasized, this aspect is about swinging them back into balance or harmony. *Honorable mention —***The Quintile:** Planets are 72 degrees apart. This spiritual indicator helps the querent express creativity based on the effects of both planets.

Zodiac Love Connections

One of the most common reasons people consult an astrologer is to assess the current state or future prospects of their love life. Yes, it's true that parents have questions about their children, the career-oriented wish to know about future promotions or job opportunities, and investors inquire about financial trends . . . but the emotion that most stirs the human heart into action is typically something to do with romantic love. These querents usually present one of two pressing questions: "Is my current partner a good match for me?" and "Could this person be *the One*, the person I will spend my life with?"

Most astrologers understand that these answers need to arise more from the querent's inner feelings, the truth of their heart—or their gut—than from the indicators offered by the stars. Yet when another person's birth sign is potentially paired with the querent's sign the results can certainly offer guidance, say a sort of roadmap, indicating factors for strong compatibility or pointing to possible bumps, hurdles, and roadblocks. It may make more sense for an astrologer to simply ask the person, "What are you looking for in a relationship?" This question then helps to identify the potentially fruitful sun signs and those the individual might wish to avoid.

To create an in-depth assessment, the astrologer will ask for the year, date, time, and location of birth of both parties, draw up a horoscopic chart that plots all the planetary and zodiac placements for each partner, and then examine how they relate to one another. There is a kind of shorthand method, however, for those who are not yet ready to seek out a real astrologer. This

method deals only with sun sign calculations and is based on the distance between the different signs. Like all generalizations, it should be taken with a grain of salt, but at least it furnishes a starting point on how a particular relationship might progress. (The information below also works as an indicator of how friends, relations, or in-laws will likely get along.)

The Compatibility Wheel

There are six primary relationships within the different zodiac signs. The querent starts by identifying their sign on a zodiac wheel and then counting the number of places to their prospective partner's sign, using the *closest* relationship, six places or under. If the querent is a Scorpio and their partner is an Aries, as a couple they are five signs apart. A Cancer and a Pisces are four signs apart, not eight.

The Same Sign

Couples who share the same sign have a similar compatibility to those who are six signs apart: that of the "instant" connection. These lovers feels like kindred spirits, each displaying many of the same qualities their partners see in themselves, both the qualities they admire and those they regret. Sometimes it's not a good thing, however, to see one's own flaws reflected in the personality of another. The realization can be jarring. Yet this insight can also provide an opportunity for personal growth. So for those who are self-aware enough to factor this in, this romantic match-up should be easy peasy, like settling onto a familiar, comfy couch.

One Sign Apart

For couples who were born a single sign apart, the relationship might become one of teacher and student. The student will feel as if they have much to learn from the teacher, and the teacher will have an understanding/ sympathy for their student that they can't quite explain. They both approach life differently, and therein lies the attraction. They have the ability to complement each other when it comes to their strengths. Balance and success in this relationship come from allowing the one who wants to take the lead to lead, and the one who wants to follow to do just that.

Two Signs Apart

With this combination of signs friendship comes easily to two people, the kind that often morphs into romantic love. Still, these two signs have enough differences between them that the couple could lapse into the "fight, break-up, make-up" syndrome without too much effort. The good news is that with the right amount of emotional attention this rough patch can be gotten past fairly quickly; the bad news is that any unresolved issues tend to keep coming back and causing discord, year after year. One

saving grace is that if the couple can maintain their strong bond of friendship, the relationship should be able to endure.

Three Signs Apart

When it comes to communicating or understanding each other, this relationship might result in some hidden tension. This couple approaches life from two differing perspectives and each person may believe their way is the right—and only—way to do something. Does he open gifts on Christmas Eve or Christmas Day? Does she think toilet paper rolls go over or under? These "silly" minor differences are often the root of major conflicts. There might also be a sense of sitting in judgment on one another. The tension that gets created could be a positive if couples let it make them more self-aware about who they are and who their partner truly is— someone different from them, but lovable nonetheless.

Four Signs Apart

This relationship often feels like it flows more effortlessly than other combinations. That is likely due to an underlying empathy that exists between the couple. They *feel* similarly. They *think* similarly. They approach

life in very much the same way. This match is statistically more successful than any of the other romantic configurations. Barring any unforeseen circumstances, this is a natural pairing that should work from the first encounter. Furthermore, these couples have the power within this relationship to clear up any misunderstandings that may come between them or threaten them.

Five Signs Apart

With this match up, an element of miscommunication or the inability to talk openly can undermine a relationship. That said, it could also be this very

tension that draws these signs together in such a compelling manner. If true caring is at the heart of this relationship, then sex can potentially bring the two together if they are feeling disconnected. There might also be a sense of each serving the other that underlies this relationship, a feeling of servility that can lead to resentment. Those who wish to remain with their partner must learn to work around it. Loyalty is the bond that will make this couple endure. If it is lacking, their chances of long-term happiness are slim.

Six Signs Apart

Couples whose signs are opposite each other on the zodiac wheel will probably feel an intense magnetism toward each other, possibly based on the theory that opposites attract. Yet these two usually have a lot in common, plus they create a team of equals, balance extremes of behavior, and offer new perspectives. Each allows the other a "bird's eye view" from a distance, which can be very illuminating. Both partners will have to stretch emotionally to accommodate their mate, making them more self-aware. The prognosis is good for romantic lovers and soul mates, as well as friends.

Consulting an Astrologer

For anyone who is seeking the counsel of an astrologer for the first time, it should help to understand how the visit might progress—and how to prepare for it.

First of all, like any interpretive art, an astrological consultation depends on the skill and intuition of the reader. A first-time querent might need to sit with several astrologers before they find one they feel is connecting with their energy. An open line of communication is very helpful for ensuring an accurate and enlightening session. If the querent has friends who have visited an astrologer and can recommend one, that is a very good place to start. Chances are if an individual's friends felt comfortable and attuned, they will as well. Speaking to a potential reader on the phone is also another way to gauge a connection.

Naturally, someone interested in booking a reading will have done their homework and become familiar with the terms and language, as well as the different types of astrology (or perhaps perused a book like this one). It also makes sense for them to download an online natal chart before the appointment, in order to prepare specific questions about the things they don't understand on the chart. Next, the querent should write down their general questions, paying specific attention to larger issues. Sure, a lot of people want to know why their partner is behaving a certain way or what the stock market will do in the next few weeks, but astrology often is more of a "big picture" process and can give indications that will have long-term repercussions. It would be beneficial, say, for someone to know which upcoming month will offer financial opportunities or at which times it is best to travel. This way the querent can focus their energy on results that will have a more widespread effect on their lives.

Also, if a client feels that they still need additional information

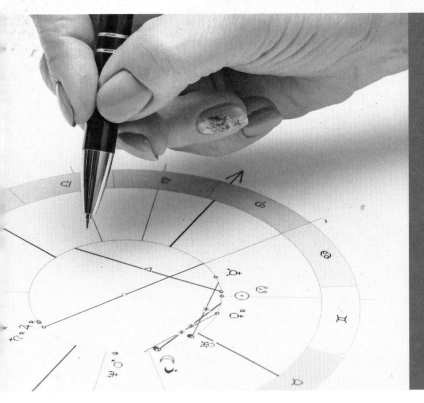

Six Smart Questions

For those who want to get to the root of life's big questions, here are six valuable things to ask an astrologer:

1. What does my natal chart reveal about my natural gifts and talents?

2. Are there aspects of my life that require more focus and commitment from me?

3. What are the lessons I'm supposed to learn from this life? (Hint: The answer is probably to be found in the North Node.)

4. Are there things I need to change about how I give and receive love?

5. What do I need to know about money and my relationship to it in order to have a secure future?

6. What types of people would make good prospects for forming a stable love relationship? What types would be the best potential friends?

at the end of one session, they should certainly schedule several more. As doors to knowledge and understanding open, it is natural that questions will multiply.

Straight Talk and Revelations

In addition to a natal reading, an astrologer can offer insight on what is happening to a person at that point in time, a process called transits and progressions. He or she will be able to translate the issues one's psyche is trying to convey both in general and in that moment.

Some people might scoff at this, but those who go . . . know: The initial consultation with an astrologer can feel personally

invasive, almost like a session with a psychologist. So a first-timer should be emotionally prepared to receive some straight talk and even criticism as their inner workings and hidden qualities are revealed. This could be a cause for anxiety or anger. It helps to remember that a reading involves a dialogue, not a one-sided lecture. Plus, a good astrologer will go over each point with a level of professionalism that eases the querent's concerns and contributes to their understanding. It is said that when the student is ready, the master will appear. Many advocates insist this is often the case with astrologers—the right one materializes on cue. Ultimately, the visit should

provide a person with the chance to add some interest to their daily routine and have a pleasant break . . . along with the added benefit of learning about their character, their inner nature, their prospects, and the best times to make a move or take a chance.

Star Points

After scanning a client's birth chart, an astrologer may realize that the questions the person came with are not the ones his or her inner self wants to ask. The birth chart may inquire more clearly about motivations and attitudes than the querent can.

Chapter Five

The Contemporary Chinese Zodiac

Aspects of a Chinese Birth Chart

Today's Chinese astrologers have retained most of the traditions established by their forebears. And even though modern-day China is bustling forward into a very technological future, many, many people in that country still rely on astrology to guide them, especially when it comes to marital and financial decisions, as well as in determining baby gender and auspicious times to move, seek a new job, or confront a problem.

Chinese astrology, which is based on birth year, called Ben Ming Nian, rather than birth day, extends for a 60-year cycle, also known as the sexagenary cycle or the Stems-and-Branches, or ganzhi. This cycle is made up of 12 yearly animal symbols each associated with five different elements. These elements are based on the Five Elements Theory, or Wu Xing, which in the East is the basis for

medicine, martial arts, fortune telling, and much more. It stems from the belief that the elements play a crucial role in the balance of the universe, and that all things that arise from and return to the universe are composed of them, forming a cycle of creation and destruction. In order the elements are Fire (huo), inspired by excitement; Earth (tu), motivated to secure foundations; Metal (jin): driven to create order; Water (shu), compelled to form emotional bonds; and Wood (mu), born with a desire to explore.

This cycle repeats every 60 years . . . and has done so since it was first used to record years in the middle of the third century BC. Although this method of numbering days and years no longer has a role in modern Chinese timekeeping, it is still used in the names of historic events and plays a key role in Chinese astrology and fortunetelling.

As with the symbols of the

Western zodiac, the animals of this zodiac all carry equal weight. Even though some animals seem less impressive than others—how does one compare a hare to a dragon or a rat to a tiger?—they are accorded the same importance by astrologers. Each has its own unique characteristics, its innate strengths, and inevitable weaknesses. Each animal is also designated as either yin (female nature) or yang (male nature).

When preparing a natal chart, a Chinese astrologer needs to know the querent's age and birth year according to the Chinese lunar calendar—for a child born in 2021 its Chinese birth year is 4719—as well as their "true animal" and the element for their birth date. The problem here is that the ancient Chinese week contained 10 days, not seven, which makes calculating these indicators quite difficult. Fortunately, there are now online calculators that translate the Chinese calendar and that will provide this data.

"True Animals"

In addition to the yearly zodiac symbols that indicate certain qualities and tendencies, Chinese astrologers can discern more detailed information by further breaking the year into months, days, and hours—together called the Four Pillars—each segment with its own representative animal. The month determines the inner animal, the day determines the true animal, and the hour indicates the secret animal. After viewing these "hidden" animals in their natal charts, people are often less confused over why certain of their traits are manifested outwardly while others remain more contained or repressed.

Month of Birth: The lunar month determines the *inner animal*, which indicates the less-obvious characteristics a person possesses but rarely shares with others. The year is divided into 24 two-week solar terms and each animal is linked to two of these solar terms.

Rat:	December 7–December 21	and	December 22–January 5
Ox:	January 6–January 19	and	January 20–February 3
Tiger:	February 4–February 18	and	February 19–March 5
Rabbit:	March 6–March 20	and	March 21–April 4
Dragon:	April 5 to April 19	and	April 20–May 4
Snake:	May 5–May 20	and	May 21– June 5
Horse:	June 6–June 20	and	June 21–July 6
Goat:	July 7–22	and	July 23 to August 6
Monkey:	August 7–August 22	and	August 23–September 7
Rooster:	September 8–September 22	and	September 23–October 7
Dog:	October 8–October 22	and	October 23–November 6
Pig:	November 7–November 21	and	November 22–December 6

Day of Birth: This indicates the querent's *true animal*, which represents the sort of person an individual will grow into as an adult.

Monday:	Sheep
Tuesday:	Dragon
Wednesday:	Horse
Thursday:	Rat, Pig
Friday:	Rabbit, Snake, Dog
Saturday:	Ox, Tiger, Rooster
Sunday:	Monkey

Hour of Birth: The time of birth indicates the *secret animal*, which signifies who a person is at their very core—their truest nature. A 24-hour period is divided into 2-hour segments each represented by a zodiac animal.

Rat:	23:00–00:59	Horse:	11:00–12:59
Ox:	01:00–02:59	Goat:	13:00–14:59
Tiger:	03:00–04:59	Monkey:	15:00–16:59
Rabbit:	05:00–06:59	Rooster:	17:00–18:59
Dragon:	07:00–08:59	Dog:	19:00–20:59
Snake:	09:00–10:59	Pig:	21:00–22:59

Western and Eastern Contrasts

Although the Chinese use a structure system to Western astrologers—one based on birth dates and time and featuring symbols located in one of 12 houses on a chart—beyond that there is little they share. Western astrology is heavily based on the position of constellations on the ecliptic at time of birth, while Chinese astrology is based on year of birth and emphasizes the lunar phase at time of birth— new moon, waxing moon, full moon, and waning moon. New moon types seek innovative environments, waxing moons are known for being hard working, full moons are diplomatic, while waning moons desire peaceful surroundings. Meanwhile, planets are treated as stars . . . Mars is even known as the Fire Star. And

only five planets are recognized— Mercury, Venus, Mars, Jupiter, and Saturn—omitting the distant trans-Saturnian examples. Furthermore, Venus is considered a masculine force completely lacking the feminine or romantic connotations of Western or Hellenic culture. Unlike Western planets, Chinese planets are associated with elements: Mercury–wood; Venus–fire; Mars–earth; Jupiter–metal; and Saturn–water.

It should be noted that Chinese astrologers do not believe that a person's fate is determined at their birth. Rather, they believe that the time and place of birth establish certain parameters and that within that framework a person has a certain amount of

choice. Whatever occurs over time is influenced by free will as well as by the family situation and cultural and economic factors.

Star Points:

According to Chinese astrology, whenever an individual's birth sign year comes around, it brings a period of back luck. It is said this happens because the person has "offended" the god of age. The experience has been compared to an entire year of dealing with Mercury in retrograde. To ward off the bad vibes, people born under that sign wear red and send red gifts to family and friends. There is nothing comparable to this belief in Western astrology

The Chinese Calendar

This calendar is traditionally broken into 24 parts or 12 fortnights, each represented by a different seasonal occurrence and based on the longitude of the sun on the ecliptic. Each pair of fortnights corresponds with one of the 12 Western zodiac signs. A calendar similar to this one is also used in Japan, Korea, and Mongolia.

Solar Terms or the 24 Periods of Ch'i

	SOLAR TERM	DATE	ZODIAC SIGN
1	Spring begins	Feb 4	Aquarius
2	Rain water	Feb 19	Pisces
3	Excited insects	Mar 6	Pisces
4	Vernal Equinox	Mar 21	Aries
5	Clear and bright	Apr 5	Aries
6	Grain rains	Apr 20	Taurus
7	Summer begins	May 6	Taurus
8	Grain fills	May 21	Gemini
9	Grain in ear	June 6	Gemini
10	Summer Solstice	June 21	Cancer
11	Slight heat	July 7	Cancer
12	Great heat	July 23	Leo
13	Autumn begins	Aug 8	Leo
14	Limit of heat	Aug 23	Virgo
15	White dew	Sep 8	Virgo
16	Autumnal Equinox	Sept 23	Libra
17	Cold dew	Oct 8	Libra
18	Frost descends	Oct 23	Scorpio
19	Winter begins	Nov 7	Scorpio
20	Little snow	Nov 22	Sagittarius
21	Great snow	Dec 7	Sagittarius
22	Winter Solstice	Dec 22	Capricorn
23	Little cold	Jan 6	Capricorn
24	Great Cold	Jan 20	Aquarius

The 60-year Cycle of Chinese Astrology

This chart shows the typical 60-year cycle of the Chinese zodiac, which is also known as the sexagenary cycle or the Stems and Branches, or ganzhi.

It consists of 12 animal symbols, each matched with one of five elements. The chart also indicates the Chinese symbols for the Heavenly Stem and

Earthly Branch. The Heavenly or Celestial Stem, are are a Chinese system of ordinals that first appeared during the Shang dynasty, c. 1250 BC,

	Years 1924-1953	Associated Element	Heavenly Stem	Earthly Branch	Stem Branch in Pinyin	Associated Animal	Years 1984-2013
1	Feb 05 1924–Jan 23 1925	Yang Wood	甲	子	jiǎ-zǐ	Rat	Feb 02 1984–Jan 21 1985
2	Jan 24 1925–Feb 12 1926	Yin Wood	乙	丑	yǐ-chǒu	Ox	Jan 22 1985–Feb 08 1986
3	Feb 13 1926–Feb 01 1927	Yang Fire	丙	寅	bǐng-yín	Tiger	Feb 09 1986–Jan 28 1987
4	Feb 02 1927–Jan 22 1928	Yin Fire	丁	卯	dīng-mǎo	Rabbit	Jan 29 1987–Feb 16 1988
5	Jan 23 1928–Feb 09 1929	Yang Earth	戊	辰	wù-chén	Dragon	Feb 17 1988–Feb 05 1989
6	Feb 10 1929–Jan 29 1930	Yin Earth	己	巳	jǐ-sì	Snake	Feb 06 1989–Jan 26 1990
7	Jan 30 1930–Feb 16 1931	Yang Metal	庚	午	gēng-wǔ	Horse	Jan 27 1990–Feb 14 1991
8	Feb 17 1931–Feb 05 1932	Yin Metal	辛	未	xīn-wèi	Goat	Feb 15 1991–Feb 03 1992
9	Feb 06 1932–Jan 25 1933	Yang Water	壬	申	rén-shēn	Monkey	Feb 04 1992–Jan 22 1993
10	Jan 26 1933–Feb 13 1934	Yin Water	癸	酉	guǐ-yǒu	Rooster	Jan 23 1993– Feb 09 1994
11	Feb 14 1934–Feb 03 1935	Yang Wood	甲	戌	jiǎ-xū	Dog	Feb 10 1994–Jan 30 1995
12	Feb 04 1935–Jan 23 1936	Yin Wood	乙	亥	yǐ-hài	Pig	Jan 31 1995–Feb 18 1996
13	Jan 24 1936–Feb 10 1937	Yang Fire	丙	子	bǐng-zǐ	Rat	Feb 19 1996–Feb 06 1997
14	Feb 11 1937–Jan 30 1938	Yin Fire	丁	丑	dīng-chǒu	Ox	Feb 07 1997–Jan 27 1998
15	Jan 31 1938–Feb 18 1939	Yang Earth	戊	寅	wù-yín	Tiger	Jan 28 1998–Feb 15 1999
16	Feb 19 1939–Feb 07 1940	Yin Earth	己	卯	jǐ-mǎo	Rabbit	Feb 16 1999–Feb 04 2000
17	Feb 08 1940–Jan 26 1941	Yang Metal	庚	辰	gēng-chén	Dragon	Feb 05 2000–Jan 23 2001
18	Jan 27 1941–Feb 14 1942	Yin Metal	辛	巳	xīn-sì	Snake	Jan 24 2001–Feb 11 2002
19	Feb 15 1942–Feb 04 1943	Yang Water	壬	午	rén-wū	Horse	Feb 12 2002–Jan 31 2003
20	Feb 05 1943–Jan 24 1944	Yin Water	癸	未	guǐ-wèi	Goat	Feb 01 2003–Jan 21 2004
21	Jan 25 1944–Feb 12 1945	Yang Wood	甲	申	jiǎ-shēn	Monkey	Jan 22 2004–Feb 08 2005
22	Feb 13 1945–Feb 01 1946	Yin Wood	乙	酉	yǐ-yǒu	Rooster	Feb 09 2005–Jan 28 2006
23	Feb 02 1946–Jan 21 1947	Yang Fire	丙	戌	bǐng-xū	Dog	Jan 29 2006–Feb 17 2007
24	Jan 22 1947–Feb 09 1948	Yin Fire	丁	亥	dīng-hài	Pig	Feb 18 2007–Feb 06 2008
25	Feb 10 1948–Jan 28 1949	Yang Earth	戊	子	wù-zǐ	Rat	Feb 07 2008–Jan 25 2009
26	Jan 29 1949–Feb 16 1950	Yin Earth	己	丑	jǐ-chǒu	Ox	Jan 26 2009–Feb 13 2010
27	Feb 17 1950–Feb 05 1951	Yang Metal	庚	寅	gēng-yín	Tiger	Feb 14 2010–Feb 02 2011
28	Feb 06 1951–Jan 26 1952	Yin Metal	辛	卯	xīn-mǎo	Rabbit	Feb 03 2011–Jan 22 2012
29	Jan 27 1952–Feb 13 1953	Yang Water	壬	辰	rén-chén	Dragon	Jan 23 2012–Feb 09 2013
30	Feb 14 1953–Feb 02 1954	Yin Water	癸	巳	guǐ-sì	Snake	Feb 10 2013–Jan 30 2014

as the names of the ten days of the Chinese week. They were also used during ancestor worship rituals as names for dead family members, who were offered sacrifices on the corresponding day of the Shang week. The Heavenly Stems, a similar cycle of 12 days, were used in combination with the Earthly Branches to produce a compound cycle of 60 days. Eventually, the Heavenly Stems no longer represented days of the week or dead kin, but they acquired other uses, the most long-lasting being their use with the Earthly Branches as a 60-year calendrical cycle. This system is still in use throughout East Asia.

	Years 1954-1983	Associated Element	Heavenly Stem	Earthly Branch	Stem Branch in Pinyin	Associated Animal	Years 2014-2043
31	Feb 03 1954–Jan 23 1955	Yang Wood	甲	午	jiǎ-wǔ	Horse	Jan 31 2014–Feb 18 2015
32	Jan 24 1955–Feb 11 1956	Yin Wood	乙	未	yǐ-wèi	Goat	Feb 19 2015–Feb 07 2016
33	Feb 12 1956–Jan 30 1957	Yang Fire	丙	申	bǐng-shēn	Monkey	Feb 08 2016–Jan 27 2017
34	Jan 31 1957–Feb 17 1958	Yin Fire	丁	酉	dīng-yǒu	Rooster	Jan 28 2017–Feb 15 2018
35	Feb 18 1958–Feb 07 1959	Yang Earth	戊	戌	wù-xū	Dog	Feb 16 2018–Feb 04 2019
36	Feb 08 1959–Jan 27 1960	Yin Earth	己	亥	jǐ-hài	Pig	Feb 05 2019–Jan 24 2020
37	Jan 28 1960–Feb 14 1961	Yang Metal	庚	子	gēng-zǐ	Rat	Jan 25 2020–Feb. 11 2021
38	Feb 15 1961–Feb 04 1962	Yin Metal	辛	丑	xīn-chǒu	Ox	Feb 12 2021–Jan 31 2022
39	Feb 05 1962–Jan 24 1963	Yang Water	壬	寅	rén-yín	Tiger	Feb 01 2022–Jan 21 2023
40	Jan 25 1963–Feb 12 1964	Yin Water	癸	卯	guǐ-mǎo	Rabbit	Jan 22 2023–Feb 09 2024
41	Feb 13 1964–Feb 01 1965	Yang Wood	甲	辰	jiǎ-chén	Dragon	Feb 10 2024–Jan 28 2025
42	Feb 02 1965–Jan 20 1966	Yin Wood	乙	巳	yǐ-sì	Snake	Jan 29 2025–Feb 16 2026
43	Jan 21 1966–Feb 08 1967	Yang Fire	丙	午	bǐng-wǔ	Horse	Feb 17 2026–Feb 05 2027
44	Feb 09 1967–Jan 29 1968	Yin Fire	丁	未	dīng-wèi	Goat	Feb 06 2027–Jan 25 2028
45	Jan 30 1968–Feb 16 1969	Yang Earth	戊	申	wù-shēn	Monkey	Jan 26 2028–Feb 12 2029
46	Feb 17 1969–Feb 05 1970	Yin Earth	己	酉	jǐ-yǒu	Rooster	Feb 13 2029–Feb 02 2030
47	Feb 06 1970–Jan 26 1971	Yang Metal	庚	戌	gēng-xū	Dog	Feb 03 2030–Jan 22 2031
48	Jan 27 1971–Feb 14 1972	Yin Metal	辛	亥	xīn-hài	Pig	Jan 23 2031–Feb 10 2032
49	Feb 15 1972–Feb 02 1973	Yang Water	壬	子	rén-zǐ	Rat	Feb 11 2032–Jan 30 2033
50	Feb 03 1973–Jan 22 1974	Yin Water	癸	丑	guǐ-chǒu	Ox	Jan 31 2033–Feb 18 2034
51	Jan 23 1974–Feb 10 1975	Yang Wood	甲	寅	jiǎ-yín	Tiger	Feb 19 2034–Feb 07 2035
52	Feb 11 1975–Jan 30 1976	Yin Wood	乙	卯	yǐ-mǎo	Rabbit	Feb 08 2035–Jan 27 2036
53	Jan 31 1976–Feb 17 1977	Yang Fire	丙	辰	bǐng-chén	Dragon	Jan 28 2036–Feb 14 2037
54	Feb 18 1977–Feb 06 1978	Yin Fire	丁	巳	dīng-sì	Snake	Feb 15 2037–Feb 03 2038
55	Feb 07 1978–Jan 27 1979	Yang Earth	戊	午	wù-wǔ	Horse	Feb 04 2038–Jan 23 2039
56	Jan 28 1979–Feb 15 1980	Yin Earth	己	未	jǐ-wèi	Goat	Jan 24 2039–Feb 11 2040
57	Feb 16 1980–Feb 04 1981	Yang Metal	庚	申	gēng-shēn	Monkey	Feb 12 2040–Jan 31 2041
58	Feb 05 1981–Jan 24 1982	Yin Metal	辛	酉	xīn-yǒu	Rooster	Feb 01 2041–Jan 21 2042
59	Jan 25 1982–Feb 12 1983	Yang Water	壬	戌	rén-xū	Dog	Jan 22 2042–Feb 09 2043
60	Feb 13 1983–Feb 01 1984	Yin Water	癸	亥	guǐ-hài	Pig	Feb 10 2043–Jan 29 2044

Birth Signs: Rat

AFFILIATES:
Chinese name: **Shu**
Years: **1912, 1924, 1936, 1948, 1960, 1972, 1984, 1996, 2008, 2020, 2032**
Polarity: **Yang**
Birthstone: **Garnet**
Colors: **Gold, blue, green**
Flowers: **Lily, African violet, lily of the valley**
Numbers: **2, 3**
Lucky days: **4th, 13th and 30th of lunar month**
Suitable gifts: **Kitchen accessories, gardening and planting books, cookbooks, bonsai trees**
Planet: **Jupiter**
Western counterpart: **Sagittarius**

Overview: The Rat is the first sign in the 12-year zodiac cycle, and so also begins a new 60-year sequence. Because the Chinese New Year is determined by the lunar calendar and does not occur on a specific date—it falls between January 21 and February 20—it is necessary to check when each new year begins. Unlike many countries, where rats are reviled, in China they are respected for their many survival skills and quick wits, and so the Rat sign indicates a courageous, enterprising person. Status and financial gratification are often their greatest motivators.

Positive traits: Rats are shrewd, clever, resourceful, and instinctive when faced with adversity. At other times they are calm and perceptive, with keen observational skills. Their honesty and loyalty make them easy to get along with. They are lively, intelligent, curious, and imaginative. Not surprisingly, they require a lot of mental stimulation or they can get restless. As the first sign in the cycle, the Rat manifests leadership qualities and is adept at handling responsibility. They also have a well-developed sense of self-preservation and are nothing if not survivors. They like stability.

Questionable traits: Rats can be opportunistic, and may even take advantage of an event or person if a goal requires it. Their egos sometimes prod them to take on more that they can handle, meaning they don't meet commitments. They dislike making small talk, pointless head games, and anything that makes them feel insecure.

Love trends: The Rat is one

Ruled by Jupiter

Jupiter, which oversees the sign of the Rat, is the planet of expansion, abundance, and benevolence. This makes sense, as rats tend to move forward with optimism and faith in opportunity. The planet is considered quite favorable by Chinese astrologers, while the sign is known for bringing luck and providing money. That makes them a winning combination.

of the four zodiac signs that is blessed in their love life. They are often more good-looking than average and have little trouble attracting the opposite sex. They place a premium on feeling secure and do not enjoy all the uncertainties a new romance may bring. Still, they are tender, caring partners, and when they finally commit to a relationship, it can become quite intense, especially in the beginning. If things cool off, however, their partner needs to reinvigorate the romance before the Rat becomes suspicious or despondent.

Best matches: Rats find they can be best friends and long-term lovers with Monkeys, Dragons and Oxes, but should probably give a wide berth to Goats, Horses, or Snakes.

Career Signposts: With their leadership qualities, Rats reign in the workplace. They rarely make mistakes due to their rigorous reviewing processes, yet they manage to maintain harmonious interpersonal relationships. Some ideal jobs for Rat people include artist, author, doctor, teacher, lecturer, marine engineer, architect, fashion designer, and photographer. They can also perform well in service industries and the fundraising and finance fields.

Notable Rats: Ovid, Diocletian, Hadrian, William Shakespeare, George Washington, Peter the Great, Galileo Galilei, Tchaikovsky, Leo Tolstoy, T.S. Eliot, Richard Nixon, Jimmy Carter, Al Gore, George H. W. Bush, John McCain, Prince Charles, Pope Francis, Eminem, Katy Perry, Cristiano Ronaldo (footballer), and Tom Holland.

Rat Elements

Elements	Characteristics
Wood Rat (1924, 1984)	Independent, self-confident, virtuous and talented, values teamwork
Fire Rat (1936, 1996)	Energetic, brave, quiet, cordial and friendly, strict with themselves
Earth Rat (1948, 2008)	Amiable, honest, flexible, modest, serious, high self-esteem
Metal Rat (1960, 2020)	Smart, talented, hot-tempered, jealous, strong sense of self-awareness
Water Rat (1912, 1972)	Talkative, shrewd, conservative, and wise

Star Points

The vitality of the Rat, including its noted high fertility and high survival rate, makes it a lucky sign for couples who are hoping to conceive.

Birth Signs:
Ox

AFFILIATES:
Mandarin name: **niú**
Years: **1925, 1937, 1949, 1961, 1973, 1985, 1997, 2009, 2021**
Polarity: **Yin**
Birthstone: **Aquamarine**
Colors: **Red, blue, purple**
Flower: **tulip, evergreen, peach blossom, rose**
Numbers: **8, 9, 3**
Lucky days: **13th and 27th of lunar month**
Planet: **Saturn**
Western counterpart: **Capricorn**

Overview: Occupying second position in the Chinese zodiac, the Ox sign reflects traditional conservative values. Lovers of the home and serene surroundings, they are loyal and compassionate to family and friends. Like their namesakes, Oxes achieve their goals by patient, persistent effort. Never flashy, they rely on their practical, sensible natures to guide them. They are also rarely influenced by those around them or by the environment, sticking to their tried-and-true methods and performing well within their own capabilities.

Positive traits: Oxes are renowned for their strength, diligence, dependability, and determination. Ox women make traditional, faithful wives who value their children's educations. With their strong personalities, they are also capable of career success. Ox men are idealistic, ambitious, and patriotic. They attach great importance to the family and to their work.

Questionable traits: Oxes are not great at communicating with others, and often decide it is not worth the effort to exchange ideas with others. They tend to be stubborn and stick to their own ways of doing things.

Love trends: Socially, Oxes are not pleasure seekers or party animals. They dislike idle chitchat and avoid parties or crowded gatherings. When they do date, they rarely flirt and are not prone to talk about their feelings, preferring to show how they feel. Anyone interested in marrying an ox may have a long wait; this sign dislikes change and must feel convinced that they are making a most suitable marriage before popping the question. Sadly, Ox marriages have a

Ruled by Saturn

This sign of the Ox is overseen by Saturn, the planet that represents tough life lessons and discipline. The things it teaches about facing up to challenges may seem harsh, but those vital lessons are something many successful people are thankful for in later years. With its strong, focused character the Ox embodies the spirit of Saturn.

tendency to fall apart, possibly because Oxes are dominant and inflexible, or because they blame others for their shortcomings. Those who are coupled with Oxes may need to coach them on how to maintain a loving relationship that is also an equal partnership.

Best matches: The Ox is most compatible with the Rat, Snake, Monkey, and Rooster.

The least promising signs are Tiger, Dragon, Horse, and Sheep. Oxes fit together quite well with other Oxes. The Pig, meanwhile, has the potential to be either a great match or a disaster.

Career signposts: Oxes are reliable, stalwart staff members who don't shirk from tackling a heavy workload. As a result, many people look up to them. They also won't take any steps on a project until they have a detailed plan in place. This places them on the track for success. Their lack of good communication skills can impact them here, however. They must learn to open up and share ideas or suggestions. Possible careers for oxes include: lawyer, doctor, teacher, author, social worker, writer, editor, government officer, policeman, technician, politician, office clerk, or consultant.

Ox Elements

Element	Characteristics
Wood Ox (1925, 1985)	Restless, decisive, straightforward, ready to defend the weak and helpless
Fire Ox (1937, 1997)	Short-sighted, selfish, impersonal, but practical
Earth Ox (1949, 2009)	Honest, prudent, strong sense of responsibility
Metal Ox (1961, 2021)	Hardworking, active, popular
Water Ox (1913, 1973)	Ambitious, tenacious, can endure hardship, strong sense of justice, keen observation skills

Notable Oxes: A number of these luminaries applied themselves with great perseverance: Napoleon, Vincent Van Gogh, Hans Christian Andersen, Charlie Chaplin, Nehru, Walt Disney, Rosa Parks, Richard Nixon, Margaret Thatcher, Barack Obama, Saddam Hussein, Peter Gabriel, Gloria Gaynor, Bruce Springsteen, Wayne Gretzky, Vivien Leigh, Clark Gable, Paul Newman, Richard Burton, Jane Fonda, Dustin Hoffman, Anthony Hopkins, Jack Nicholson, Robert Redford, Meg Ryan, Meryl Streep, George Clooney, and Sigourney Weaver.

Star Points

In Chinese folklore there are many stories about the ox, or ox-like gods interacting with humans. Some feature the ox as the major character, in others the ox is more subsidiary. Myths may also reflect oxen-related subjects like plowing or ox-powered carts.

Birth Signs: Tiger

AFFILIATES:
Mandarin name: **hu**
Years: **1926, 1938, 1950, 1962, 1974, 1986, 1998, 2010, 2022**
Polarity: **Yang**
Birthstone: **Sapphire**
Colors: **Blue, gray, orange**
Flowers: **yellow lily, cineraria, anthurium**
Numbers: **1, 3, 4**
Lucky days: **16th and 27th of lunar month**
Planet: **Uranus**
Western counterpart: **Aquarius**

Overview: Primarily, the Tiger is a sign of power. Those born under this sign are courageous, determined, and persistent, but also cautious. With their sharp senses and keen observation skills they make good leaders at work and in sports, and because they are both frank and fair, they are able to help others sort out their problems. Openly speaking out about their feelings . . . they quickly gain the trust of others.

Positive Traits: People born in a year of the Tiger are brave, competitive, and confident. They are very charming and well-liked by others. But sometimes they are likely to be impetuous, irritable, and overindulged.

Questionable Traits: Tigers are authoritative and stubborn . . . and rarely go back on a statement. In social relationships, they always try to take a dominant role. Even in other relationships, they may display a high-handed manner. Once they make up their minds, they are hard to dissuade from a course of action. They are not good communicators and don't do well at networking or business socializing. They either talk to much or don't talk at all. And even thought they typically know a lot of people, they have very few truly close friends. They may also be unpredictable. Most people who are close to Tigers know that understanding, patience, and tact are often needed.

Love trends: Some Tigers have trouble showing deep affection to their partners because they lack a sense of romance. Other Tigers can be tender in love and even sentimental. They enjoy the feeling of being loved, but

Ruled by Uranus

This sign is under the sway of Uranus, the planet connected with individuality and freedom. This fits the Tiger to a T . . . as the rebel of the Chinese zodiac, the tiger, like Uranus, is all about questioning authority and instituting change. Yet Tigers are also the humanitarians of the zodiac, courageously standing up for what they believe in and making positive changes to the world.

can become too enthusiastic, which can make their partner uncomfortable or overpowered. Male tigers know how to impress girls with their air of command. Females are more judgmental, with a strict sense of right and wrong. Tiger partners need to remain active to keep up with this sign's need for adventure.

Best matches: Tigers pair

Tiger Elements

up well with Dragons, Horses, or Pigs, but should probably steer clear of Oxes, other Tigers, Snakes, or Monkeys. A Tiger-Tiger match is not recommended because it can generate a lot of conflict.

Career Signposts: In China the Tiger is known as the "king of animals," and so it makes sense that Tiger signs are considered strong candidates for management positions. As senior staff members, they are respected by others and also enjoy being the center of attention. In their early years, however, Tigers are prone to have rocky careers that smooth out as they gain maturity. This is when they find their true direction and soon acquire wealth. With their boundless enthusiasm, Tigers expend a lot of energy at work, which means they need to take time to refresh themselves outside of work—or risk burning out. Promising careers for Tigers include: advertising agent, office manager, travel agent, life coach, sports coach, actor, writer, artist, pilot, flight attendant, musician, comedian, and chauffeur.

Element	Characteristics
Wood Tiger (1914, 1974)	Compassionate, expansive, and open
Fire Tiger (1926, 1986)	Optimistic and independent; poor self-control
Earth Tiger (1938, 1998)	Adventurous and realistic, with strong sense of faith
Metal Tiger (1950, 2010)	Females are very enthusiastic; males are indecisive, stubborn, and feminized
Water Tiger (1962, 2022)	Strong sense of self-esteem and learning ability

Notable Tigers: Among these headliners are a number of natural leaders: Marco Polo, Karl Marx, Emily Dickinson, Beethoven, Emily Brontë, Beatrix Potter, Isadora Duncan, Dwight D. Eisenhower, Elizabeth II, Joe Louis, Usain Bolt, Joe DiMaggio, Evander Holyfield, Jerry Rice, Tenzing Norgay, Derek Jeeter, Ray Kroc, Harper Lee, Rafael Nadal, Marilyn Monroe, Jerry Lewis, Alec Guinness, Tom Cruise, Leonardo DiCaprio, Jim Carrey, Penelope Cruz, Joaquin Phoenix, Jodie Foster, John Candy, Bill Murray, Garth Brooks, Kenny Rogers, Stevie Wonder, Drake, Lady Gaga, and Hugh Hefner.

Birth Signs: Rabbit

AFFILIATES:
Mandarin name: **tù**
Years: **1927, 1939, 1951, 1963, 1975, 1987, 1999, 2011, 2023**
Polarity: **Yin**
Birthstone: **Pearl**
Colors: **Red, pink, purple, blue**
Flower: **plantain lily, jasmine**
Numbers: **3, 4, 6**
Lucky days: **26th, 27th, and 29th of lunar month**
Planet: **Neptune**
Western counterpart: **Pisces**

Overview: The Rabbit may seem like an unexciting sign. After all, pet rabbits are sweet, cuddly, and fuzzy. But in the wild, rabbits are clever, fast, agile, and vigilant—skilled at surviving the threat of predators, as well as adapting to the encroachments of civilization on their meadow habitats. They persevere when they encounter difficulties; rarely feeling discouraged, they keep working on solutions until they achieve success. These are all enviable characteristics.

Positive Traits: Rabbit signs tend to be gentle, quiet, sensitive, and elegant, yet they are also alert and quick. They can be quite intuitive, have good memories, and enjoy using humor to communicate. Because they can't stand to be bored, they are good at organizing special occasions or creating romantic moments. Male Rabbits are polite and sincere, greeting others with a smile that makes them appear safe and reliable. Female Rabbits, who are often quite pretty, are demure and good-hearted. Rabbits are also considered one of the luckiest signs—each month has three lucky days, the 26th, 27th, and 29th, when chances for good fortune, wealth, or improved relationships will increase.

Questionable Traits: Rabbits can be superficial, stubborn, and melancholy. Although rabbits are open to those around them, they are overly discreet and rarely reveal their thoughts to others. They are prone to anxiety and often seek ways to escape reality. Meanwhile, they if are too cautious or conservative when they need to act, they miss legitimate opportunities.

Love trends: Rabbits are

Ruled by Neptune

This sign is overseen by Neptune, the planet of healing and intuition. This makes sense, as the Rabbit sign dislikes conflict or disruption in the home. Rabbits are also gifted healers, who are happy to nurture others and place their needs first. The gentle, humble nature of the Rabbit reflects the qualities of Neptune, which helps with the transition from the physical into the spiritual.

known for their fertility and the frequent couplings that achieve this. This might explain why this is one of the four signs that is blessed in love relationships. Rabbits may be quiet, gentle, but they are usually quite good-looking, with polished manners and dignified behavior. They are favorites with the opposite sex and never have trouble meeting potential partners, even though

Rabbit Elements

Elements	Characteristics
Wood Rabbit (1915, 1975)	Clever, quick-witted, selfish, lively in appearance, but shrewd at heart
Fire Rabbit (1927, 1987)	Broad-minded, smart, and flexible, with unique views
Earth Rabbit (1939, 1999)	Frank, straightforward, ambitious, hard-working; slightly reserved
Metal Rabbit (1951, 2011)	Kind-hearted, conservative, lively and enthusiastic
Water Rabbit (1963, 2023)	Gentle, amicable, adjusts readily to different conditions; weak mindset and principles

they can be shy at first. Male rabbits value a stable home with few conflicts. Female rabbits are outgoing and quite social, although they are thoughtful and treat everyone well.

Best matches: This sign pairs well with Ox, Goat, Snake, and Pig. Rabbit and Rat matches can be iffy, but compelling if they work out. Rabbit-Rabbit matches can feel like magic, like the perfect tasteful romance. The downside is that the couple will spend a lot of time fretting about finances and should engage a good accountant to ease their minds. Matches with the least potential are Rooster, Monkey, and Horse.

Career Signposts: In work situations, Rabbits are intelligent, skillful, kind, patient, and very responsible. And quick, which is always a welcome virtue on the job. Still, they are not nearly as competitive as some signs, and rely on their merits to rise up the ladder. Some Rabbits can be creative, with finely a developed artistic and literary sense.

Others are good at handling precision work or overseeing quality control. Possible career choices include: literature or art teacher, psychologist, nurse, writer, minister, judge, dog or cat breeder, electronics engineer, business consultant, translator, quality inspector, and nanny.

Notable Rabbits: Some of these celebrities can thank their Rabbit cleverness, determination, or agility for their success: Queen Victoria, Albert Einstein, Tiger Woods, Michael Jordan, Maria Sharapova, David Beckham, Orson Welles, Roger Moore, Charlize Theron, Orlando Bloom, Johnny Depp, Angelina Jolie, Brad Pitt, Drew Barrymore, Mike Myers, Tobey Maguire, and Tina Turner.

Birth Signs:
Dragon

AFFILIATES:
Mandarin name: **lóng**
Years: **1928, 1940, 1952, 1964, 1976, 1988, 2000, 2012, 2024**
Polarity: **Yang**
Birthstone: **Amethyst**
Colors: **Gold, silver, grayish white**
Flowers: **Hyacinth, bleeding heart, dragon flower, snapdragon**
Numbers: **1, 6, 7**
Lucky days: **1st and 16th of lunar month**
Planet: **Mars**
Western counterpart: **Aries**

Overview: The fifth sign of the Chinese zodiac animals is the only supernatural creature in the group. Due to this, it is considered the most vital and powerful sign in the zodiac. In Chinese culture dragons traditionally symbolize power, nobility, honor, luck, and success. These positive qualities are often combined, however, with a hot temper and a sharp tongue. In past times, Dragons were thought to be natural leaders due to their ambition and dominant natures.

Positive traits: Dragons exhibit courage, tenacity and intelligence along with enthusiasm and confidence. They face up to challenges and are not afraid to take risks. These are the people you want on your team—at work or play.

Questionable Traits: Dragons are sometimes seen as aggressive, and when angry, they are definitely not open to criticism. They rarely consider themselves irritating and arrogant, though those around them may disagree.

Love trends: The Dragon in love can be surprisingly idealistic, generous, and even passive. Unfortunately, they unrealistically seek perfection in every aspect of life, including romance. Many hopeful lovers pursue Dragons, which makes them smug. Yet they often marry late. They seek partners who are elegant, intelligent, and

Ruled by Mars

The Dragon, a powerful sign respected for its courage and determination, is fittingly ruled by Mars, the planet of passion and strength. Mars also represents self-empowerment, while Dragons are all about growing into their power and learning to wield it out in the world.

compassionate. Praise is sure to win them over.

Best matches: Dragons get along well with Rats, Roosters, and Monkeys. Far less successful are matches with Oxes, Goats, or Dogs. Dragon-Dragon matches are more promising for lasting friendships than for love connections.

Dragon Elements

Elements	Characteristics
Wood Dragon (1964, 2024)	Introverted, less enthusiastic, lacking in strong relationships
Fire Dragon (1916, 1976)	Smart, unreliable, easygoing
Earth Dragon (1928, 1988)	Smart, ambitious, hardworking
Metal Dragon (1940, 2000)	Natural and straightforward; unpredictable with continually changing emotions
Water Dragon (1952, 2012)	Persevering, farsighted, and vigorous

Career signposts: Repetitive jobs are not suitable for Dragons, who need more scope to utilize their many talents. Jobs related to imagination or creativity are right up their alley. With their strong ability to communicate they might consider careers in teaching, journalism, broadcasting, or writing. They also thrive in leadership positions such as managers or department heads. As team players, however, they can sometimes lack a spirit of cooperation. Suitable jobs include architect, politician, economist, doctor, quality inspector, financier, pharmacist, electrician, priest, athlete, artist, or actor.

Notable Dragons: The combination of power and ambition has given these Dragon the keys to success: Joan of Arc, Louisa May Alcott, Sigmund Freud, Florence Nightingale, Susan B. Anthony, Pearl Buck, Frank Sinatra, John Lennon, Dr. Seuss, Salvador Dali, Che Guevara, Bruce Lee, Rihanna, Liam Neeson, Nicholas Cage, Robin Williams, Russell Crow, and Sandra Bullock.

Astrology Meets Feng Shui

The ancient Chinese philosophy called Feng Shui (*fnng shway*) generates good fortune through the study of auspicious environments. This technique can be utilized by different zodiac signs to improve their chances of receiving lucky blessings. Each sign has a favored direction and these may come into play.

Feng Shui's history goes back more than 3,500 years, when it was first used by early Chinese people selecting dwelling sites. By the Han dynasty (220 BC–AD 220) the practice was studied alongside geography and astrology. The term means "wind-water," and the philosophy states that energy, qi (chee), exists in all things found in the universe. The core concept of good Feng Shui is creating harmony between humans and nature, which in turn generates good fortune. Bad Feng Shui produces bad luck. Advocates of this philosophy believe it can effect the destiny of a person or even the fate of nations.

Feng Shui utilizes two traditional theories: Yin-Yang Theory posits that everything in the universe is made of two opposed, but deeply connected forces—yin (negative, dark, or feminine) and yang (positive, light, or masculine). Feng Shui attempts to find a balance between the two. Five Elements Theory states that five elements—fire, earth, metal, water, and wood—are critical for defining Feng Shui in a space. Each has a certain characteristic and represents an aspect of life. The following list offers advice on how each sign of the Chinese zodiac can improve their Feng Shui and bring improved fortune to relationships, finances, and their health.

The Rat

The Rat sign needs to add a water element, perhaps a bowl of goldfish or a small fountain, to the north section—their lucky direction—of their office or home work space.

The Ox

This sign requires a strong fire element in order to increase luck. Oxes should add a few ceramic bowls or figurines to the office or bedroom. This works as a fire element because ceramics are heated at extremely high temperatures.

The Tiger

In order to gain good fortune, the Tiger sign should bring an earth element, perhaps a potted plant or terrarium, into their living area. Plants generate oxygen in the home, which is an added benefit.

The Rabbit

Rabbits need an invisible earth element to help them receive a financial boon. Hiding a jade stone in the northeast corner of the bedroom, their lucky direction, may do the trick.

The Dragon

Northwest is the lucky direction for those born under the Dragon sign. They require water in the northwest corner of the bedroom—a water basin with a handful of soil and several lotus flowers growing in it may bring long-lasting fortune.

The Snake

The Snake sign needs to add a metal element, maybe a pewter candlestick or brass vase, somewhere in the west portion of the home. Wearing gold or silver ornaments can ensure that basic expenses will always be met, even if a fortune is not in the stars.

The Horse

Horses need to place a metal element in the northwest area of the bedroom, perhaps a bronze version of the lucky three-legged toad, Jin Chan. This figure can almost guarantee a change of fortune for the better.

The Goat

To gain the maximum benefit people born in this year should place a wood element, like a small maple or walnut box, in the north of their office and then place a career-related object inside—a fountain pen for a writer, for instance.

The Monkey

For those born in the year of the Monkey, the direction west points to promising things. These people should place a tall plant, ideally taller than they are, in the west area of their living space.

The Rooster

To ensure good luck, the Rooster should plant grass seeds in a non-metal container (red enamel over earthenware works well). As the grass sprouts, it provides limitless possibilities and the chance to acquire a fortune.

The Dog

Those born in the year of the Dog should avoid water and earth elements. Instead they can arrange peach tree branches in their office for luck, but not place them in water or soil.

The Pig

The Pig sign needs the fire element to gain good fortune. A set of kiln-fired ceramic dishes (including a tray) in the living space will help accomplish this.

Birth Signs: Snake

AFFILIATES:
Chinese name: **shé**
Years: **1929, 1941, 1953, 1965, 1977, 1989, 2001, 2013, 2025**
Polarity: **Yin**
Birthstone: **Opal**
Colors: **Black, red, and yellow**
Flowers: **Orchid, cactus**
Numbers: **2, 8, 9**
Lucky days: **1st and 23rd of lunar month**
Planet: **Venus**
Western counterpart: **Taurus**

Overview: According to Chinese culture, the Snake is the most mysterious and intuitive of the zodiac animals. They act upon their own judgement and because they are so private, they rarely talk about their motivations or their reasons for any decisions. Very goal oriented, they dislike failure and really strive to avoid it at all costs. Snakes are quite fond of material pleasures and prefer the best quality items, but they also happen to hate shopping.

Positive Traits: Snakes are thought to be intelligent and wise, usually well-educated, as well as decent, sophisticated, and humorous. They are good communicators even though they usually say only what is necessary to convey an idea. In leadership roles they show creativity and responsibility.

Questionable Traits: Like snakes in nature, zodiac Snakes have a reputation for malevolence. What is more likely to be true is that they are catty, harsh, suspicious, and stingy when it comes to money. They are prone to over spending and not being able to maintain a budget. They also go through lazy, low-energy periods just like snakes do when molting.

Love trends: At first the Snake in love may be romantic, enthusiastic, and loyal. Alas, they also have intimacy issues—Snakes do not have a lot of friends, mainly because they are hard to know and keep many of the their feelings bottled up inside. Yet once a Snake is committed to a partner, he or she will open up and become responsive. If they become too connected, they have to watch out for jealous or obsessive behavior.

Ruled by Venus

This sign is overseen by the Morning and Evening Star, otherwise known as Venus, the planet of love and beauty. Those born under the Snake sign are often viewed as the most physically beautiful, and they also have a fondness for the aesthetic things in life. The Snake's charm and enchanting manner draws others to them.

Best matches: Snakes have a high level of compatibility with Dragons and Roosters. They don't share good chemistry with Tigers, Rabbits, Goats, or Pigs. A Snake-Snake match usually works well because they can trust each other and build on that foundation.

Career Signposts: Snakes are in demand in jobs that

require creativity and diligence. They tend to become job-hoppers, however, if they get bored, which happens frequently. They are clutch performers who enjoy jobs that offer complex problems to solve and tight deadlines. They prefer to work alone, however, and can get stressed by team dynamics or group demands. When starting a business, they do better after taking on a partner to handle the "meet and greets." Good career choices for Snakes include research scientist, analyst, investigator, politician, mediator, teacher, painter, potter, jeweler, astrologer, musician, dietician, psychologist, or sociologist.

Notable Snakes: Many of these Snakes used their creativity and intelligence to rise to the top: Elizabeth I, Abraham Lincoln, Charles Darwin, Pablo Picasso, Anne Frank, Martin Luther King Jr., Muhammad Ali, Mahatma Gandhi, Indira Gandhi, Jacqueline Kennedy Onassis, Audrey Hepburn, Kim Basinger, Liv Tyler, Daniel Radcliffe, Bob Dylan, Carole King, Neil Diamond, Burt Bacharach, Ann-Margret, and Martha Stewart.

Snake Elements

Elements	Characteristics
Wood Snake (1905, 1965)	Orderly, intelligent, with refined taste and a gift for appreciating others who succeed.
Fire Snake (1917, 1977)	Smart, insightful, communicative; active and fond of the limelight
Earth Snake (1929, 1989)	Calm. strong, steadfast, and diligent in work
Metal Snake (1941, 2001)	Determined, courageous, confident, and able: a born leader
Water Snake (1953, 2013)	Clever, creative, lively, and communicative, but sentimental

Birth Signs:
Horse

AFFILIATES:
Mandarin name: **ma**
Years: **1930, 1942, 1954, 1966, 1978, 1990, 2002, 2014, 2026**
Polarity: **Yang**
Birthstone: **Topaz**
Colors: **Yellow, green**
Flowers: **Calla lily, jasmine**
Numbers: **2, 3, 7**
Lucky days: **5th and 20th of lunar month**
Planet: **Mercury**
Western counterpart: **Gemini**

Overview: The horse appears in many Chinese myths and legends as a figure of admiration or strength . . . and so it it fitting that the zodiac sign of the Horse is one of high charisma with a rare ability to overcome obstacles. Horses can liven up social occasions or bring harmony to a heated discussion with their verbal skills. Due to an excess of energy, they may be unruly or rebellious as children, but soon mature into focused achievers.

Positive Traits: Horses possess great vitality, zeal, and passion, showing interest in a wide range of pursuits. Warmhearted and generous, they make friends easily. They often provide positive role models for younger members of their family and social circle.

Questionable Traits: Horses love to spend money. Creating a savings account to prepare "for a rainy day" can be very difficult for them. They are also too frank at times, not considering the other person's feelings when they speak out. Horses are very bad at keeping secrets, which can affect their business dealings. If they don't achieve something quickly, they have a tendency to give up. They are also vain and clothes-proud.

Love trends: Horses are noted for falling in love quickly, but once in love they can be torn by indecision . . . they yearn for their childlike freedom but enjoy connecting with another person so intimately. (This is a common problem for Horses, who love independence and being around people. In fact, that independent streak sometimes acts as a lure for the opposite sex.) Once a Horse has accepted the relationship, he or she will make

Ruled by Mercury

It makes sense that this energetic sign is overseen by Mercury, the planet of intelligence and information. Mercury allows Horse signs to think on their feet during a crisis, and gifts them with the ability to communicate effectively. Plus, Horses know how to get their ideas across in a charming manner. They are often talented artists or writers.

a point to display their strength and confidence to their partner. Male Horses can be especially romantic, often creating surprises for their mates. Women born under this sign are flirtatious but rarely promiscuous. Faithfulness is part of their nature. Horses enjoy touching, but are not especially sexual, not in the steamy bedroom-marathon sense. They are more interested in romantic wooing and in making their partner feel special.

Horse Elements

Elements	Characteristics
Wood Horse (1954, 2014)	Freedom-loving, diligent, passionate and careful in character; also hot-tempered, impulsive, and impatient.
Fire Horse (1966, 2026)	Smart, energetic, acute, and cautious.
Earth Horse (1918, 1978)	Pure and kind-hearted; puts the needs of others first
Metal Horse (1930, 1990)	Full of affection; bold, open, outgoing character
Water Horse (1942, 2002)	Kind, mild, and helpful; can view things in another's shoes

Best matches: Horses pair up best with Tigers, Rabbits, and Goats. They should avoid Rat and Ox partners. Horse-Horse matches have a lot of potential—they are extremely compatible at first, but may find that their mutual dislike of housekeeping leads to a messy house—and maybe a messy breakup. Horse-Dog connections also start out well, but Dogs may soon judge Horses to be fickle and superficial.

Career Signposts: The Horse's high levels of energy, ability to learn new things, and strong leadership skills may allow it to rise early in its career. Horses can be shrewd, intent on self-improvement and meeting their goals. They know they can rely on the friends they made on the way up to always have their backs. Possible career choices include architect, scientist, sales rep, events planner, publicist, politician, entrepreneur, art gallery manager, public speaker, journalist, translator, securities trader, performer, or tour operator.

Notable Horses: The following are strong, admirable, accomplished members of the Horse clan: Genghis Khan, Isaac Newton, Rembrandt, Chopin, Davy Crockett, Theodore Roosevelt, Ella Fitzgerald, Jackie Chan, John Travolta, Kobe Bryant, Denzel Washington, Harrison Ford, Barbra Streisand, Oprah Winfrey, Paul McCartney, Aretha Franklin, Jerry Seinfeld, Sandra Day O'Connor, and Leonard Bernstein.

Birth Signs: Goat

AFFILIATES:
Mandarin name: **yáng**
Years: **1931, 1943, 1955, 1967, 1979, 1991, 2003, 2015, 2027**
Polarity: **Yin**
Birthstone: **Emerald**
Color: **Brown, red, and purple**
Flower: **Carnation, primrose**
Numbers: **2, 7**
Lucky days: **7th and 30th of lunar month**
Planet: **Moon**
Western counterpart: **Cancer**

Overview: Sometimes known as the Sheep, this sign typically indicates a gentle or mild-mannered soul, one who prefers to travel in groups, but avoids the center spotlight. They are not pushovers, however, and know how to defend themselves against attack.

Positive Traits: Goats are calm and dependable, with kind hearts and good minds. Although they may seem passive, never underestimate the interior toughness of a Goat. When they have a goal in mind, they can persevere, and when knocked down, they have the resilience to recover and get back up. Their opinions are usually well thought out, and they tend to stick to them. One reason they seem quiet is that they like being alone with their own thoughts. They are surprisingly fashion conscious and enjoy following the latest styles, but are not snobbish about wealth.

Questionable Traits: This sign can be moody and vain, and resists spending money. They often judge things by their surface appearance and find it difficult to reveal emotions. Goats value their privacy and have trouble opening up.

Love trends: Even when Goats fall in love, they can still have trouble expressing their feelings. The men make sincere, romantic lovers, but they can also act childish. The women are attractive and considerate of their partners, but they also are too polite to refuse suitors who don't appeal to them. They tend to take any criticism to heart. Both genders need encouragement from caring partners to open up and create true intimacy.

Best matches: This sign has the best chance at romance with a Rabbit, Horse, or Pig. The worst matches may be

Ruled by the Moon

The Moon is the planet of feelings and nurture, which explains why Goats are the most creative creatures in the Chinese zodiac—the moon allows them to tap into the subconscious, the source of ideas, innovations, and solutions. The moon is also responsible for this sign's remarkable intuition and their outflow of emotions, always guided by a heart of gold.

with Ox, Dragon, Snake, or Dog. A Goat-Goat match has traditionally been considered an almost perfect pairing by Chinese astrologers—both parties will enjoy giving their opinions about art and music, planning for their home, and even sharing work as colleagues.

Career Signposts: Goats are creative and intuitive, always a valued combination in the workplace. They are quick to acquire professional skills, but prefer working in a team, especially with Horse signs. Status and power don't really motivate them. They are not quick to volunteer, but will lead a group if asked. Career options include pediatrician, actor, daycare or grade school teacher, interior designer, florist, hairstylist, musician, editor, illustrator, and art history professor.

Notable Goats: These Goats found enough moxie to break away from the safety of the group and gain success: Michelangelo, Mark Twain, Thomas Edison, Orville Wright, Arthur Ashe, Joe Frazier, Rudolph Valentino, Katherine Hepburn, Bruce Willis, Robert De Niro, Mel Gibson, Nicole Kidman, Chow Yun-fat, Nat King Cole, George Harrison, Mick Jagger, Jim Morrison, John Denver, Kurt Cobain, Isaac Asimov, Bill Gates, and Steve Jobs.

Goat Elements

Element	Characteristics
Wood Goat (1955, 2015)	Amicable, gentle, and compassionate
Fire Goat (1907, 1967)	Friendly, frank, and honest, always making everything clean and tidy
Earth Goat (1919, 1979)	Righteous, honest, straightforward; will never harm their friends
Metal Goat (1931, 1991)	Ambitious and kind-hearted; strong sense of responsibility at work; sometimes too stubborn
Water Goat (1943, 2003)	Always ready to help out; can sacrifice their own interests for others

Goat, Sheep...or What?

Even in China, astrologers are not sure about the answer to this question. In the Chinese language the word 羊 (yáng) is a generic term and can refer to a sheep (羊), goat (山羊), ram/buck (公羊 male sheep or goat), antelope (羚羊), etc. Throughout the country's history there has been a lack of clear definition on the zodiac Goat. Still, folklorists favor the term Goat, in part because the Han people invented the Chinese zodiac and they were noted for raising goats. Another reason is that the Goat often appears on postage stamps and New Year paper decorations and paintings. Thirdly, it is a goat, not a sheep, that is found among the 12 bronze figures of the zodiac at the Old Summer Palace in Beijing.

Birth Signs:
Monkey

AFFILIATES:
Mandarin name: **hóu**
Years: **1932, 1944, 1956, 1968, 1980, 1992, 2004, 2016, 2028**
Polarity: **Yang**
Birthstone: **Peridot**
Color: **White, blue, gold**
Flower: **Chrysanthemum**
Numbers: **4, 9**
Lucky days: **14th and 28th of lunar month**
Planet: **Sun**
Western counterpart: **Leo**

Overview: Those born under the Monkey sign are smart, cheerful, and energetic, but their curiosity and playfulness also incline them to mischief. Like their animal namesakes, they are also known for being adaptable and flexible. Although they can be clever and creative, they don't always choose the proper ways to display their talents.

Positive Traits: Monkeys are considered loyal, wise, and caring, Their characteristic insight, intuition, and forethought often appear while they are still quite young. With their upbeat, amiable personalities, they raise the mood of a room just by entering it.

Questionable Traits: Restless monkeys may become impatient and irritable around those who are less active, and they are easily

frustrated. These masters of hijinks look for opportunities to have fun with others, but their pranks can go overboard and hurt people's feelings. Monkeys can't always "read" their audience. They can be eccentric or sly, which does not endear them to everyone.

Love trends: Monkeys attach great importance to love and tend to be optimistic when in a relationship. Male Monkeys are willing to help their partners in both life and work. Their good humor and joy for life helps to dispel any gloom. But they do require their loved ones to create an atmosphere of affection and caring at home. Female Monkeys dislike being restricted or giving up their freedom. It takes a powerful attraction and a promise of stability for them to change and become part of a

Ruled by the Sun

The sun, which oversees the Monkey sign, represents self-identity and ego. As a result of this influence Monkeys often seem to brim with confidence and can easily hold their own in the spotlight. The sun breathes warmth and energy into Monkeys, giving them passion and the desire to be seen and heard.

loving team. Both genders need partners who can stimulate them and keep them from getting complacent or bored.

Best matches: Statistics show that a Monkey's best chances for happy, harmonious pairing are with Ox, Dragon and Rabbit signs. Rats are also possibilities— they push the Monkey to succeed in business. Unpromising combinations are with the Tiger, Pig, and Snake signs. Monkey-Monkey matches start out very

Monkey Elements

Elements	Characteristics
Wood Monkey (1944, 2004)	Eager to help others; strong self-esteem, but stubborn
Fire Monkey (1956, 2016,)	Ambitious and adventurous, but irritable
Earth Monkey (1968, 2028)	Frank, optimistic, and fearless
Metal Monkey (1980, 2040)	Smart, confident, but irritable and stubborn
Water Monkey (1932, 1992)	Quick-witted, fond of the limelight, but haughty

well, with lots of shared traits, but both partners need to realize that egotism and jealousy could shake them out of their bliss.

Career Signposts: Monkeys are competent, goal-oriented performers who show strong leadership potential. These quick learners and innate problem-solvers can be surprisingly scheming when it comes to moving up the ladder at work. Monkeys tend to be short-sighted; if they become distracted or bored, they can lose sight of project goals. Careers that play to a Monkey's strengths include most types of freelance work such as editor, artist, or journalist, also entertainer, musician, DJ or emcee, event planner, social director, linguist/translator, shop owner, stockbroker, teacher, or athlete.

Notable Monkeys: Lots of Monkey creativity and energy can be found among these renowned individuals: Julius Caesar, Leonardo da Vinci, Betsy Ross, Lord Byron, Charles Dickens, Annie Oakley, Eleanor Roosevelt, Harry S. Truman, Bette Davis, Elizabeth Taylor, Michael Douglas, Will Smith, Halle Berry, Tom Hanks, Owen Wilson, Daniel Craig, Mick Jagger, Diana Ross, Miley Cyrus, Celine Dion, Nick Jonas, Christine Aguilera, Alice Walker, Yao Ming.

Still Starstruck...
the Continuing Presence of Astrology

Astrology is increasingly popular throughout the world, with practitioners and advocates in America, Canada, Great Britain, South Africa, Australia, much of Europe, and the Middle East.

Yet in those places, astrology is still not an intrinsic part of the culture, not like it is in Asia, especially in countries like India, Sri Lanka, China, Burma, or Singapore, where it engenders an almost religious fervor.

Astrology is probably most popular in India, which holds the top spot for astrology-related Google searches—many of them no doubt seeking Dr. Sohini Sastri of Kolkata, who currently holds the record of "most searched astrologer in India." Sastri works with Bollywood divas but offers equal attention to less-illustrious clients. India's Vedic system of astrology is used to arrange marriages, pick the best time to launch a business, and even predict international political events.

In Sri Lanka, likewise, astrology plays a large part in everyday life. In fact, more Sri Lankans subscribe to the top astrology magazine than to the daily newspaper. Everyone, including the government, takes horoscopes seriously, to the point that an astrologer was arrested in 2009 for predicting the country's current leader would be overthrown.

The astrology-mad Nepalese have made Basudev Krishna Shastri, a TV astrologer with his own show, into a major celebrity. And considering that an estimated 99 percent of Nepalese astrologers are men, female astrologers have recently been making strides to change that unequal dynamic.

In Burma (Myanmar), the exact moment for the establishment of Burmese independence was chosen by an astrologer. That is how seriously this country takes its stars, to the point where they got up before dawn at 4:20 AM on January 4, 1948. The current leaders still plan their itineraries based on the guidance of astrologers; they even moved the capital from Yangon (Rangoon) to the middle of the jungle based on the position of the planets. Sadly, their astrologers need to shape up. Since 1948, Burma has gone from being the second wealthiest country in the region after Japan, to a financial and economic disaster ruled by a repressive regime. Perhaps these dire results are because their astrologers are not incorporating the modern planets into their horoscopic charts.

Naksti is an ancient eastern version of astrology that is a blend of Indian/Western traditions, or Kartsi, and

Astrology's Top Ten Cities Worldwide

The following results are based on Google trends.

1. **Chennai**, India
2. **Bangalore**, India
3. **Delhi**, India
4. **Mumbai**, India
5. **Toronto**, Canada
6. **Vancouver**, Canada
7. **Los Angeles**, California, US
8. **New York**, New York, US
9. **San Francisco**, California, US
10. **Seattle**, Washington, US

Opposite: Parrot astrology in Mahabalipuram, Tamil Nadu, India

Chinese traditions. Yet it remains uniquely Buddhist, based as it is on the Kālakakra Tantra, an ancient, divergent, astrological school of Buddhism. Until recently, most practicing Naksti astrologers were monks. Naksti horoscopes are calculated along four major themes: a person's life span; physical condition; economic and political power; and overall luck in business and work. They also draw on the Arising Vowel System, dByangs-'Char, which assigns a different vowel for each day of the month, factoring its effect on both individuals and nations. Typically, when a child is born, their Naksti chart can anticipate which problems will occur at certain ages. That way that the

parents will know the rituals needed to remove the negative karma.

In spite of Singapore's air of worldly sophistication, the populace still turns to astrology to guide their lives . . . and to parrots for delivering the details. Originating in India, "parrot astrologers" use green parrots or parakeets who pick a lucky card for the querent. In Singapore, these parrot astrologers originally catered to the Indian population, but they soon became popular with many communities, even the city's edgy young people who seek advice on romantic matters or career decisions. Parrot astrology is usually a family business.

Birth Signs: Rooster

AFFILIATES:
Mandarin name: **ji**
Years: **1933, 1945, 1957, 1969, 1981, 1993, 2005, 2017, 2029**
Polarity: **Yin**
Birthstone: **Citrine**
Color: **Gold, brown, yellow**
Flower: **Cockscomb**
Numbers: **5, 7, 8**
Lucky days: **4th and 26th of lunar month**
Planet: **Mercury**
Western counterpart: **Virgo**

Ruled by Mercury

Just like the Horse, the Rooster is ruled by the planet of information and intelligence. And like Horses, Roosters are also highly communicative, but they are more expressive in how they reach out. Never subtle, people always know when a Rooster is in the room. They are great talkers, as well as having engaging and dynamic personalities.

Overview: Roosters are natural mixers, and with their active, amusing, talkative personalities, it is no wonder they are popular. They tend to be very attractive and are quite comfortable being the center of attention. Still, in spite of seeming strong and courageous, Roosters need reassurance and validation from those close to them. In ancient times these feisty birds were thought to ward off evil spirits.

Positive Traits: Roosters are hardworking, resourceful, and creative, as well as loyal to friends and family. These deep thinkers are typically honest, bright, ambitious, capable, and warm-hearted. Few things can sidetrack them when engaged on a mission; if thwarted they can be fierce.

Questionable Traits: Roosters can be demanding, expecting others to listen while they speak and then becoming agitated if they are not heeded. This habit of always needing to command attention can be very wearing to friends. Sometimes vain or boastful, Roosters like to brag about their achievements, crowing like their namesakes. They can be perfectionists who will criticize anything they believe does not meet their standards.

Love trends: When Roosters fall in love, they become very caring. This tenderness often makes their partners grow infatuated with them. They are good communicators but not when it comes to romance; they have to let their behavior do the

talking. This sign finds refuge and contentment in the family setting, and their potential mates should be forewarned that they believe the more family members the better.

Best matches: Roosters and Dragons form the most compatible pair, with Roosters willing to support the Dragons and back them up; meanwhile Dragons' accomplishments make Roosters proud. Roosters and Snakes, can discuss the

Rooster Elements

Elements	Characteristics
Wood Rooster (1945, 2005)	Active, vibrant, overconfident, tender, unstable
Fire Rooster (1957, 2017)	Trustworthy, with a strong sense of responsibility at work
Earth Rooster (1909, 1969)	Generous, trustworthy, popular with their friends
Metal Rooster (1921, 1981)	Forceful, brave, persevering, hardworking
Water Rooster (1933, 1993)	Clever, quick-witted, tenderhearted, caring

secrets of life and pursue dreams together. Ox's honesty and conservativeness meshes with the Rooster personality. The least successful pairings are Rabbit, Dog, and other Roosters, which should be obvious . . . there just can't be two centers of attention in one relationship.

Career Signposts: Roosters do not really care about making money. They earn it and quickly spend it. Still, they take their jobs very seriously and usually make good career choices. Their communication skills allow them to shine in interactive positions. They have a strong sense or self-respect and rarely rely on others to get things done. Roosters should consider working as a police officer, diplomat, athlete, cosmetologist, intelligence agent, speech writer, teacher, actor/actress, politician, diplomat, tour guide, or fashion designer.

Notable Roosters: These celebrities used their outgoing personalities to make their mark: Catherine the Great, Rudyard Kipling, Amelia Earhart, Groucho Marx, Jennifer Aniston, Elijah Wood, Natalie Portman, Matthew McConaughey, Anna Kournikova, Diane Sawyer, Serena Williams, Cate Blanchett, Matt Damon, Justin Timberlake, and Elton John.

Birth Signs:
Dog

AFFILIATES:
Mandarin name: **gou**
Years: **1934, 1946, 1958, 1970, 1982, 1994, 2006, 2018, 2030**
Polarity: **Yang**
Birthstone: **Diamond**
Color: **red, green, and purple**
Flower: **Rose, cymbidium orchid**
Numbers: **3, 4, 9**
Lucky days: **7th and 28th of lunar month**
Planet: **Venus**
Western counterpart: **Libra**

Ruled by Venus

Like the Snake, the Dog is overseen by Venus. But whereas the Snake shares Venus's love of beauty and pleasure, the Dog is more concerned with the planet's values. Dogs are driven by justice and balance and have strong moral characters. They want to make the world a better place. Venus gives them the clarity to see the beauty around them, but also the areas that need work.

Overview: This is an upstanding sign that values justice and sincerity and is popular as a friend who dispenses good advice. Dogs tend to be happy individuals who are active at sports. They don't chase the almighty dollar and so are more relaxed than most at work and at home. This inner peace makes them resistant to illnesses.

Positive Traits: Dogs are loyal, amiable, and industrious. Men born in Dog years are no-nonsense and genuine; they are usually energetic, though somewhat pessimistic. They are deeply attached to their families, to the point that any stubbornness in their character disappears when they are dealing with those they love. Women are naturally cautious, giving their trust only sparingly, and highly protective of their families. They enjoy any activities that bring them outdoors and into nature.

Questionable Traits: Unlike their animal namesakes, which can convey a message to their human by just the expression in their eyes, those born under the Dog sign are not great communicators. Often nervous or worried on the inside, Dogs still tend to stick to their decisions. Men can be very opinionated and quick to correct others. Women are often openly indifferent toward those they don't like.

Love trends: Dogs have trouble giving their hearts away and can take longer than normal to open up emotionally, even with someone they are attracted to. Yet once they trust the other person enough to commit, they will become completely faithful and loyal. Even if they suffer a lot of emotional ups and downs, devotion is their watchword.

Best matches: Those born under the Dog sign pair up best with Rabbits; all the other signs can be somewhat problematic for romance. Dogs matched

Dog Elements

Elements	Characteristics
Wood Dog (1934, 1994)	Reliable, considerate, understanding, patient
Fire Dog (1946, 2006)	Intelligent, hardworking, genuine
Earth Dog (1958, 2018)	Communicative, serious, responsible on the job
Metal Dog (1910, 1970)	Conservative, desirable, ready to help others; cautious
Water Dog (1922, 1982)	Brave and well-versed in financial issues; self-centered, even selfish

with other Dogs may first think they have found the perfect complement, but when faced with their equally high standards, the couple will need to work out how to relax and be comfortable together. The worst pairings are with Dragon, Goat, and Rooster.

Career Signposts: Loyal, obedient Dogs often do well at jobs where they look after or serve others. They make valuable and valued employees who typically give their all to a job. They are easy to get along with and they often help share the workload, something that does not go unnoticed by their superiors. During heavy work periods, they need to make sure to get enough restorative rest. Potential career paths might include police officer, scientist, defense attorney, judge, hospitality worker, event planner, nurse, EMT, counselor, interior designer, professor, political aide, priest, or sales clerk.

Notable Dogs: These people overcame potentially poor communication skills to rise to the top of their fields: Confucius, Socrates, Voltaire, Benjamin Franklin, Herbert Hoover, George Gershwin, Winston Churchill, Golda Meir, Bill Clinton, Donald Trump, Prince William, Andre Agassi, Ellen DeGeneres, Jane Goodall, Madonna, Jennifer Lopez, Queen Latifah, Shirley MacLaine, Susan Sarandon, Mariah Carey, Michael Jackson, and Justin Bieber.

Birth Signs:

Pig

AFFILIATES:
Mandarin name: **zhu**
Years: **1935, 1947, 1959, 1971, 1983, 1995, 2007, 2019, 2031**
Polarity: **Yin**
Birthstone: **Ruby**
Color: **yellow, gray, brown, gold**
Flower: **Hyacinth**
Numbers: **2, 5, 8**
Lucky days: **17th and 24th of lunar month**
Planet: **Pluto**
Western counterpart: **Scorpio**

Ruled by Pluto

This sign is overseen by Pluto, which is known as the planet of transformation. Although those born under the Pig sign can appear to be simple, cheerful souls, there is depth to their character. Pluto serves as a reminder that things are not always what they seem outwardly, and that, because life is short, those inner qualities should be revealed and not hidden away.

Overview: Unlike America, where pigs are viewed as unclean, lazy animals that eat too much, in China pigs are revered for their calm demeanor and as symbols of luck, wealth, and prosperity. Those born under the Pig sign are known for their diligence, compassion, and generosity. Ultra responsible, they keep their eyes on the goal and never flag, no matter what the obstacles. Even though they rarely seek help from others, they are quick to volunteer to lend a hand.

Positive Traits: Pigs combine a number of admirable qualities: they are kind-hearted, even-tempered, considerate, and very loyal. They are accommodating and gallant, never seeking to harm others. They project a calm, stable appearance that reflects their steady natures, but they may occasionally be impetuous.

Questionable Traits: Because they are so straightforward themselves, Pigs rarely suspect trickery and so are easily taken advantage of. They believe that money is very important and can buy peace of mind. They may shower a love object with gifts as proof of their feelings. Pigs can sometimes be slow-witted or hesitant, or, conversely, hot-headed and rash.

Love trends: Pig signs in love are usually sensitive, refined, and affectionate, with an almost old-fashioned attitude about what to expect from a romance. Their courtship can be defined as sweet rather than sensual, and they show their attraction by caring actions, not sexy moves. Men of this sign speak of craving a passionate marriage, yet they often act shy, thinking it will attract the woman they have chosen. This behavior causes them to occasionally miss a potentially loving connection. Women born under this sign may act fragile or passive during courtship, but their real thoughts are often veiled. They may just be in it for the presents! If they do fall in love, they make excellent mothers, although they still enjoy being taken care of by their husbands.

Best matches: The optimum pairings for Pigs are Goats, Tigers, and Rabbits. These signs are attracted to each other and, most importantly, know how to please one another. As a married couple they admire each other's merits and are willing to work hard for the family. The worst matches for this sign are Monkeys and Snakes. At the most these couples are polite to each other, but lack the deep connection that a lifelong union requires. A match between two Pig signs will probably be quite compatible and sensual, but they run the risk of becoming so fixated on each other, and on pleasing their partner, that the outer world fades away. They can also get into a criticism/counter-criticism loop that is dangerous to their harmony.

Career Signposts: Pigs have great concentration and stay calm whenever there is an emergency or crisis. They work well in groups and are accustomed to relying on others. Many enjoy working with animals, plants, and nature, as well as in public service and in medical or creative fields. They

should stay away from jobs that require strict schedules or are based on a lot of competition. Some career options include: veterinarian, forester, engineer, civil servant, police officer, doctor, livestock breeder, professor, artist, singer, dancer, or human resource counselor.

Notable Pigs: Many of these people displayed the calm, hard-working character that the Pig is known for: Oliver Cromwell, Henry Ford, Ernest Hemingway, Alfred Hitchcock, Ronald Reagan, Arnold Schwarzenegger, Magic Johnson, Lucille Ball, Woody Allen, Hillary Clinton, Stephen King, Mahalia Jackson, Amy Winehouse, and Julie Andrews.

Pig Elements

Elements	Characteristics
Wood Pig (1935, 1995)	Sweet-natured, attractive, easy-going, generous; brave but irritable
Fire Pig (1947, 2007)	Ambitious, persevering; can be impatient
Earth Pig (1959, 2019)	Communicative, popular, a strong sense of time keeping
Metal Pig (1971, 2031)	Open-minded, amicable, and willing to help others
Water Pig (1923, 1983)	Mild-mannered, modest, sincere, responsible

Chapter Six

Astrological Branches

Mundane Branch | Electional Branch
| Horary Branch | Feature: Gallery of
Zodiacs | Medical Branch | Relationship
Branch | Psychological Branch |
Evolutionary Branch

Mundane Branch

Considering the number of people who are actively practicing natal astrology, it should be no surprise that its sister branches are now generating interest.

Some astrologers who have grown too familiar with Western horoscopic or Chinese astrology—or feel the need to break new ground—are beginning to tap into these other branches, especially the ones with long histories that might offer new insights to age-old questions.

Mundane astrology focuses on predicting world events and politics. Naturally, it was quite popular during the eras when emperors, kings, and caliphs were attended by personal astrologers who helped them to rule successfully. The name comes from the Latin *mundus*, meaning "the world." At some point it branched off from judicial astrology and is likely one of the oldest forms of the main discipline.

Practitioners believe there is a correlation between events in nature such as earthquakes or storms and the movement of the celestial spheres as they relate to things here on earth. This branch assesses the patterns of history, determines what purpose these happenings served, and predicts future events and how they will affect the world. It provides a cautionary message so that courses can be changed and catastrophes avoided. During the Middle Ages, this branch was referred to as Revolutions, because it signified upheaval. Mundane astrology uses a chart that is drawn up for a nation or country.

Planetary Representations

The Sun symbolizes leaders: prime ministers, aristocracy, magistrates, judges; heroes, champions.

The Moon represents the common person; its position on a chart indicates where public attention is focused.

Mercury, planet of communication and transport, represents the literary world: publishers, newspapers, books, intellectuals.

Venus symbolizes women, birth rate, marriage, children; entertainment, the arts, sports, musicians; peaceful resolutions of problems.

Mars represents war and opposition: military, navy, soldiers, attacks, disputes, conflicts, fire.

Jupiter represents the religious and the judicial world: priests, religious leaders, bankers, judges.

Saturn represents the elderly and the nation's death rate; deadly epidemics, state funerals;

Uranus represents political tension; rioting, fascism, individualism, right wing political ideas; scientific discoveries.

Neptune represents left wing political ideas such as socialism and communism; covert plots, fraud, illicit activities, and loss; change and rebirth.

Pluto represents change and rebirth.

Electional Branch

Also known as event astrology, the electional branch zeroes in on choosing opportune times for business ventures and other important events.

It differs from horary astrology in that the horary branch is used to find the answer to a specific question, while the electional branch allows astrologers to determine an auspicious period of time that offers the best outcome.

Throughout history, this branch has been used to schedule battles; plan uprisings, political coups, or revolutions; or arrange dates for certifying independence. It has also been used in business and family arenas such planning mergers, buyouts, or other deals, or arranging weddings, trips, or reunions.

An early form of electional astrology was practiced in Babylon after the 16th century BC, and along with other forms of astrology was passed to the Egyptians and Persians. Early Vedic astrologers also used a more sophisticated form, Muhurta, for determining the timing of yajnas (fireside rituals), trips, wars, marriages, and, recently, filmmaking. The modern version traces back to Dorotheus of Sidon's treatises, the oldest writings on this branch.

Even though modern discoveries on the real nature of planets and stars have eroded confidence that their motions affect a nation's or person's luck, and empirical evidence points to the inaccuracy of many predictions over the centuries, quite a few Asian cultures still depend on electional forecasting.

Planning Ahead

In electional astrology, the querent tells the astrologer of an event they wish to schedule, and the astrologer calculates the best time for the event to take place. Elections are typically divided into three categories, depending on the type of event. Radical elections are based mainly on the natal chart of the querent. Mundane elections involve using prominent mundane horoscopes that are currently in force to pick a time. With ephemeral elections, by far the most popular, the chosen day is based on highly favorable celestial placements, sometimes in combination with the querent's birth chart.

Creating Talismans

Ephemeral elections have a long history of being used to make talismans and seals, thus imbuing these items with the qualities of the auspicious time at which they were created. Instructions for preparing these types of "lucky charms" are often found in medieval literature.

Horary Branch

Horary astrology is an ancient branch of horoscopic astrology, the lowest of the four main branches.

Unlike natal astrology, which is based on a birth date, here the astrologer attempts to answer a question by constructing a horoscope for the exact time that the question was received and understood by the astrologer. The answer might be a simple yes or no . . . or it might be complex and full of insights. It might even examine the motives of the questioner or the motives of those involved in the matter; it will usually reveal the options open to them.

Some astrological principles are unique to this branch. The position of and aspects to the moon are key factors. The querent is represented by the ruler of the sign the first house falls into on the chart. Leo in the first house means the querent is ruled by the sun. The planetary aspects to the house cusps are given more weight than with other branches. Other elements include the lunar nodes, the planetary antiscia (symmetrical openings equidistant from each cardinal point), the fixed stars, and the Arabic parts (mathematical points based on the ascendent). As can be seen, this branch is no cakewalk for a novice astrologer.

Before the chart is read, the item being asked about, the quesited, is assigned to a particular house. If the question is about a lost pet, it would be represented by the sixth house, which governs animals smaller than a goat. A question about a parent would be in the fourth house. The cusp of the querent's house will be in a particular sign, say Cancer. Cancer is ruled by the moon, so that would be the lost pet's *significator.* The moon's state in the horoscope would then give clues about the animal's wellbeing, and its placement would relate to the pet's location. Calculating the correct house in terms of the context of the question is critical to correctly interpreting a horary question.

Below is a brief list of houses and their possible associations in terms of determining a significator.

First House: The querent. The querent's physical appearance, temperament, mental state.

Second House: The querent's finances, wealth, material and financial possessions. Any moveable possessions. Allies or supports, such as a lawyer. Questions about the value of possessions.

Third House: Siblings and neighbors. Concern about relatives. Communications and contracts. Comings and goings, short journeys. Letters, emails, paperwork. Cars in matters of travel are in third house; in matters of value or buying or selling are second house. Lower education—elementary, junior high/middle, high school.

Fourth House: Parents. Immovable possessions, e.g. houses, gardens, orchards. Mines, oil, buried treasure, anything from the "bowels of the earth."

Fifth House: Children, love affairs, romance, sex (pleasure and procreation). Gambling, speculation, arguments, games, pleasure. Venues that cater to pleasure or fun: restaurants, clubs, casinos, bars, music venues.

Sixth House: Illness and disease or sickness. Servants or anyone querent employs: plumber, electrician, tutor, etc. Pets and animals smaller than a goat (larger animals are twelfth house). Work and work environment. People with whom querent works in some kind of agreement.

Seventh House: Marriage, partners and partnerships— both business and personal. Competitors and opponents of all kinds. This is the house of open enemies, which means enemies querent is aware of. Hidden enemies are the twelfth house. If no other house suffices, use the seventh house to represent "any old person."

Eighth House: Death, fears, anxiety; now also known as the "house of other people's money."

Ninth House: Long-distance travel, trips to unknown or "exotic" locations. Foreigners and foreign lands. Universities, students with a higher education: doctors, lawyers, priests, astrologers. Visions, dreams, religion, churches, philosophies. Books. Spiritual pilgrimages or journeys.

Tenth House: Career and persons of authority. Heads of state, the government, judges, royalty. Indicates the property belonging to a partner or opponent.

Eleventh House: Friendships or groups. Wishes, hopes and aspirations. This is the house of "Good Fortune," the house of friends and acquaintances.

Twelfth House: Secrets, hidden motives and enemies, captivity, imprisonment and self-undoing. Things not yet known. Magick, witchcraft, or any manner of secretly undermining the querent.

Gallery of Zodiacs

Above: Prince Elector John Georges and **alchemist Leonard Thurneysser; Opposite, left: Druids** celebrating the Summer Solstice at Stonehenge, England; **Opposite, right:** Drummers parading during celebrations to mark the **Yoruba Olojo festival** in Osun State, Nigeria.

In addition to the different branches of astrology still practiced today and featured in this chapter, some astrologers use zodiacs or horoscopic methods that differ from the two most familiar ones: the Western zodiac, with 12 birth signs per year, and the Chinese zodiac with its 12 yearly animal signs.

The totems or symbols employed in these alternative zodiacs often reflect aspects of the culture in which they evolved . . . Druids revere trees, for instance, so it makes sense that a Druid zodiac would feature different types of trees.

Arabic Zodiac

This zodiac has twelve signs, all bearing the names of medieval weapons: Spear, Sling, Ax, Dagger, Club, Mace, Knife, Scimitar, Machete, Chain, Poniard and Arch, each with a lucky number associated with it. The Arabic method of creating a horoscope appeared a century before the birth of Christ, but it was not until about 900 years later that it emerged in the form that is known today.

Alchemist Horoscope

This method of casting combines numerology and metals; it consists of ten signs associated with elements of the periodic table. Centuries ago, certain metals were believed to contain positive and negative energies and this system plays off that theory. The horoscope is calculated by adding the digits of the date of birth, and the result, which will have two figures, is added together until there is one single digit or a number that ends in 0. The element indicates the querent's personality traits.

(1) Silver: seductive, very independent; reactive to insult, not tolerant of jealousy

(2) Iron: attractive, freedom-loving; restless, frank

(3) Mercury: sociable, funny, adaptable; often possessive

(4) Zinc: impulsive, sensitive, supportive; naive at times

(5) Tin: dynamic, wilful, determined; not always responsible

(6) Lead: shy, honest, loyal; sometimes rigid in character

(7) Platinum: multi-talented, lucky, selective; often cold or distant

(8) Nickel: born to lead, original, imaginative; capricious

(9) Gold: passionate, faithful, generous; profligate with money
(0) Copper: Generous, supportive, energetic; prone to resentment

Celtic Zodiac

This zodiac variation has the most signs: a total of 21, all of them tree names. If an individual is born under the guardianship of a certain tree, they obtain its protection and characteristics. There are two trees for equinoxes, September (Olive) and March (Oak), and two for solstices, June (Birch) and December (Beech). The remaining 17 trees are Fir, Poplar, Maple, Hazel, Hornbeam, Chestnut, Cedar, Cypress, Ash, Fig, Apple, Walnut, Elm, Pine, Willow, Rowan, and Linden.

Druid Zodiac

The druids, high-ranking figures in ancient Celtic culture, were tasked with watching over divine things. Their astrology praises nature and the seasons and therefore their zodiac has tree names. Its 13 signs are associated with lunar phases and are Birch, Rowan, Ash, Alder, Willow, Hawthorn, Oak, Holly, Hazel, Vine, Ivy, Cane, and Elder.

Gypsy Zodiac

Gypsies, also known as travelers, are lauded for their divinatory skills, especially cartomancy and palmistry. Besides these, they have their own zodiac. The signs are represented by inanimate objects and assigned to each person according to their date of birth: Cup, Chapel, Knife, Crown, Candlesticks, Wheel, Star, Bell, Coin, Dagger, Axe, and Horseshoe.

Orisha Zodiac

A traditional religion of Africa and the New World, Yoruba employs the Orisha zodiac, which has a dozen signs that use names of dieties: Ogun, Oko, Eleguá, Oshun, Shango, Yemanyá, Obatalá, Orula, Babalú Aye, Agayú Solá, Oshosi and Inle. These names are related to Cuban Santeria, a religion that seeks equivalance between Christianity and the Yoruba faith. For example, Eleguá is related to San Antonio de Padua, Yemanyá with the Virgin of Regla, and Babalú Aye to San Lázaro.

Wuykü Zodiac

This zodiac has the fewest signs—four—represented by animals sacred to Buddhists, with each representing three months of the year. The Spider rules January, February, and March and is considered beautiful on the inside. The Ant covers April, May, June, and oversees material activities. Scorpions represent July, August, and September, and stand for cognitive ability and pride. The Turtle is responsible for the final three months and represents consistency and patience. This method of forecasting goes back about two millennia before Christ, and first emerged in the Tibet region of China.

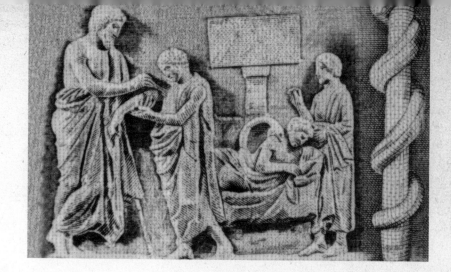

Medical Branch

This branch of astrology has deep, ancient roots, going to back to the Hellenic period in Greece. Even during later eras when predictive astrology was condemned, medical astrology was still accepted and in some cases mandated by law. Until 1666, it was required for European physicians to pass astrological exams in order to practice medicine.

Astrologers believed that the planets and constellations provided information on how different body parts function; the 12 sun signs were said to govern these parts, starting with Ares at the head down to Pisces at the feet. If a person were suffering from a painful stomach—ruled by the sign of Virgo—the astrologer/physician would determine which planet was in Virgo at the time. Was fiery Mars causing indigestion or the moon creating a depression that affected the appetite? Once the sign and planet were identified, the physician would then prescribe specific herbs or treatments. (*See* Feature: Influence over Body Parts on p. 152).

Subtle Influences

Even without the aid of a medical astrologer, the home stargazer can look for links between certain body parts and their accompanying signs and planets. The influences may be subtle but detectable, if not always medical. If Mercury, the planet of communication, is in Gemini, the sign that oversees the hands, a person may suddenly start using more gestures during conversations or find they are using their fingers to mark the lines they are reading in a book. Or, becaues Mercury is a hot little orb, their hands may experience feelings of warmth at that time.

Although it is no longer utilized to any great extent—after all, a patient doesn't hand the doctor their astrological birth chart before an examination—medical astrology still has insights and benefits to offer. And in case someone wants to consult a medical astrologer, the practice hasn't died out completely. Furthermore, there is still interest in this branch among naturopaths, practitioners of holistic medicine, and even an occasional MD.

Planetary Effects

Below are the effects the planets and key indicators may have on the body or the psyche if they are somehow restricted on an astrological chart.

Sun: fatigue
Moon: anxiety, gloom
Mercury: uncertainty
Venus: discomfort
Mars: irritation
Jupiter: misfortune
Saturn: complication
Uranus: confusion
Neptune: hypochondria
Pluto: malfunction
Ascendant: neglect
Medium Coeli: doubt

Relationship Branch

This is branch of the discipline is concerned with compatibility, also known as synastry.

A couple's compatibility is determined by comparing their two birth charts, which show the positions of the planets and sun signs, as well as the rising signs, moon signs, and aspects. The aspects are angles that represent the positive and negative relationships between planets . . . which in turn may describe the relationship between the two people under consideration. There are three main methods used to calculate compatibility: Western astrology, Chinese astrology, and Vedic astrology.

Western

Western astrologers use the sun signs as the main determinant when evaluating a match between two people—calculating points where the two signs will blend and points that indicate discord. The signs' relationship on the zodiac wheel is also a factor. Astrologer-approved connections have a good rate of success, but this might be due to a querent's suggestability, that being told he or she is compatible with another person makes them more likely to find or emphasize attractive traits.

The success of astrological matches was demonstrated by psychiatrist Carl Jung in his book *Synchronicity*. While exploring the nature of coincidence, Jung was offered 400 pairs of horoscopes of married couples. He randomized half of the pairs and attempted to find the couples who were actually married. He discovered a correlation between the married couples that matched astrological prediction. As there was no causal relationship to explain his correlations, he called synchronicity an "acausal principle."

Vedic

In Vedic astrology, romance is influenced by the constellations in the ascendent (Lagna) at the couple's birth. Indicators to be considered by the astrologer include longevity, sexual character, widowhood, poverty, progeny, body status, planetary nature and afflictions, time of query, auspicious time for marriage, etc. The ancient books caution, however, that these compatibility checks are to be used only for arranged marriages. When two people are in a committed relationship, the match of minds already exists, and love overrides all other indicators.

Chinese

Chinese astrologers are frequently consulted about suitable partners as well as the best times to propose or marry. Their calculations are based on birth signs years; there is a belief that four years apart for two signs is very good, while six years apart often spells trouble.

Psychological Branch

Swiss psychologist **Carl Jung**

Many people turn to astrology when their emotions are in turmoil or they are unable to make critical decisions that affect their future. This is not so different from the reasons people visit psychologists or psychiatrists—to find answers, identify guideposts, and ease their minds.

At some time around the 1970s, traditional astrology became much more oriented to the subconscious mind, resulting in a new branch—psychological astrology. Also known astropsychology, it grew from the cross-fertilization of the fields of astrology with depth psychology, humanistic psychology, and transpersonal psychology.

This process started in the early 1900s with Alan Leo, who used astrology to evaluate characteristics of personality rather than predict upcoming events. This new application of astrology bolstered the concept of autonomy and free-will rather than restricting it. The baton was then taken up by other astrologers in the UK and US, who espoused a concern with personal experience and insight on one's life purpose.

This new approach to astrology was only one part of a larger spiritual movement associated with the Neptune-Pluto conjunction of that era, which witnessed a reshaping of modern understanding of both the psyche and cosmos. Other influential factors included the decline of traditional religions, the resurgence of occult practices, the revolution in physics— including relativity and quantum theory, the emergence of depth psychology, and the introduction of Eastern concepts to the West. A major contributor to this cultural and spiritual renaissance was Swiss psychologist Carl Jung. His work had a profound effect on 20th-century astrology and was initially promoted by Dane Rudhyar, then by Jung himself.

> **Psychological astrology offers a meaningful tool for coping with the trials of daily life.**
>
> **1. Allows** a better understanding of self by acknowledging the less favorable aspects of birth signs.
> **2. Increases** empathy for the situations of others, eliminates judginess, and promotes an appreciation for the differences between people.
> **3. Enables** individuals to forgive themselves for acting out or letting bad traits take control; also, by understanding one's basic nature, it is possible to refine it.
> **4. Creates** more confidence in intuition and fosters the making of critical decisions without waffling or confusion.
> **5. Reminds** people that everyone is part of the larger picture and that even when things seem out of control, there are always cosmic energies to work with.

Evolutionary Branch

Evolutionary astrology relates to the progression of the human soul. It asks the questions, "Why am I here?" and "What are the lessons I am meant to learn?" It looks back to the development and maturation of the soul, especially into past lives, if one's beliefs incline that way. In any case, every adult has been through experiences in their youth that may still be affecting them.

Often those "early chapters" in a person's life story can explain the dynamics behind troublesome characteristics or bad habits they might wish to shed. Examining the soul's past, looking for hidden motivators, can be critical to achieving a balanced mental state and making positive changes that may have previously been

difficult to accomplish. The concepts of this form of astrology were consolidated by Steven Forrest and Jeffrey Wolf Green around 2000 with a set of core perceptions.

The focal point of evolutionary astrology is the position of Pluto, the "soul" planet. It is a source of insight that can explain the evolutionary path, evoke the soul's truest feelings and deepest yearnings, and empower an individual to create a satisfying, fulfilling life. Perhaps the best way to understand this branch is to experience a reading with an evolutionary astrologer.

The Lunar Nodes

In addition to Pluto, the Lunar Nodes are important to this branch. They are mathematical points found opposite each other on a birth chart, the glyphs for each node resembling

horseshoes. The South Node and North Node respectively provide information about past habits and the current direction of a person's life, not from the viewpoint of ego, but rather from the perspective of the soul's growth. This branch uses the Porphyry house system (not the more common Placidus system), which was developed in the 4th century by a Christian mystic and Neo-Platonist named Porphyry. Using alternate house systems is tricky: they shift the position of the planets to different houses and affect trisecting the quadrants and the house cusps a planet lands on. One reason Porphyry is the preferred system here is because it reflects the Natural Law of the Trinity, which can be said to represent the past, present and future. It is also the house system that Indian Vedic astrologers use, no small recommendation.

Chapter Seven

Lessons from the Masters

Generating a Birth Chart | Feature: An Astrologer's Toolkit | Creating a Daily Horoscope

Generating a Birth Chart

When an individual sits down to prepare a natal chart—either their own or someone else's—they become part of a tradition that is thousands of years old.

Stargazers have long used the movement of the constellations, the planets, the sun, and the moon to indicate character traits, provide guidelines toward personal growth, and suggest future events. In modern times, astrology is often used as a creative tool for self-discovery rather than a predictive process.

But regardless of the motivation or desired result, the creation of a birth chart requires several basic steps.

Creating a Natal Chart

A natal chart is laid out in a circle like a clock, except that it is read counterclockwise. It begins at 9 o'clock, with whatever zodiac constellation is in the First House, which then becomes the querent's rising sign. Underneath that, below the "horizon," are the Second House, Third House, etc. Within each house may lie planets and constellations.

Starting with the Seventh House, which is positioned opposite the First House, the houses are now arranged above the "horizon." Along with the chart there will be a key or legend featuring a lot of symbols; each one signifies a planet, constellation, lunar nodes, the MC (the Medium Coeli or midheaven point, the southernmost high point above the horizon at time of birth), or other factors.

Once the natal chart is cast, it is up to the astrologer to interpret the results. This may include an explanation of what the sun sign

A Sample Natal Chart

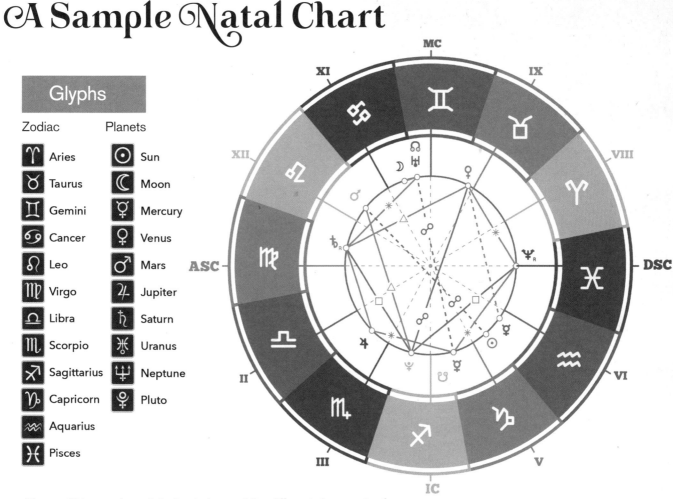

Glyphs	
Zodiac	**Planets**
♈ Aries	☉ Sun
♉ Taurus	☽ Moon
♊ Gemini	☿ Mercury
♋ Cancer	♀ Venus
♌ Leo	♂ Mars
♍ Virgo	♃ Jupiter
♎ Libra	♄ Saturn
♏ Scorpio	♅ Uranus
♐ Sagittarius	♆ Neptune
♑ Capricorn	♇ Pluto
♒ Aquarius	
♓ Pisces	

Above: This sample **natal chart** shows all the different placements of zodiac signs, planets, and other influential factors that are taken into account during a reading.

means and how the other signs and planets are affected by the houses they are in. The querent might discover what dignities the various planets possess. Are any of them in detriment, in fall, or peregrine? What are the aspects in relation to each other? The complexity of this process explains why many astrologers spend years studying the reading and interpretation of star charts . . . and still fall short of complete understanding. No wonder the

study of astrology can involve a lifetime's worth of work.

The Main Placements

Many recreational astrologers focus on the meaning of the three main placements: sun signs, moon signs, and rising signs.

The sun sign represents a person's basic character and the core of who they are. It is simply based on the day of birth, which

reveals which constellation the sun was in at that time.

The moon sign represents who a person is when they are alone and acts as a window to their emotional side. It is determined by which constellation of the zodiac the moon was in on the day of birth and to be downloaded from an online calculator.

The rising sign, or ascending

sign, reflects how other people first see the querent and how he or she appears outwardly. It is based on the zodiac constellation that was on the eastern horizon at the time of birth. This also needs to be downloaded. Also factored in are the effects of the 12 houses and their impact on romance, family relationships, finances, and future goals. More arcane or complex data, like dignities, detriments, or aspects may appear on a computer-generated chart, but interpreting them could be beyond the scope of many novices.

There are a number of online sites that will calculate an individual's entire natal chart with a bare-bones explanation for free—with the option of paying a reasonable fee for a more detailed, multi-page interpretation.

Other influencers on the chart include the eight true planets, which reflect mental function, and the two lunar nodes, which indicate past behavior and possibilities for the future.

Hemispheric Divisions

Yet other influencers on the chart include the four hemispheric divisions—Northern, Southern,

Eastern, and Western, which are positioned counterintuitively, with Southern above Northern, and Eastern before Western—and the two lunar nodes, North and South.

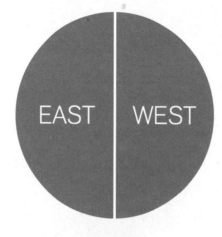

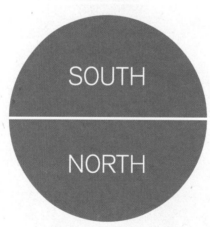

If the signs or planets are clustered below the horizon in the lower or Northern Hemisphere (Houses 1 through 6) they are in the subjective, personal area of the chart. The querent may face inner battles or challenges.

If there is a cluster of planets or signs above the horizon in the upper or Southern Hemisphere (Houses 7 through 12) they are in the objective, social portion of the chart. It means the querent is concerned with outside events and their issues are primarily expressed in public.

If a cluster occurs in the Eastern Hemisphere (Houses 1, 2, 3, 10, 11, 12) this represents freedom, a future that is a blank slate, indicating the querent is self-motivated and has free will to create their life.

If the cluster is found in the Western Hemisphere (Houses 4, 5, 6, 7, 8, 9) this represents fate. The querent considers the needs of others before taking action; their life will be more predestined, more pre-determined.

The North and South Lunar Nodes indicate levels of spirituality and emotional opportunity. They lie opposite each other, so if the North Node only is represented, the South can be found directly across the chart. The position of the South Node represents the overdeveloped traits in a person's life, things they may wish to jettison. If this node is in Leo, say, the person's time as a showboat may be ending, perhaps ushering in a period of more quiet self expression. The North Node represents the potential of the future, traits that may need to be developed if the querent seeks balance in their life. The node opposite Leo would be in Aquarius, a sign that rejects conventionality and is known for nonconformity.

Astrological Symbols

The "shorthand" language of the natal chart is written in hieroglyphics, also known as glyphs. Most of the symbols originated with Byzantine codices—ancient manuscripts typically dealing with religion, science, and medicine—in which many ancient Greek horoscopes were preserved.

For instance, in the original Greek papyri, the sun was represented with a circle with the V-shaped glyph for "shine" emanating from it, while the moon was represented by a hollow crescent. The symbols for Mercury, Venus, Jupiter, and Saturn have been traced to this same source. The current symbol for the sun, a circle with a dot in it, first appeared during the

Renaissance. Other symbols of the zodiac were also simplified at this time. Obviously new symbols were devised for the more recently discovered trans-Saturnian planets. Some, like Uranus and Pluto, ended up with multiple symbols. For a planet with retrograde motion, the symbol is a capital R with a stroke through the tail. The same symbol has been used for medical prescriptions, indicating the word "recipe," and in the Catholic missal to mark a "response." A number of astrological glyphs are the same as astronomical symbols because of the long historical overlap between the two fields.

Interceptions

When checking a natal chart in order to determine the elements for a reading, astrologers often find two house cusps within the same sun sign, This is called an "interception"—when another sign appears halfway through a house and throws off the house's cusps. It is not a negative indicator, it just happens to be the way the signs fell. Additionally, if one house was intercepted, its opposite on the zodiac wheel will show an interception as well. This is not uncommon, and the result is that two of the 12 signs get swallowed up inside the two opposite houses and do not have a house of their own to govern. Even though all 12 signs appear in the chart, an interception makes it seem like two signs disappeared. The glyph for the missing signs is found between two house cusps.

An Astrologer's Toolkit

Contrary to public impressions, most astrologers don't live in a tent along a carnival midway or in a kiosk on the beachside boardwalk. They are normal people who live in normal homes, and many of them consult from that space or from a small storefront or office.

And just like any professional who takes their job seriously, they require certain tools and support materials to help them decipher the movements of the stars and planets. No matter what form or branch of astrology an individual pursues, or whether they are a novice or seasoned practitioner, the materials they need are basically the same.

Ephemeris

Widely recommended by astrologers, this desktop almanac gives the future trajectory of naturally occurring astronomical objects and satellites. From an astrologer's standpoint it provides the planets' positions, retrogrades, eclipses, and other useful information about what the Solar System is getting up to, making it invaluable for researching horoscopes. Ephemerides are also available online.

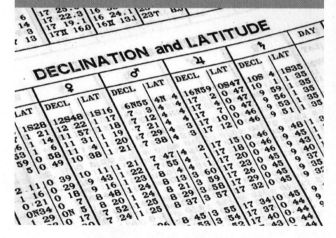

Blank birth charts and colored pencils

Many astrologers enjoy creating their own birth charts rather than simply printing them out from the internet. Using different colors to indicate planets, signs, and aspects makes reading the chart a lot easier. Yellow is traditionally used for highlighting the ruling planet wherever it appears; when it comes to aspects, blue is for trines, red for squares, and green for quincunxes (planets that are 150 degrees apart).

Astrology journal: Keeping a desktop journal can prove quite useful, plus it supports the multiple-input method of learning. It can be a place to keep reference charts, like the meaning of glyphs or sun signs or to collect information from reference materials and articles. It might be somewhere to jot down new interpretations of charts or one's thoughts on a reading, or notes for an upcoming article or talk. Look for attractive journals in gift shops, stationery shops, or online . . . or create your own "cosmic" cover.

Going High Tech

Even astrologers who prefer to go old school, appreciate the ease of creating a birth chart on the computer. For one thing, it allows more time for translating the placements. (Even if the software provides an interpretation, many astrologers like to do their own assessment or augment the original reading.) They are also excellent for calculating support secondary progressions, solar arcs, solar returns, and transits.

Computer software

There was a time when astrologers required numerous charts and books full of tables in order to ascertain what had been happening in the sky at the time of a querent's birth. Fortunately, today there are a number of superior software programs designed help everyone from practicing astrologers to curious beginners perform the calculations required to prepare a thorough chart. These companies also offer licenses for astrologers to print out their reports and sell them through a website or directly to clients.

Matrix Win*Star: Provides all types of wheels, graphs, and aspects.

Astrolabe's Solar Fire: The pioneer in Windows astrology software.

Streamlining a Natal Chart

Experienced astrologers understand that not all placements and influencers need to be taken into account when creating a natal chart. The following list of traditional and more modern factors offers a guideline of what to consider and what might not be useful.

Helpful: Planets, constellations, elements, houses, modalities, polarities, planetary order, planetary speed and retrogradation, aspects, midpoints, Koch houses (midheaven at time of birth turned back to the ascendent), tropical signs (traditional but inaccurate positions of the zodiac).

Occasionally helpful: The dwarf planet Chiron and the four major asteroids—Ceres, Vesta, Pallas, and Hygiea; fixed stars; finer aspects such as 5, 7, 11, 13, called harmonics; arc transforms, which are derived from harmonic charts.

Not helpful: Imaginary Uranian planets; super-outer planets that go slow; heliocentric, local space; esoteric astrology; sidereal or Vedic systems (accurate but non-traditional positions of the zodiac).

Toolkit Sources

There are numerous places where budding astrologers can shop, both in person and online. New Age stores, health food stores, and "head" shops often carry astrological paraphernalia. Online, in addition to Ebay and Amazon, Etsy offers a whole section of astrology support materials—charts, maps, notebooks, research materials, and essential oils, as well as beautiful zodiac-related décor and jewelry. Astro-seek. com provides free tools, books, and tables.

Kepler: Intended for those with any level of experience.

Janus 4: Designed for pros and beginners.

WOW World of Wisdom: Requires no previous knowledge of any astrological techniques.

Astro Gold A chart-calculating app for iPhones.

Creating a Daily Horoscope

Safe to say, the majority of people in the US have at some point looked up their horoscope in a magazine or newspaper or online. And maybe that nugget of astrological information prompted a shift in attitude, raised the possibility of a new relationship or job, or simply made the person feel better about their prospects . . . and themself.

A daily horoscope differs from a birth chart horoscope in that it deals with the outlook for the here and now rather than going back to the day or year of birth. Obviously, professional astrological writers cannot prepare detailed horoscopes for each of their readers, so they create 12 individual charts, each with one of 12 birth signs in the first house, and then drop in the remaining signs. By comparing these individual charts to the transiting planets—and because the moon moves very fast—there is likely to be contact between the moon and one of the planets on each chart. This type of horoscope once required an experienced astrologer versed in researching transits, but now that data can be accessed online.

The Changeable Moon

The reason most published horoscopes are based on the position of the moon is because earth's satellite changes signs every 2 to 2½ days and so affects people's moods and emotions on an almost daily basis. As an example, with sun sign Leo positioned at 9 o'clock and with the moon in Virgo, the astrologer would refer to whichever house was ruled by Virgo to see which area of life would be affected. Virgo rules the 6th house, the House of Health concerned with strength, energy, and routines, so those are the issues that would be addressed in the Leo horoscope. If the moon on an Aquarius chart were in Capricorn, which rules the 10th house, that horoscope would deal with professional achievements and career advancement.

Monthly horoscopes are written using the positions of Mercury, Venus, Mars, and the sun. These planets change every month or every few months. Often astrologers will identify which planets are moving through a given sign in their monthly horoscopes.

Yearly horoscopes use Jupiter and Saturn because Jupiter remains in one sign for a year, while Saturn can remain for 2 to 2 ½ years. Again, the horoscope will often mention which house the planets are moving through for a particular birth sign.

Long-term horoscopes use the slow-moving, or generational, planets like Neptune, Uranus, and Pluto. These trans-Saturnian planets take many years to move through a single sun sign and are able to influence an entire generation over the course of a decade or longer. This explains why some generations tend to act alike or hold similar beliefs.

The Transit of Venus across the Sun in 2012

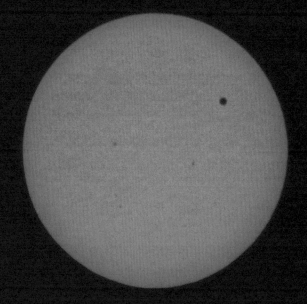

Transits and Returns

In astronomy, a transit occurs when a celestial body passes between a larger body and an observer and appears to be moving across the larger body's face. Astrologically speaking, transit refers to the ongoing movement of the planets, in contrast to their "fixed" positions at one's birth. Transits are connected to the current reality, therefore are useful for calculating contemporary trends. One significant transit, or transit period, is known as the planetary return. This occurs when a planet has completed a whole circuit of the sky and resumes the position it occupied at a person's birth, thus initiating a new cycle in their life. The two most significant returns are Jupiter—occurring roughly every 12 years and heralding a time of growth and development, and Saturn—which returns approximately every 30 years and ushers in a new phase of the aging process.

Augmenting the Horoscope

Those familiar with their birth charts are able to widen the breadth of a published horoscope: after perusing the results for their sun sign, they should check out the reading for their rising sign. Say, their rising sign is Capricorn. This means that whatever comments or cautions fall under that heading should also resonate with them and offer some insights. Many people are shocked to discover that their rising sign, rather than their sun sign, is often more aligned with what they consider their true nature.

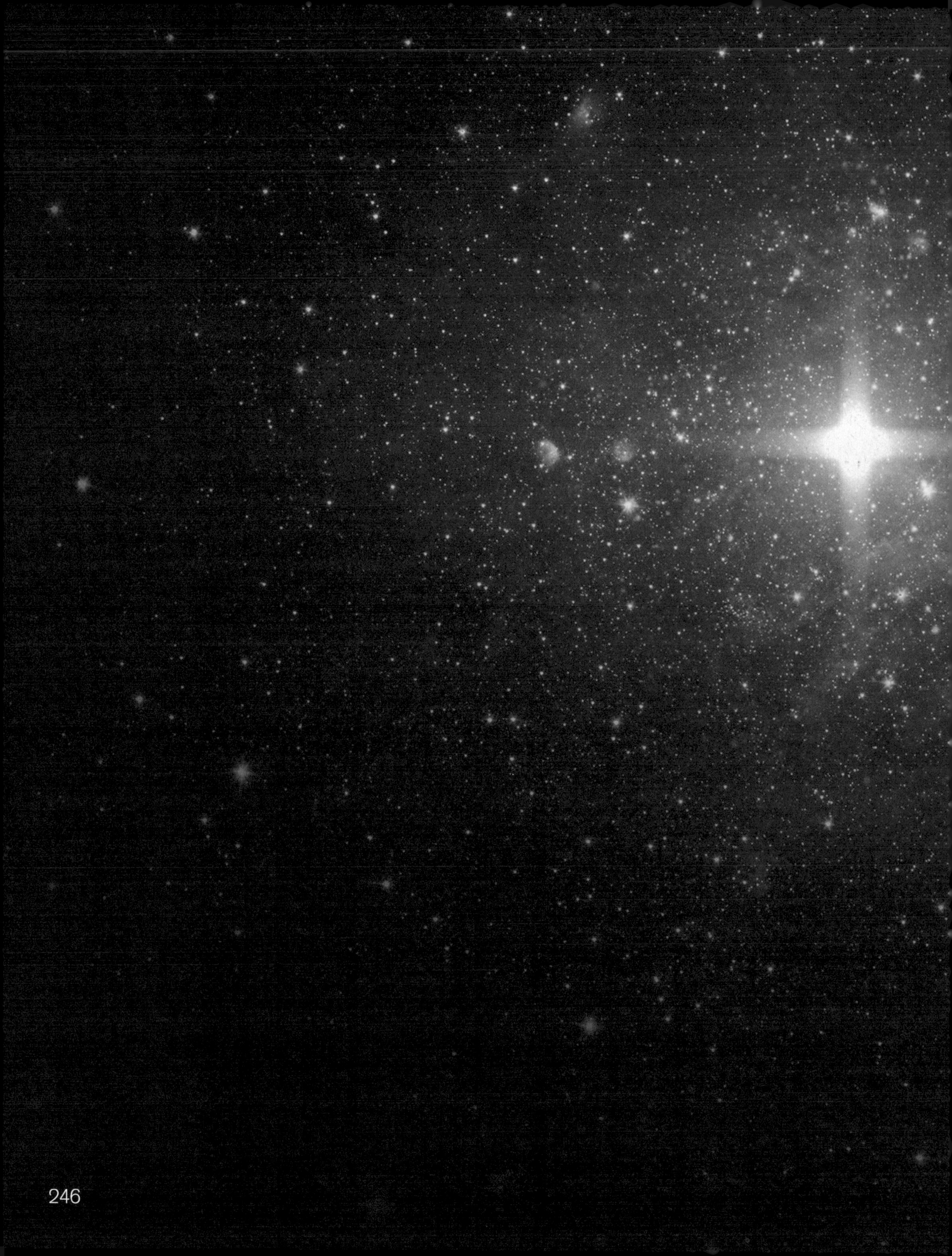

Appendix

Glossary | Index | Credits

Glossary

afflicted: Unfavorable planetary

air signs: Signs possessing the qualities of the element Air (intellect, thought process, etc); Gemini, Libra, and Aquarius.

aneric degree: The final degree of a sign (29th). Also referred to as the degree of fate.

angles: The lines of the chart wheel which lie at 0 degrees (Ascendent), 90 degrees (I.C.), 180 degrees (Descendent), and 270 degrees (M.C.). These major points represent Cardinal Qualities.

Aquarian Age: 2000 year period influenced by the qualities of Aquarius starting approximately at the new millennium.

arc: An angular measurement between two celestial planets or points. Any part of a circle, measured around its circumference.

ascendent: The rising sign. The degree at which the zodiac rests over the horizon of the birthplace at the time of birth. The ascendant represents the persona and image to the world. One of the four major angles of a birth chart. The other three are the descendent (at the cusp of the 7th house), the IC or Imum Coeli at the cusp of the 4th house, and the midheaven or Medium Coeli at the cusp of the 10th house.

aspect: Squares, Oppositions, and Quincunxes: The angular distance, calculated in specific number of degrees of the chart wheel, between two celestial points or planets. It shows the nature of the relationship between planets.

astrolabe: ancient hand-held astronomical instrument.

birth chart: A diagram showing the exact positioning of the planets in the signs at the moment of birth.

cardinal signs: One of the three qualities or modalities, these are related to the change of the seasons; Aries, Cancer, Libra, and Capricorn: Represents initiative.

celestial: positioned in or relating to the sky or outer space.

combust: When a planet is very near the Sun in the birth chart. It is theorized that the planet loses some of its force.

composite chart: Two individual charts which are merged to form one. It shows the relationship between two individuals.

configuration: An aspect that has three or more planets.

conjunction: Two or more planets sitting next to each other. A conjunction gives great strength to the energies of the interacting planets.

constellations: Arrangements or patterns of stars seen by ancient civilizations as resembling or representing gods, humans, animals, or objects.

cosmos: the universe seen as a well-ordered whole.

cusp: A line dividing each of the twelve houses. The midway point between two signs.

cycle: The time it takes a planet or point to make one complete revolution in the heavens.

decante: The division of each sign into three equal parts of 10 degrees each.

declination: The distance of a planet north or south of the celestial equator.

degree: 1/360 of a circle.

descendent: The opposite point from the ascendant located at the cusp of the 7th house. Describes a person's interaction with another. One of the four major angles of a birth chart.

detriment: A planet is said to be in its detriment when placed in the sign opposite the sign that it rules.

dignity: Essential dignity is the idea that the sun, moon, and planets are more powerful and effective in certain signs.

earth signs: Signs with the qualities of the element Earth (practical, etc.); Taurus, Virgo, Capricorn

ecliptic: great circle on the celestial sphere representing the sun's perceived path during the year; the plane of earth's orbit around the sun.

electional astrology: a branch of astrology in which favorable times are elected, or chosen, in advance.

elements: Four-fold division of the zodiac: Fire, Earth, Air, Water. Signs of the same element share qualities of that element.

ephemeris: Astrological almanac listing zodiacal positions of the planets, future trajectories, and other astronomical data.

equator: The imaginary line drawn around the earth, dividing it into the northern and southern hemispheres. When this line is extended into space, it is called the celestial equator.

equinox: A time of equal day and equal night occurring twice a year at the beginning of spring and autumn.

exaltation: Certain planets are strengthened when the occur in their sign of exaltation: Saturn (Libra), Sun (Aries), Venus (Pisces), Moon (Taurus), Mercury (Virgo, although some disagree with this classification), Mars (Capricorn), Jupiter (Cancer).

fall: A planet in the sign opposite its exaltation is said to be in its fall and subsequently weakened.

feminine signs: The earth and water signs. Feminine signs are referred to as negative and indicate passive and receptive energy.

feng shui: practice that uses energy forces to harmonize humans with their surroundings.

fire signs: Signs with the qualities of the element of Fire (willful, energetic, etc.); Aries, Leo, and Sagittarius

fixed signs: One of the three qualities or modalities; fixed signs occur in the middle of season; Taurus, Leo, Scorpio, and Aquarius. Indicates stability and stubbornness.

geocentric: The convention that the earth, rather than the sun is at the center of the Solar System or universe.

glyphs: these are the symbols used for the astrological signs, planets and luminaries, and aspects.

grand cross: Configuration in which four planets form mutual squares. This creates a lot of tension.

grand trine: When three planets meet each other to form a triangle. This is a harmonious configuration.

great year: The period when the pole makes a complete circle.

H

hard aspect: Squares, oppositions and quincunxes. Aspects which create tension and/or friction.

hemisphere: Each half of the birth chart divided either vertically or horizontally when determining hemispheric influences.

Hermeticism: a philosophy that explores the nature of duality based on the work of the legendary Hermes Trismegistus, a combination of the Greek god Hermes and Egyptian god Thoth.

horizon: On a birth chart the horizontal diameter line represents the horizon, with six signs above the horizon and six signs below it.

houses: The celestial sphere is a 360 degree circle that is divided into 12 sections called houses. They are numbered counterclockwise, with the first house, or the ascendant, in the 9:00 position. Each house represents certain aspects of life, and each adds another layer of interpretation to the planet-sign formula

I

IC (Imum Coeli): One of the four major angles of a birth chart. It is at the beginning or cusp of the 4th house and is a very personal point in a chart.

Inquisition: a group of institutions within the Catholic Church whose aim was to combat heresy.

J

joys: Places in the zodiac where planets, being harmoniously located, have the most beneficial effect. Rarely used in modern astrology. According to William Lilly, the joys of the planets are: Saturn joy in Libra; Jupiter joy in Sagittarius; Mars joy in Scorpio; Sun joy in Leo; Venus joy in Taurus; Mercury joy in Virgo; Moon joy in Cancer.

judicial astrology: Relates to the forecasting of principal events that will befall a country and public conditions that will prevail.

Juno: The queen of the gods. An asteroid seen by modern astrologers as significant.

Jupiter: The king of the gods, a planet symbolizing matters to do with the law, religion, authority, the higher mind and so on. Ruler of Sagittarius and Pisces. Exalted in Cancer. The greater benefic.

Jyotish: Indian (Vedic) astrology. This is based on the sidereal zodiac, as opposed to the tropical zodiac favored by most contemporary Western Astrology.

K

key words: Words that encapsulate the meaning of an astrological factor. For example, Cancer: "I feel."

Ketu: Name for the Dragon's Tail, in Indian Astrology.

kite: A Grand Trine with one of the planets making an opposition to a fourth planet which in turn makes sextile aspects to the two others of the Grand Trine.

L

latitude (celestial): Measurement of distance of any planet or star north or south of the ecliptic. The Sun never has any latitude.

latitude (terrestrial): Degree of distance of any place north or south of the Earth's equator.

Leo: This regal sign is the fifth sign of the zodiac. Ruled by the Sun. The exaltation of Pluto. Leo's symbol is the lion.

Libra: The seventh sign of the zodiac, Libra is the sign most concerned with relationships. Cardinal and Airy. Ruled by Venus. The exaltation of Saturn. Libra's symbol is the scales, or balance

lights: Sun and moon.

Lilith: The "Black Moon." a supposed invisible satellite of the Earth, also an energy vortex in the Sun-Moon-Earth system. There is as well an asteroid called Lilith. Lilith, the Dark Goddess, is a Hebrew name for Caput Algol, the Demon Star. In mythology, Lilith was the first wife of Adam, formed like him from the earth, rather than from his rib, like Eve.

logarithms: Tables by which when a planet's motion is known its position at a given time may be readily calculated.

long ascension: Signs of long ascension take longer to ascend than others. Cancer, Leo, Virgo, Libra, Scorpio, Sagittarius. Long and short ascension are reversed in the Southern Hemisphere.

longitude (celestial): Measurement along the ecliptic in terms of signs and degrees from the point of the vernal equinox (0° Aries). The longitude of a planet in the 126th degree of the zodiac is 6° Leo.

longitude (terrestrial): Distance in degrees, minutes and seconds of any place east or west of Greenwich, England. Also measured in hours, minutes and seconds.

luminaries: Another name for the sun and moon in their role as zodiac "planets"

Luna: The Moon. More about the Moon .

lunar mansions: 27 traditional sectors (nakshatras) of the zodiac, where the Moon spends her time on a day by day basis. Each mansion, of 13° 20' duration, has a specific influence, especially if Moon, Sun, Ascendant, or Ruling Planet are placed there. This system is mainly used today in Indian (Vedic) astrology. There are also ancient Chinese, Arabic and Renaissance systems, using 28 lunar mansions of 12° 51' 26" of arc.

lunar node: See Nodes

lunation: A lunar period, measured from one place in the zodiac until the Moon's return thereto. For example, the time taken by the moon from one conjunction with the Sun until the next, 29 days, 12 hours, 44 minutes and 3 seconds, is called a synodical lunation. Lunation is also used to describe different aspects of the moon to the sun, thus accounting for her phases. The new moon is also called a lunation. A chart made for the moment the moon conjoins the sun is called a lunation chart.

M

MC (Medium Coeli): Also known as the midheaven, one of four major points in

Glossary

the birth chart, it lies at the top of the chart (beginning of the tenth house). It represents public life and reputation.

masculine signs: Aries, Gemini, Leo, Libra, Sagittarius, and Aquarius. Masculine signs are assertive and self-assured.

meridian: The meridian at Greenwich. The point from which time and space is measured. It divides longitude into east and west.

midpoints: The midpoint between two planets or angles and sometimes house cusps.

modalities: Cardinal, fixed, mutable. These represent the sign and element's ability to move and evolve over time. Also called qualities.

mutable signs: One of the three qualities or modalities, these fall at the end of a season; Gemini, Virgo, Sagittarius, and Pisces. Indicates a flexible nature.

N

natal: Birth. The natal chart refers to a chart for the time of birth.

nodes: The North and South Nodes of the moon are those points on the ecliptic where the moon crosses it going either north or south.

O

opposition: An opposition is when planets are exactly opposite each other in the chart wheel. Oppositions create stress.

orb: The space in the chart wheel measured in degrees, between planets and points, by which an aspect may vary from exactness and still remain effective.

P

peregrine: When a planet in a birth chart lacks any essential dignities.

Platonism: A view that such things as abstract, non-physical objects exist, but not in time or space.

Pluto: Once the ninth planet, now classified as a dwarf planet; continues rulership of Pluto and the Eight House of the Zodiac.

polarity: Each sign has a relationship with its partner across the zodiac wheel; opposite signs affect each other. May also refer to masculine or feminine designations.

progression: A method of advancing the planets and points of a natal chart to a particular time after birth.

Q

quadrants: there are 4 "quadrants" in a chart; each starts at the cusp of the first, fourth, seventh, and tenth houses.

qualities: Cardinal, fixed, and mutable; they represent the sign and element's ability to move and evolve with time. Also known as modalities.

quincunx (inconjunct): An arc of 150 degrees. An uneasy aspect with karmic lessons.

quintile: An aspect of 72 degrees. An easy aspect representing accomplishments.

R

retrograde: When a planet appears to be traveling backward from Earth's perspective. The energy of a retrograde planet is less assertive.

rulership: Different signs are "ruled" by different planets and their influences can be affected by this.

S

sidereal time: Time reckoned by the stars rather than by the sun.

solstice: When the sun reaches its maximum declination. This occurs twice a year, at the beginning of summer and winter.

stellium: A group of planets gathered in one area of the zodiac; sometimes, a multiple conjunction.

sublunar: Having to do with events within the moon's orbit and subject to its influence; on the earth.

sublunar sphere: Plato's concept of a region in the geocentric cosmos below the moon and consisting of the four classical element: earth, water, air, and fire.

sun sign astrology: As seen in newspaper and online astrology columns, predictions for the day, month or year ahead based on solar birth signs.

supralunar: Having to do with events that take place beyond the moon, in outer space.

synastry: Comparing natal charts to find strengths and weaknesses in the area of compatibility.

T

transit: A planet's movement in the sky, aspecting another planet or moving into a new house or sign. At least a few transits happen on any given day.

trans-Saturnian planets: The more recently discovered planets of Uranus, Neptune, and formerly Pluto, which is now classified as a dwarf planet.

U

under the sun's beams: Within 17 degrees of the sun. Any planet here is weakened, though more so if combust (within 8 degrees 30 minutes). Not so important in natal astrology.

Uranian planets: Planets postulated to lie beyond the orbit of Pluto.

Uranus: Formerly known as Herschel, after its discoverer, this planet was not discovered until 1781. It has been deemed to rule Aquarius. It stands for unexpected disruptions and sudden catastrophes.

V

Vedic: An ancient type of astrology practice in India.

void-of-course: A term describing a planet that does not make a major aspect before changing signs. It is primarily with respect to the moon.

W

water element: One of the four astrological elements. A feminine element, it stands for emotion, feeling, matters to do with intuition and so on. The other elements are Fire, Air, and Earth.

water signs: Signs with the qualities of the element Water (sensitive, sentimental); Cancer, Scorpio, and Pisces.

Y

yod: A powerful aspect.

youth (phase of): The period of life from birth up to the first Saturn return (roughly 30 years).

Z

zodiac: From the Greek zodiakos, meaning "circle of animals." A band in the heavens divided into twelve signs, each containing 30 degrees of longitude and acting as a barometer for various human traits.

Index

Index

Index

Credits

All imagery is courtesy of SHUTTERSTOCK.COM, with the exception of: p13, Magic 8-Ball, courtesy **"By greeblie from US"**; p15, Dr John Dee, courtesy **the Ashmolean Museum** Oxford, England; p17, The Ecliptic Path, courtesy **WikiCommons**; p25, Tintoretto, *The Origin of the Milky Way*, c.1575 courtesy **the National Gallery**, London; p26, Taurus and Orion's Belt in the Caves of Lasceaux, courtesy **Somewhereville.com**; p27, *Planisphaerion Coeleste,* courtesy **WikiCommons**; p41, the Dendera Zodiac, Courtesy of **Alamy**; p42, *Petosiris's Circle,* courtesy **TheDigitalRambler.com**; p.47, Roman Coin with Capricorn, courtesy **Catawiki**; p50, Chinese coin with zodiac stamp, courtesy of **Pinterest**; p51, courtesy **WikiCommons**; p61, from the *Tres Riches Heures du Duc de Berry,* courtesy **Wikipedia**; p67, Chinese coin with Zodiac, courtesy **Powerhouse Museum Photolibrary**; p70, courtesy **Alamy**; p80, Crab Nebula, courtesy of **WikiCommons**; p95 *Terrarum Orbis*, courtesy **Barry Lawrence Ruderman Inc.**, **raremaps.com**; p97, courtesy **the Royal Australian Mint**; p101, courtesy **the Polynesian Voyaging Society**; p104, Zoroaster, courtesy **Alamy**; p109, Emperor Tiberius, courtesy **Alamy**; p115, Ptolemy, courtesy **Alamy**; p119, Paracelcus, courtesy **Alamy**; p121, Nostradamus, courtesy **Alamy**; p126, Kepler's Supernova, courtesy **WikiCommons**; p131, Susan Miller, cover art of *Planets & Possibilities*, courtesy **Amazon**; p135, illustration in Conan Doyle's *Spiritualism*, courtesy **Alamy**; p194-195 Elements of graphs taken from **Wikipedia**